Wolves at Our Door

Wolves at Our Door

The Extraordinary Story of the Couple Who Lived with Wolves

Jim and Jamie Dutcher

with James Manfull

POCKET BOOKS

NEW YORK LONDON TORONTO SYDNEY SINGAPORE

All insert photos by Jim and Jamie Dutcher except for the following: page 2, top and bottom right: Bob Poole; page 8, bottom: Jake Provonsha; page 12, bottom, and page 16: Shane Stent; page 15, top: Franz Camenzind.

Photo of the authors by Garrick Dutcher.

Map drawn by Evelyn Backman Phillips.

POCKET BOOKS, a division of Simon & Schuster, Inc.
1230 Avenue of the Americas, New York, NY 10020

Library of Congress Cataloging-in-Publication Data

Dutcher, James.
    Wolves at our door / Jim and Jamie Dutcher with James Manfull.
        p. cm.
    ISBN 0-7434-0048-8 (alk. paper)
        1. Wolves—Behavior—Anecdotes. 2. Dutcher, James. 3. Dutcher, Jamie.
I. Dutcher, Jamie. II. Manfull, James. III. Title.

    QL737.C22 D883 2002
    599.773'15—dc21

                                                          2001052084

First Pocket Books hardcover printing February 2002

10 9 8 7 6 5 4 3 2 1

POCKET and colophon are registered trademarks of
Simon & Schuster, Inc.

For information regarding special discounts for bulk purchases,
please contact Simon & Schuster Special Sales at 1-800-456-6798
or business@simonandschuster.com

Designed by Joseph Rutt

Printed in the U.S.A.

For the Sawtooth Pack, as we remember them.

Wildlife films are not scripted. The story takes shape after a great deal of observation, as the animal's behavior reveals itself. The shooting schedule always allows room for experimentation and improvisation, and everyone on a crew, from the producer to the production assistant, contributes to the creative process. Living and working creatively alongside a tight-knit crew is what I enjoy most about making films, and something I sorely miss when I am between productions. I have spent some of the best hours of my life sitting beside the woodstove with the crew, hatching ideas, pinning notecards to a storyboard, and letting our energies and imaginations flow together. For the quality of my films, I owe my crews a great deal. For the memories I have of hard work, collaboration, and especially friendship, I owe my crews everything. Most of all, I am grateful to my wife, Jamie, who changed her life to join me by that woodstove. *Wolves at Our Door* would not have been what it was without her talent, spirit, and love.

Jim Dutcher

Acknowledgments

Jim and Jamie wish to thank the following people for providing support, ideas, and advice on the care of wolves, on the making of two documentaries, and on the writing of this book: Randy Acker, Margo Aragon, Ed Bangs, Mitra and Frederic Boloix, Tom Brandau, Peter Bricca, Ken Britton, Dave Dickie, Lisa Diekmann, Barbara and Corneil Dutcher, Gaynelle Evans, Joe Fontaine, Steve Fritts, Nelson and Renée Funk, the Furey family, Gary Gadwa, Jim and Lucia Gilliland, Kay Sprinkle Grace, Jed Gray, Gordon Haber, Jude Hawkes, Teresa Heinz, Kate Hopkins, Maurice Hornocker, Idaho Department of Fish and Game, Glenn Janss, Mike Jimenez, John Jolley, Jomo, James and Patricia Jones, B. A. Kempler, Lois and Michael Kempler, George Klingelhofer, Erich Klinghammer, David Knotts, Suzanne Laverty, Irwin and Rita Liptz, Helen and Lowell Manfull, Grant Mauer, Kathy McCormack, Mission:Wolf, the Nez Perce Tribe, David O'Dell, Chris Palmer, Carl Pence, Karen Penn,

Mabel and Pierro Piva and family, Charlie Pomeroy, Mike Quattrone, the Racine family, Mose Richards, Harriet and Barry Rosenberg, Debbie Rothberg, Sandy and Bob Sallin, Brent Snider, Mark and Margaret Stewart, Brian Sturges, John Tait, Pat Tucker, United States Forest Service, Diana and Mallory Walker, Bruce Weide, Jan Wygle, and Erik Zimmen.

And a very special thanks to the crew of *Wolf: Return of a Legend* and *Wolves at Our Door*. These individuals lived and worked with us at wolf camp as part of the film-making team or as caretakers for the Sawtooth Pack (the lines between the two jobs were often blurred): Val Asher, Sarah Bingaman, Franz Camenzind, Christina Dutcher, Garrick Dutcher, Johann Guschelbauer, Janet Kellam, Keith Marshall, Karen McCall, Megan Parker, Bob Poole, Jake Provonsha, Patty Provonsha, Jan Roddy, Laurie Schmidt, Vanessa Schulz, Burke Smith, Shane Stent, and Suzie Wrentmore.

James Manfull, our production manager, spent many hours working with us to shape our story into this book. We're grateful for his talent and for his help.

We would also like to thank Norma Douglas, who believed in our story and supported us in making this book happen, including finding our extraordinary literary agent, Geri Thoma.

Lastly, the wolf project and the films would never have happened without the support and vision of two very important people to whom we owe a special debt of gratitude: Dennis Kane and Karin Rundquist.

Contents

Wolves at Our Door

trapper's cabin

lodgepole
pines

fir
trees

meadow
where wolves
played

willows where
lakota hid

chemukh's
den

makuyi's
hiding place

aspen groves

N

where cou
jumped fen

©2001 E.B. Phillips

Home
of the
Sawtooth Pack
1990-1996

NW gate

beaver ponds

wolf camp

willows

pup enclosure

lock off

SE gate

old yurt

gate

old tent camp

structures and fencing not to scale

Introduction

JIM AND JAMIE DUTCHER

Clouds form and dissolve in an uncertain April wind. They gather around the mountain peaks, cloaking everything in gray, then part for a moment, revealing a sudden flash of granite, snow, and blue sky.

From the mountains to the valley floor, the ground is blanketed in white, yet the wind carries the rumor of spring, the smell of moss and damp earth. Lodgepole pines creak and groan, as though awakening from a long sleep. By a swollen stream, the bough of a spruce tree rocks back and forth. Black-capped chickadees hop among the bare red willow branches, looking for insects. Below them, tiny rivulets join and diverge, etching a latticework in the retreating snow.

This pattern is interrupted by a straight line of tracks, direct and full of purpose. Dark prints of mud stain the clean white surface, then fade away as the trail moves from the willow bog into the spruce grove.

Rhythmic footsteps whisper in the snow. She proceeds with a graceful and easy lope, gliding over the surface. When she reaches the forest, she pauses to glance back, checking to see if she is being followed. Then in a single fluid motion, her dark form is absorbed by the shadows.

She moves through a landscape where her kind have been absent for over fifty years. But the wolf knows nothing of this. The purpose that fills her gait has nothing to do with reclaiming her ancestral land. The call that drives her forward is even more urgent, as ancient and mysterious as life itself. She stops and then doubles back, inspecting the area, looking for signs of intruders. Then she crouches and slips into a dark hole hidden beneath a fallen tree.

For many hours all is silent. The sun drops behind the jagged ridge of the mountains and all goes dark. Then, in the icy stillness of the night, a soft staccato whining, a chorus of tiny voices, rises from within.

A new day dawns, bright and cold, but immediately the sun goes to work on the frozen snow pack, turning the icy crust to slush. The worn ground outside the den is a bustle of activity. Other wolves gather at the opening, quivering and whining in excitement. These are the mother's family, her pack. They peer into the hole and sniff the air, taking in the smell of new life.

Several yards away, a woman stands motionless. She wears headphones and points a long microphone in the direction of the activity, holding steady. After a few minutes, she leans the long pole up against a spruce tree and glances toward her husband, who crouches behind a movie camera nearby. Sensing her question, he looks up from his eyepiece and nods. Carefully, as if in slow motion, the woman brings her gear to him and then walks over to the den. Kneeling down, she peers into the darkness. Surrounded by wolves, she is calm. They make way for her, and one greets her with a gentle lick on the cheek. They seem to be aware that she means no harm, that she shares their curiosity and excitement over the newborn pups.

The mother wolf is aware as well. She pokes her head out of the den for the first time since the previous day, then crawls out completely and sits beside the young woman. Wolf and woman regard each other, perhaps trying to read each other's intentions. The mother's eyes show no fear, only curiosity and intelligence. She is as calm as if one of her own pack were approaching her young.

The woman slowly reaches into the pocket of her coat and withdraws a small flashlight. She shows it to the mother, giving the wolf time to inspect it and make sure that the unfamiliar object poses no threat. Then the woman lowers herself onto her belly, delicately inches herself into the cavern, and clicks on the light.

Imagine you are hiking deep in the wilderness, somewhere in the Rocky Mountains, in one of the few places in the lower 48 states where wild wolves still live and hunt. If you are alert and your eyes are sharp, you might catch sight of something, a flicker of motion a hundred yards away. You fumble for your binoculars, speculating on what it was that caught your eye—a large coyote, a young bear? Zeroing in on the spot where the motion was, you instantly make out a doglike form.

If you've spent time in the Rockies, most likely you've seen your share of coyotes; but this animal is different, larger and more muscular, with a wider face and shorter ears and muzzle. He has stopped and is already staring straight at you, having become aware of your presence while you were still strolling along, admiring the scenery. You can see him only because he is allowing you to. The moment you take another step forward, or shift your weight from one foot to the other, he is gone, absorbed into the landscape like melting April snow.

Most sightings of wolves in the wild are fleeting glimpses made from a great distance, the animal already turning tail and fleeing the perceived danger. The wolf is one of North America's least observed and least understood creatures. It is also one of its most persecuted.

For centuries, Europeans and their descendants in North America have accepted as conventional wisdom that wolves are ferocious man-eaters, animals to be feared, hated, and destroyed. To be sure, wolves are adept hunters who bring down prey in a violent, moblike fashion. But that alone cannot account for the hatred we have harbored for this animal since the beginnings of remembered history. Naturalists speculate on how the wolf became the enemy of early Europeans, and there is probably some truth in every theory. Human beings and wolves have been competing for the same prey ever since our ancestors came down from the trees; yet among hunting cultures, the wolf was often seen more as a teacher to be emulated than a competitor to be annihilated. The agricultural revolution altered man's relationship with nature such that the wolf quickly developed a reputation as a murderer of sheep and cattle.

Wolves, being intelligent and opportunistic, did indeed pose a threat to domestic livestock. They also capitalized on periods of war and pestilence during early Christian Europe. Occasionally wolf packs raided battle-fields and the shallow graves of plague victims to feast on human corpses. Visions of a savage mob of wolves fighting over the grizzly spoils like a hoard of barbarians helped to paint the wolf as an attendant of the Devil.

To complete the image, some enemies of early Christians held to ancient beliefs that often included the wolf as a powerful symbol. From the wolf cults of the late Roman Empire to the Norse armies that ransacked medieval England, the fearsome wolf preyed on the "Lambs of God" (Bomford, p. 24). It was a clear-cut battle between the Christian forces of good and the Pagan forces of darkness. More damning than its reputation as a killer of livestock, the wolf found itself the victim of religious symbolism.

In a context so clouded by misinformation and religious fury, it isn't surprising that very few people were able to see what the animal was really all about—a highly intelligent and social mammal that lived in a large family unit and depended on cooperation for its survival. The darker side of wolves was the only side to appear in folklore, fables, and literature. Misunderstanding bred fear and fear bred hatred.

When Europeans began to settle North America, they brought their centuries-old attitude toward wolves with them to the new and untamed land. The early colonists found themselves huddled in small enclaves surrounded by a seemingly limitless wilderness. The Devil was represented in the New World by all the things that 17th- and 18th-century settlers feared: bloodthirsty beasts and wild men prowling the dark forests, just beyond the pale glow of colonial fires. The new wilderness was, by definition, a godless place, a land to be feared and to be conquered.

Immediately upon arrival, the colonists began raising livestock—pigs, cattle, sheep—and almost as quickly, some of those animals were lost to predators. Already wearing the brand of evil, the wolf was nearly always blamed for these deaths, even though the colonies themselves were the source of a burgeoning population of feral dogs that were frequently the real culprits (Lopez, p. 175). Economic loss made wolves a convenient target for even greater religious wrath, causing age-old distinctions between good and evil to resurface with newfound zeal. Religious and secular attitudes reinforced each other, trapping the wolf in a vicious circle. It didn't take long for the first bounty to be placed on a wolf's head.

Whatever the motivation, Americans have traditionally measured their success by how much of the wilderness they are able to tame and turn into productive pastures, farms, and towns. As civilization rushed west to the Pacific coast, and trickled into all the small pockets of unsettled land that remained, the wolf didn't stand a chance. What is difficult to comprehend, however, is why so many wolves were killed, even after they ceased to be a meaningful cause of livestock loss. Regardless of the fact that disease, storms, injury, and other causes were taking a far greater toll on livestock, the cry was still loudest against the wolf, perhaps because it was the one adversary that could be decisively controlled.

As the country continued to grow, the measures of predator control became more and more severe. Expert wolf hunters appeared with tool kits of poison and complicated snares. State veterinarians introduced canine diseases, such as mange, into wolf communities. The all-out war against the wolf escalated, even as wolf populations were dwindling. The national opinion of wolves went far beyond a dislike for an animal that killed livestock; it was a hatred that bordered on the pathological. Eventually so many wolves were killed that the numbers could hardly be estimated. Many wolf bounties were lifted, not so much because of changing attitudes but because there were not enough wolves left to make them worthwhile.

Not until the second half of the 20th century was there an inkling in any but the most enlightened minds that we might be doing something wrong. The passage of the Endangered Species Act, first drafted in 1967 and reinforced in 1973, was the first step of a change in our national attitude toward wildlife. Species with more winning reputations, like the bald eagle, have seen a marked improvement in their numbers. But unlike the noble eagle, wolves compete with human hunters for deer and elk. People are simply unable to change their minds about an animal they have hated for thousands of years.

In spite of this, the federal government took the new spirit of protection a step further when, in the early 1990s, it reintroduced wolves to a few selected areas in the United States. Many applauded the idea. Others were outraged that the government would bring back a varmint that they had only just succeeded in getting under control. It remains one of the most polarizing environmental controversies in history.

The wolves that now live in the lower 48 states are a far cry from their ancestors who once ruled the forests and plains, nearly uncontested. They are a mix of reintroduced newcomers from Canada combined with the few surviving members of the original population who were cunning enough to avoid traps, guns, and poison. Today's wolves are elusive and fearful, well aware that they are in constant danger. Their secrecy, born of self-preservation, now frustrates our attempts to learn more about them. Thus are the old myths difficult to dispel.

Common knowledge regarding wolves continues to be a mixture of fact and mythology. People understand that they are predators, but many still do not know the other side of wolves, a side that the animal does not readily reveal.

Our goal was to listen to the wolf, not as scientists but as social partners. First and foremost, we are filmmakers. We knew in advance that seeing wolves at all is a rare enough occurrence; to see them demonstrate their social structure, their methods of communication, and their intimate family life requires special conditions. On the edge of Idaho's Sawtooth Wilderness we created an environment where a pack of wolves could open their lives to us and accept us as just another part of their world. We called them the Sawtooth Pack, and set out to capture their intimate lives on film—to dispel myths and show a side of them so often overlooked by scientists and politicians. What we encountered was beyond our greatest expectations.

The Den

JAMIE

I flicked on the flashlight and slithered down the passageway into the den. There, my beam of light found a furry black mass huddled against the earthen wall. The pups looked almost like little bear cubs, jet black with flat faces. As their newborn eyes were still tightly closed, they could not make out just who or what I was, but I'm sure my human scent revealed me as something new and unfamiliar. With a boldness afforded only to the very young and innocent, the pups sniffed the air and chirped at me, perhaps hoping I was there to feed them. I couldn't help thinking that this was exactly how they would have regarded a wolf hunter in the 1920s as he pulled them from their den.

I turned off the light and backed my way out to where Chemukh, their mother, was waiting. She looked at me, cocking her head, listening to my voice as I gently congratulated her, then giving me a reassuring lick on the nose.

Only two years had passed since I had raised

Chemukh herself from puppyhood, taking over the role of her mother, feeding and cleaning her so that she would be at ease around human beings. From the time she was three months old, however, she had run with a real wolf pack, living in their society and obeying their laws with very little human intervention.

I was amazed at her display of absolute trust, allowing me to crawl right into her den and inspect her precious litter, the first pups born to the Sawtooth Pack and, by all known accounts, the first wolves to be born in the Sawtooth Mountains for fifty years or more.

The birth of pups is a momentous event and the excitement within the pack was electric. The other wolves were intensely interested in seeing the new arrivals. Although pups are born to the alpha male and female, the leaders of a wolf pack, they really belong to the group as a whole. Every wolf in a pack is part of the extended family. All share in the joy when pups are born and all play a role in their upbringing, from feeding, to education, to discipline. What was truly remarkable was that Chemukh allowed me to crawl into the den, a privilege that she did not extend even to the other wolves. To her, I was not a stranger who might harm her pups or steal her food, I was a familiar and trusted friend.

For as long as I can remember, I have had a passion for wildlife. My grandmother used to tell me that the first recognizable picture I drew was not a house or a stick person, but an elephant. My treasured books were not Nancy Drew mysteries but animal stories. When I was a young girl, the woods behind my Maryland house, just outside of Washington, D.C., served as the great wilderness; the walks I took among the oaks and hickories, looking for salamanders and white-tailed deer, were my safaris. I remember, at the age of seven, hearing that someone had seen a black bear in nearby Rock Creek Park. For days I searched the woods, wondering if the bear might stop by, hoping to not only see him but befriend him. I figured he would like me as much as I knew I would like him.

Of course, when we are young we have many dreams and fantasies. When we grow up, some come true and some do not. I never did make friends with a wild black bear, but here I was, so many years later, sitting side by side with a wolf—an animal that has such a traditional fear of humans that few people ever see one. Yet I was welcomed into her pack and treated to a glimpse of her family's private life, invited to share in the excitement of birth.

This experience and new life of mine, observing wolves, recording their howls, and documenting their family structure would never have come about were it not for the vision of one man. In 1990, filmmaker and naturalist Jim Dutcher had an idea, a way to film an elusive animal up close without disturbing its natural behavior. He envisioned creating a balance between a captive and wild state in which wolves were raised in a huge enclosure, but with minimal interference from humans. While they could not hunt or roam without boundaries, they were free to build their own society, choose their own leaders, and sort out their own disputes.

In the beginning, this was just an idea for a film, a one-hour television documentary. He never dreamed that the project would last for six years or that these wolves would become famous throughout the world. Nor could either of us ever have imagined that it would affect us so personally and so deeply, bringing us so much wonder and joy, and so much heartache.

Jim and I are not scientists. This book is about the years we spent filming, observing, and living with wolves. It is not a scientific treatise but rather an account of what we experienced, learned, and felt as filmmakers and as human beings. This at times allowed us a freedom of speculation that no scientist could afford. Conversely, we were very careful not to let ourselves be blinded by fantasy, making these animals out to be more than what they are: neither demon nor deity, but simply wolves, incredible and inspiring in their own right.

Inspiration

JIM

The horses had spent the night in a meadow below the Continental Divide, grazing contentedly on the damp grass and dozing in the cool mountain air. Once the sun came up in the morning to warm them, they would grow restless and start to wander. It was my job to arrive at first light and drive the herd back to the ranch and into the corral for the day.

The year was 1959, and I was a 16-year-old Floridian with a dream summer job—the chance to play cowboy and get paid for it. The chilly morning air, the sense of responsibility, the freedom: it was all so exhilarating that most days I'd bolt out of my bunk and be among the horses well before dawn, gathering them together and weeding out any confused moose that had joined the herd during the night.

One particular day, the herd was more agitated than usual. By the time I arrived at the meadow, a handful of horses had strayed into the forest. The buckskin mare I'd been given to ride for the summer knew her job so well that she nearly did it by herself. With almost no effort I rounded up the bulk of the herd, guided them the two miles back to the ranch, then set out to collect the strays. It was always the same few malcontents that would break away from the rest. Earlier in the season I had put bells on these few to make them easier to track down. As the day began to heat up, my mare and I followed the faint tinkling of the bells out of the meadow and up onto higher ground.

The Diamond G Ranch sat perched at 9,200 feet, beside Brooks Lake on the southwestern edge of Wyoming's Absaroka Range. A steep road winds through Togwotee Pass, across the Continental Divide, joining the valleys of the Snake River to the west and the Wind River to the east. Because most of the human attention fell on nearby Grand Teton and Yellowstone National Park, Togwotee was then, as now, largely forgotten, serving as a route of travel rather than as a destination. Once off the main road, the landscape quickly became wilderness.

Rounding up stray horses meant the chance to spend the morning riding alone, exploring the backcountry. It was not unusual to surprise a herd of shy elk, see bald eagles soaring above the gray cliffs, or catch a black bear foraging for berries and grubs, and I was always catching glimpses of skittish coyotes. Everyone who worked the ranch, myself included, was under instructions to shoot any and all coyotes seen but I soon learned that I didn't have the stomach for it. Even so, the coyotes seemed to know that they were a marked animal and were quick to disappear whenever they caught sight or smell of me.

Thus I was quite surprised when I entered a small meadow at the base of a cliff and found myself staring at a very large coyote who didn't seem the least bit frightened by my presence. Instead of darting off into the forest, he stood his ground, boldly staring at me as I stared at him. He was huge, with longer legs and a wider face than any coyote I'd seen. Even at a distance, I could sense his yellow eyes watching me. Suddenly I felt the hair on the back of my neck stand up and I found myself in the grip of some primal understanding as my instinct suddenly grasped what my brain was slow to comprehend. Although I had never seen one before, I realized I was in a face-off with a gray wolf. My heart was pounding. Here, embodied in one creature, was all the mystery, the savagery, the beauty of the American West. Slowly I coaxed my horse forward and to the side, trying to get a closer look without appearing too threatening. The wolf didn't seem to have any fear of me, exhibiting instead what looked like a cool curiosity. His confidence is what I still remember most about that meeting, the way he stood his ground and regarded me as an equal.

As I circled the edge of the clearing, the wolf did the same, so that we ended up on opposite sides of the meadow, each standing where the other had been. He seemed to have a keen interest in inspecting the area where my horse had trampled the grass, trying to figure out what we were and if we were a threat.

After we stared at each other for a minute more, he seemed to tire of the meeting and casually trotted off down the hill and into the trees. I didn't know enough about wolves to be aware of it at the time, but in 1959 I had seen something so rare that only a few dozen of his kind existed in the entire U.S. Rocky Mountain range. It would be thirty years before I'd see another.

The most profound changes in life are often the ones that pass slowly and unnoticed. A life-transforming event can lie dormant, waiting to be made complete. This was the case with the wolf in the Absarokas. That experience stayed with me, remembered but unimportant, until a final ingredient gave it meaning.

When I returned to the ranch in 1990, it had become a guest lodge and I was a guest. I was there on vacation, taking a break after completing a three-year film project entitled *Cougar: Ghost of the Rockies*. The film had been something of a new direction for me. Instead of trying to film a secretive predator in the wild, I had teamed up with biologist and big-cat expert Dr. Maurice Hornocker to build an enclosure in a natural setting and bring the predator to us. The enclosure would allow Dr. Hornocker to conduct research on a female cougar as she raised her cubs. It would allow me to get intimate footage of an animal that was hard enough to *see* in the wild, let alone film. I had always held reservations about intruding on a wild animal's home, habituating it to a human presence and eroding its natural fear, especially when the creature is legally hunted. The next time someone pointed something at that animal, it might not be a lens.

For me, the technique was a revelation, a way to bring

an audience closer to the animal than in any film I had made before. I felt that if I gave people an intimate look at something as beautiful and majestic as a mountain lion, I could make them value and protect a creature that they might never see firsthand. I didn't know what subject I would tackle after *Cougar*, but I knew I wanted to capture that same intimacy with another elusive animal. There were so many options. I decided that what I needed was to get out into nature with a stack of books, to hike and fish and research the possibilities.

The place where I really thought I could clear my mind was the old ranch in the Absarokas. Something about that place always brought me a sense of peace. Perhaps it was the fact that, while I was thirty years older, the land hadn't changed all that much. The sharp cliffs still loomed above Brooks Lake. Below, the sweeping alpine meadows, so broad and empty, still defied one's sense of distance.

I had only been there for a day when I received a message from my executive producer, Dennis Kane, informing me that *Cougar: Ghost of the Rockies* had been selected to launch his *World of Discovery* series for its premiere season. It was an incredible honor and I was ecstatic. There was an old favorite climb of mine, an incredibly difficult scramble up a steep rocky slide that I hadn't made since I was sixteen, but upon hearing the news from Dennis, I found myself darting up the slope with the sudden energy of a boy. I zigzagged through a stand of white pine and clawed my way over the brittle rocks toward the peak. At the summit, I stood up to gaze at the rocky spires of

Pinnacle Buttes, but when my view cleared the crest, I froze in my tracks. There, below me on a gentle slope of alpine tundra, stood a gray wolf.

Memories of that thrilling day in 1959 came flooding back, only I knew enough not to mistake it for a coyote this time. There was no way of telling, but I thought perhaps this could be a descendant of that wolf I had seen as a boy, one of the few remaining members of a thin family line that still managed to survive in a land where its kind were hated, feared, and shot. It seemed as if thirty more years of extermination at the hands of man had taken its toll on this wolf's trust of humans. Unlike its cool, curious, and unafraid ancestor years before, this wolf showed unmistakable fear. I barely had a moment to bring my binoculars to my eyes for a closer look before he saw me and took off like a shot. But the moment was long enough for me. My next film had found its subject.

Unlike the Absarokas, the Sawtooth Mountains of Idaho hadn't seen wolves for over fifty years. This range of jagged peaks, running southeast out of the town of Stanley, is prime wolf country, or at least it could have been at one time. It was the perfect location to film a pack of wolves for my new documentary. My plan was to set up a huge enclosure, as I had for the cougar film, and raise a pack of wolves in this wild setting. As I paced off the area below Williams Peak that would become the pack's home, I noticed the remains of a tiny log cabin a short distance away. Pine saplings had grown thick on the cabin floor, well fed by rotting timber, and only a portion of the four walls remained. The cabin's only resident was a porcupine who scurried under a nearby log and waited for me to leave.

There was hardly enough left of the place to warrant a second look, but for me it still resonated with an eerie significance. Toward the early part of the 20th century, someone—a fur trapper or hunter perhaps—had built and lived in that tiny single room, suffering bitter cold and staggering loneliness for weeks or even months at a time. This person, whoever he was, was perhaps also the one who put the last of the wolves of this region to death.

The only clue to his existence came from several scattered jars that had once contained cloves, an old-time toothache remedy. I imagined him, stalking through the forest, chin bandaged and sucking on a mouthful of cloves, training his rifle on the final members of a dwindling wolf pack, thinking of the money he would earn (to buy more cloves, no doubt) for their thick fur, and from the bounty that the state paid for their deaths.

So, months later, when I walked through the gate of the completed Sawtooth wolf enclosure, cradling a sedated female wolf named Makuyi in my arms, it was not without a hint of nostalgia and pride. Wolves were back in the Sawtooths. Although they were not free like their wild ancestors, perhaps these wolves would act as ambassadors and educators, guiding us to a better understanding of their species and helping us learn from our mistakes. But before then, I had a considerable amount of learning to do myself, and many mistakes to make.

When I saw Makuyi in a Montana wolf shelter, I instantly fell in love with her. She was a beautiful wolf with the slender build of a female: long graceful legs, deep amber eyes, and a wonderfully sweet disposition. I was, in fact, caught completely off guard, never expecting to be so captivated by her. It was my first inkling that I was about to embark on something very special.

Her owner, Karin Rundquist, had managed to rescue a group of wolves from a research lab in the 1980s and had built a pen on her property where they could live. Makuyi was the offspring of two of those wolves. Karin had recently seen *Cougar: Ghost of the Rockies* and loved the idea of a similar film that would educate people about wolves. She agreed to provide the five-year-old female and four unrelated puppies to start my project. Karin and I were slightly concerned that Makuyi suffered from cataracts, but when we watched the spry wolf sprint around her small enclosure without any trouble, her vision seemed fine. She would become the alpha female of a new pack, I thought, to be paired with an alpha male who would arrive in a matter of days.

Janet Kellam, my associate producer, located a male, Akai, in Ely, Minnesota, where he was part of a small wolf organization under the care of Laurie Schmidt. Janet and I both thought we would need an expert, someone with experience in handling wolves, so when Laurie offered to fly out with Akai and stay with us for three days, we were thrilled. In August 1991, the project was fully under way.

Meanwhile, I was frantically devouring every piece of

literature on wolf behavior and socialization I could find. Dr. Erich Klinghammer of the Wolf Park Institute of Ethology in Indiana had established techniques for raising wolves in captivity. He sent me his manual, *The Management and Socialization of Captive Wolves,* probably the definitive work on the subject. While Akai was on his way from Minnesota and plans were already laid to bring Makuyi to Idaho, I went to the post office and picked up Klinghammer's manual, casually leafing through it as I waited in line to claim another package. As I absentmindedly skimmed paragraphs on the raising, feeding, and handling of wolves, my eye fell on the following passage:

Although rare, confrontations with a particular wolf can occur. In that case, once grabbed, most people have a tendency to pull in the opposite direction in which the wolf is pulling. This natural reaction is nevertheless wrong because it merely results in more tearing of skin and muscles . . . one should follow the wolf, who has a tendency to shake the head or yank. This reduces the strain, throws it off balance, and will sooner or later cause it to let go to get a better grip. Watch for this, and then quickly pull back AND STAND PERFECTLY STILL, AND AVERT YOUR GAZE. Now is the time for one of two maneuvers if one has no weapon of any kind. The first is to make a fist and shove it down the wolf's throat as deep as possible; then grab its windpipe with the other hand and choke the wolf. We have a policy that no one goes into the wolf enclosure alone. There should always be at least two, if not more, experienced handlers for backup. . . .

"My God," I thought, "what am I getting myself into?" In one glance I had gone from making a film about the social life of an intelligent animal to fending off a savage beast who has decided that tearing my arm off would be a good way to exhibit a touch of dominance.

Despite the initial terror that it produced, I could see the ultimate sense in Dr. Klinghammer's methods. His approach took into account the innate sensitivity and intelligence of the wolf. I was nevertheless disappointed at the amount of socializing and strict control of the animals that he considered necessary. I was concerned that too much manipulation would jeopardize the very qualities that I wanted to film. The last thing I wanted to do was turn the wolves into tame animals.

Next, I met with Dr. Erik Zimmen, a wolf expert and manager of his own laboratory and pack in Bavaria. Dr. Zimmen's approach involved less handling than Klinghammer's, but he still maintained that I would need to bond the wolves to me in order for the project to work. Trust, he said, was the most important ingredient in a safe and healthy pack, and this trust could only be achieved by living with the wolves as a social partner. I had hoped that, as in my work with the cougar, I could simply leave these animals alone and they would reveal all their secrets to me. Now it appeared that I would have to be involved in their lives more than I ever anticipated. Every expert I spoke to said or implied the same thing: these wolves must trust me absolutely or my work would be impossible.

With Akai and Makuyi safely in the enclosure, I returned my attentions to another matter. We had four tiny wolf pups to raise, who, together with the adults, would form the pack. My staff and I hand-raised the puppy pack all summer long, first at my home in Ketchum, about an hour south of Stanley, then in a separate fenced-off area near the main enclosure. Initially I wanted to introduce them to Akai and Makuyi within a few weeks, allowing the pair to raise the adopted family in a natural setting. I had learned that adult wolves will care for young pups even if the pups are not their own. After listening to the advice of Karin Rundquist, Erik Zimmen, and others, however, it now seemed that I would have to raise the pups myself for the first fourteen weeks. Adult wolves, even if they themselves were socialized to human beings, would teach very young pups to fear us. These wolves would eventually need to be around a film crew and caretakers, and they would need to be given shots required by state and federal regulations. I could not afford to risk any fear between wolves and staff. So, despite my original desire not to intervene in their upbringing, I decided to hand-rear the pups.

There were four in all, ten days old, with eyes newly opened. Two of my staff, Karen McCall and Janet Kellam, thought up the idea of giving the pups Native American names. Given the frequent presence of the wolf in the mythology of many Native American cultures, and the realization that both were original inhabitants of this continent who had suffered greatly after the arrival of Europeans, the idea seemed fitting. Karen and Janet pored over dictionaries of the Blackfoot and Lakota Sioux languages and came up with names that not only sounded beautiful but gave the wolves a suitable air of dignity and mystery. Of course, we never made any attempt to teach the wolves their names; we used them only among ourselves as a means to tell them apart.

The two males, nearly identical, with typical gray and black markings, were named Kamots, the Blackfoot word for freedom, and Lakota, the Lakota Sioux word for friend. Their sister was coal black in color with a skittish and vocal personality. We named her Aipuyi, the Blackfoot term for "one who speaks a lot." The last pup was a mysterious and shy female with a coat of black and brown. We gave her the name Motaki, the Blackfoot word for shadow.

In my Ketchum home, the pups began their lives in a small pen in the mud room and later, as spring turned to summer, in a fenced-in area behind the house. I have always made an effort to keep my property as wild as possible. A spring-fed creek widens to a pond a few yards behind the house, forming a little ecosystem unto itself. Under the cover of tall native grass, it attracts an incredible array of animals. Deer browse the banks and foxes hunt for mice among the willows. Wood ducks, goldeneyes, and mallards arrive every year to spend the summer on the pond. They are watched from above by a pair of red-tailed hawks that have nested in the same tree for ten years. I keep a suet feeder stocked for a family of piliated woodpeckers, and every once in a while, a black bear strolls in at night to tear the whole thing down. Now added to this mini-wilderness were four gray wolf pups.

The presence of the pups turned my home into a round-the-clock nursery, and the resulting chaos soon enveloped my children and a small collection of friends who turned up day or night to help feed and clean the irresistible little balls of fur. As caretakers, my small crew and I had to imitate everything a mother wolf would do. This went way beyond nursing. A mother wolf is constantly grooming and attending to her young. We simulated a mother's care as best we could with warm damp rags to imitate her tongue, laps and blankets to replace her cozy fur. Young wolf pups have to be fed a modified canine puppy formula every four to six hours. The crew began to work in shifts so that there would be someone with the puppies at all times. After finishing their meal, the pups, well fed and warm, would fall asleep in our laps.

It was during these moments, I believe, that the real connection took place, when the young wolves really began to trust us and form a relationship that went beyond simply accepting our presence. They bonded with us and, as practical and scientific as we tried to be, we bonded with them.

Wolf Camp

JIM

My career began underwater, but it evolved onto land. Before turning to cougars and wolves, I spent many years documenting the coral reefs around Florida and the Caribbean. From my very first dive, at the age of eight, I was enthralled by the mysterious and strange undersea world. My earliest films were really an attempt to bring an audience into this foreign realm and show them something they might not otherwise see. In the creation of every film I have made since, whether on land or under the sea, this has remained my goal.

A major change in my career occurred during the filming of my first full-length documentary, titled *Water, Birth, the Planet Earth*. The story was about the evolution of life and its immutable connection to water. Like the first amphibious pioneers that ventured out of the sea, the film starts in the ocean, then surfaces and works its way up the rivers and streams to finally stand on firm ground. Thus in one film, my subjects evolved from aquatic animals to terrestrial ones, and my career followed suit. For my next project, I decided to explore the mountains that I had learned to love as a teenage wrangler. So far, I haven't returned to the sea.

My next project was to produce a film about a mammal, one common to the Rocky Mountains, that lives both a terrestrial and an aquatic life. My intentions in making *A Rocky Mountain Beaver Pond* were the same ones behind my underwater films: to show the hidden world of an animal, one that is famously difficult to observe.

Beavers are secretive animals, spending much of their time either underwater or inside a fortified lodge constructed of logs and hardened mud, venturing onto land to chew down trees, often under cover of darkness. I wanted to make a film in which I would reveal their private world, but how could I do so without tearing apart a beaver lodge and scaring them out of their pond and halfway across the state? The answer to this problem became the technique that I would use in all my future films.

Today our production office is a cozy little log cabin next to my home in Ketchum, but it was not always this way. Once it stood in a rough and unfinished state, populated by dragonfly larvae, salamanders, chipmunks, and, most importantly, a pair of beavers. The cabin was fitted with huge terrariums, aquariums, and tables for macrophotography, but the centerpiece was a large beaver den that could be gently opened on two sides for filming. The den, which was fabricated of real beaver-cut wood and mud-colored concrete, was connected by means of a tunnel through the cabin wall to an outside swimming and feeding area.

Inside the den lived a pair of beavers that I had purchased from a fur farm. They accepted the presence of people and lights as just another part of their world, carrying on as they would if we were not there at all. They just beavered away, eating leaves and bark from the branches we placed in their swimming area. To create a seamless portrait of a beaver's life, I also filmed a pair of wild beavers in a pond near my home, and cut the wild and captive footage together. In late winter the captive pair mated. After we spent an exhausting thirty days of observation, the female finally gave birth, and we were there to film it. It was a sequence never before seen on television and one that would have been completely impossible to film in the animal's natural habitat.

I took this technique to the next level with the filming of *Cougar: Ghost of the Rockies* for ABC/Kane television. Cougars are seldom seen in the wild, hardly enough to make a film about them. The project was primarily a study of a mother's care of her cubs: innate versus learned behavior and the vocalizations of a generally silent animal. Again, the chance to peer into the animal's private life was what made the film successful.

The wolf project was to be much more ambitious, allowing for year-round living and constant filming. I needed to find the perfect spot. I needed a location that was accessible to an equipment truck—to ferry in and out the fence materials—but remote enough that strangers could not easily find it. I needed a place that was picturesque and had a variety of vegetation and topography in which to film. For the wolves, it needed to have a good balance of sunlight and shade and a consistent water source that wouldn't dry up in the summer.

I had little idea just how hard it would be to find the right place. Starting in October of 1990, Janet Kellam and I made seventeen trips into the backcountry of central Idaho, either by four-wheel-drive, on foot, or by snowmobile. We looked into all the surrounding mountain ranges: the Pioneers, the Boulder/White Clouds, and the Sawtooths.

A month into our search, we began to investigate the Sawtooth National Recreation Area. Jed Gray, a native of Ketchum who had spent his life exploring the backcountry, was our guide for these excursions. Jed knew every inch of the land, and the people who lived nearby. He knew the local politics and how probable it was that I would be allowed to set up my project in a given area. It was Jed who had found the location for my cougar camp and, true to form, he tipped us off to a place called Meadow Creek, a pretty little clearing in the forest a short distance away from two large ranches. One morning in early October, we set off for the Sawtooth Mountains.

The trip to Meadow Creek was decidedly uninspiring. The jeep trail wound across ranchlands through dull fields of sage. Although the mountains formed a majestic backdrop, the land itself was flat and dry. We parked the truck where the dirt track ended and walked toward the mountains. As the elevation began to rise slightly, the landscape started to change. The ground was suddenly interlaced with tiny streams; sage gave way to willow and grass.

After a short hike, we found ourselves standing in the middle of a wide, grassy meadow. To one side ran a mountain brook, to another was a grove of aspen. In front of us was a deep forest of lodgepole pine and spruce, out of which soared the gray walls of the Sawtooths. It was absolutely perfect. Of course there was a lot more to finding the right spot than planting a flag in the ground and declaring, "This is it." Next came trips on snowmobiles and snowshoes, to see how passable the trail would be in winter, and another trip in the spring to see if the marshy areas flooded. After nearly a year of thorough investigation, we were finally convinced that we had found the perfect setting.

Not only did Jed find the location, he went to bat on my behalf with the neighboring landowners, putting together an agreement that enabled me to cross their land freely to access the site. In May of 1991, the U.S. Forest Service issued me a permit to set up a camp and enclosure in Meadow Creek. With the cougar project, I had earned a valuable reputation for taking care of the land. The Forest Service planned to use the new wolf enclosure as a showcase project demonstrating nonconsumptive use of public lands.

In May, I marked off approximately 25 acres, trying to encompass a wide variety of terrain and vegetation. For another month, the area remained too wet to do any construction—a four-wheel-drive vehicle would have cut deep scars into the soft ground—but by June it was dry enough to start erecting the fence.

In hindsight, I sometimes have to laugh at how secretive we were about the whole thing. For example, we contracted a company from Montana to erect the fence because we didn't want local residents to know exactly where it was. My overcautiousness was mostly due to the fact that the political climate was—and still is—anything but friendly. To say that the ranching and hunting communities of Idaho had a certain dislike and fear of the wolf would be a grave understatement. At this time, the U.S. government was just beginning the process of selecting regions in which to reintroduce wolves. One of the areas they had chosen was the Frank Church River of No Return Wilderness, which lay just to the north. Many local ranchers and hunters pledged to adopt a policy of "shoot, shovel, and shut up" if they ever came across a wolf. A captive pack, nestled in the Sawtooth Mountains, was seen by many as a political tool to gain sympathy for a loathsome predator.

Mike Jimenez, a U.S. Fish and Wildlife biologist, acted as one of our consultants. He warned us of how easy it would be for someone to shoot through the fence, or, even more likely, to throw strychnine-laced meat into the enclosure. Mike himself had watched helplessly as a pack of Canadian wolves he was researching were mysteriously poisoned, so he was justifiably concerned. The last thing I wanted was for my project to become ground zero in a war between hunters, ranchers, biologists, and environmentalists.

It wasn't just the wolf-haters who concerned us, but the wolf-lovers as well. I feared that people might get wind of "friendly" wolves in the Sawtooths and hike in to commune with the pack. Although I loved the idea of an educational visitor center, I was liable for any injury that happened to anyone as a result of my project, even if a foolish stranger decided to climb the fence for a one-on-one visit. In the agreement that Jed Gray had worked out with the ranchers whose land bordered my project, I had promised to be as unobtrusive as possible, keeping traffic on their dirt road to a minimum.

Most importantly, I wanted to create an atmosphere in which the wolves would be as relaxed and natural as possible. An unwanted visitor, whether friend or foe, would distract the wolves and make them run to investigate, or run away in fear. Either way, it would alter the wolves' behavior and perhaps jeopardize their trust in me.

I looked into many possible security options, but on the edge of wilderness with only the electricity produced by a few solar panels, what kind of security could we have? Ultimately our best protection was the area itself. The only way to reach Meadow Creek from the main road with any type of vehicle was over a gated jeep trail that passed through private land.

Despite the stereotype of ranchers at war with wolves, the three ranchers whose land I had to cross to get to Meadow Creek were intrigued by my work. One of them actually agreed to be interviewed on camera and expressed, if not enthusiasm for the wolf's return, at least a willingness to accept a few of these predators in the wild and at my camp. If I achieve one thing through my projects, I hope to create a bridge between ranchers and wolves. I have always had great respect for ranching and its heritage in this country. After all, it was a ranch that brought me west in the first place. When we imagine the Western landscape, with its dramatic vistas and wide open spaces, we often forget the debt we owe to ranching, for ranches often protect the land from rampant development. I would not be a wolf advocate if I didn't believe that there was room in the West for both wolves and ranchers.

Nevertheless, I understand that not everyone feels this way. Thus, I was hardly surprised when the hate mail and threatening phone messages began to arrive. It was nothing new. I had been receiving threats of bodily harm as a result of my work with cougars. *Cougar: Ghost of the Rockies* contained a sequence of a mountain lion hunt that painted cougar hunters and outfitters in a less than favorable light. I hadn't resorted to any editorial trickery; I'd just turned the camera and microphone on the hunters and let them do the rest. The outfitter's team of radio-collared dogs tracks and trees the big cat, holding it at bay until the paying hunter, following the radio signal, can catch up on an all-terrain vehicle. Arriving upon the terrified and exhausted cougar, the hunter shoots the animal with a .45-caliber pistol at point-blank range.

My personal opinion about this type of hunting was something I chose not to belabor in the film, but it came across loud and clear all the same. One indirect result was that organizations hoping to ban cougar hunting in California, Oregon, and Washington began using clips from the film in their campaigns. Many of these campaigns were successful and, at least in California, dog-assisted cougar hunting was outlawed. The community of hunters in the West would never forgive me for that. When a cougar hunter leaves a threatening message on your answering machine, it is pretty hard to brush off, especially when you know the guy carries a gun.

The Idaho Department of Fish and Game has a historically strong partnership with hunters and was understandably less than enthusiastic about issuing me a permit to keep wolves. After all, by allowing me to keep a captive cougar they had facilitated the making of a film that had made hunters look barbaric, resulting in some strained relations between the department and powerful hunting groups. At the same time, environmentalists criticize Fish and Game for allowing such a brutal form of hunting in the state. The department had taken heat from both sides of the issue and wasn't keen on repeating the process. Some department heads swore that my days of producing films in Idaho were over.

The Fish and Game offices are located in Boise in a cold cinder block building. In an effort to add some gaiety to the sterile environment, they have decorated the halls and offices with the stuffed heads and bodies of almost every Rocky Mountain animal imaginable. The centerpiece of the building is aptly called the "trophy room." At the start of the wolf project, I found myself in this room, pleading my case for a permit to keep captive wolves.

At a large folding table, five stone-faced Fish and Game commissioners sat beneath the mounted heads of some of Idaho's principal game mammals: mule deer, mountain goat, moose, bighorn sheep, and pronghorn antelope. Humorously, from where I sat in the conference room, each commissioner had a corresponding animal head directly above his own, complete with a name tag emblazoned on the wall. My gaze kept shifting between the faces of man and beast. Despite my best efforts to ignore this distracting coincidence, each bureaucrat began to take on the countenance and mannerisms of the animal above him.

Moose, the largest and most aggressive official, said, "We've been looking into your past, Dutcher." He was concerned about the pair of cougar cubs, born to the adult female in *Cougar: Ghost of the Rockies,* that Dr. Maurice Hornocker and I had released into the wild. He believed that Idaho Fish and Game had not approved the release, which, of course, they hadn't. Dr. Hornocker captures and releases cougars under a research permit. It is part of his job.

Goat was more upset with the cougar-hunting controversy. He suggested that I had purposefully filmed the shadiest, most unscrupulous outfitters and hunters in Idaho and demanded to know how I had found them. My answer was that I had simply called Idaho Fish and Game and requested the names of local outfitters. This bit of information was hard for even a goat to swallow.

Mule Deer was concerned (as a mule deer ought to be) about what would happen if the wolves escaped. Who would be held responsible, and how would that person be punished, if the beasts killed a deer. Licensed hunters in

Idaho are very proprietary about their deer. They wouldn't stand for a rogue wolf killing a deer that was intended for their crosshairs. He insisted that the wolves be tattooed with an identification number and that I be held personally responsible for any havoc they might cause.

I was actually surprised that they issued me a permit. I think they did because, ultimately, they couldn't find a valid reason not to. In a state that allows just about every exotic animal to be kept as a pet, there could be no grounds for prohibiting me from keeping wolves for a film and research project. My care of the animals had always been exemplary; rather, it was the subject matter of my films that irked them. And everyone in the room understood that trying to silence a filmmaker simply because his films were irritating would have been censorship, pure and simple.

With permits secured from the U.S. Forest Service and Idaho Fish and Game, I was free to start building the enclosure. When the land dried out in the summer of 1991, a large flatbed truck sputtered up the dirt trail. As roll after roll of chain link was unloaded and stacked in the grass, it became clear to me just how huge this undertaking was going to be.

Fence construction was an exercise in paranoia and could be intensely maddening. Everytime I looked at the fence, I kept imagining something going over it, under it, or through it. As I had on many projects before, I enlisted the help of my good friend Jake Provonsha, a carpenter and designer. Not only was Jake able to conceive and build just about anything, but he was an excellent sounding board for filmmaking ideas. His attention to detail was invaluable. For my film on beavers, Jake designed and constructed the elaborate beaver den that enabled us to film the mother beaver giving birth. Later, as my production manager, he helped me design and build the camp for *Cougar: Ghost of the Rockies*. I knew that with his expertise I could create the safest, most inconspicuous enclosure possible.

The first thing we had to decide was how high to make the fence. It was not unusual for the area to amass five or six feet of snow during the winter. In the early spring, the surface of the snow melts and then refreezes, making it crusty and firm. A wolf, with its huge wide paws, can easily stand on the surface. Particularly hard snow could provide enough resistance for a wolf to make a good jump. In the warm months, the ten-foot fence looked like overkill, but in the winter, with five feet of snow on the ground, we were glad to have it. Sometimes I wished for even more.

At each entrance, we constructed a small double-gated section that jutted into the enclosure, like an airlock on a spaceship. By closing the first gate before opening the second, we eliminated the chance of ever having an open passage to the outside. Unfortunately, in solving one problem we created a second. These sections formed a number of right angles in the fencing. We suspected that, if a wolf wanted to, it could brace itself against the opposing walls and climb the fence, so we immediately had to construct overhangs to fortify the corners. This in turn created yet another problem, as the first winter found us having to sweep snow off the overhangs to keep them from buckling under the weight. It was a pure case of "learn as you go."

Far more than its climbing ability, the wolf's reputation as a digger concerned us. Along the bottom of the fence line, we attached an extra section of chain link that curved into a six-foot horizontal apron extending inside the enclosure. If a wolf were to try to dig under the fence, it would have to excavate a six-foot-long tunnel under the apron—an exceptional feat of engineering, even for an animal as smart as a wolf.

Where any two pieces of fence met, an overlapping seam was created. An enterprising wolf could possibly pry open a hole at one of these spots. To eliminate any possible chink, we clamped a total of 32,000 "hog wires" along these seams by hand, one by one.

At the section of the enclosure nearest the camp, we built a large "lock-off" that could comfortably accommodate all the wolves at the same time. If we ever needed to repair the fence or remove one of the wolves for medical reasons, the pack could be held in this area for a short time. All our second-guessing paid off. In the end, we had built the largest enclosure ever constructed for a wolf pack. It included every example of terrain and vegetation that Meadow Creek had to offer. We must have done something right, for later the design was employed in Yellowstone as the basis for "soft release" enclosures, where reintroduced wolves could acclimatize to a new area.

Ultimately, we found that the wolves never demonstrated any desire to leave. They never paced along the fence line or tried to break through the barrier. They accepted it as their home, and with so much space in which to roam, they always had a selection of places to explore. There were vast sections of their territory where they didn't spend much time at all. They practically ignored the deeper lodgepole forest and much of the swampy willow area, preferring to spend most of their time in the grassy meadow, the aspen grove, or by the pond. Even so, with my signature on countless government permits, and with a less than friendly political climate, I was happy to have so much security.

After the fence was up, it was time to begin work on the finer points of the camp. It was a huge leap in complexity from the cougar project. The wolf enclosure was five times larger, and although we spent a considerable amount of time with the cougar, we did not actually live there in every season. The new camp would be bigger, so as to accommodate more supplies and year-round living.

The most wonderful aspect of creating the camp was that everyone involved added a little bit of knowledge and experience to the design. I based the overall plan on the safari camps I had seen in Africa. Jake brought years of technical drawing and building experience working with natural materials. Janet Kellam, who in addition to being my associate producer was also an accomplished mountain guide and avalanche expert, taught us techniques of cold weather survival and introduced us to a type of tent called a yurt. This wonderful lodging has its origins among the nomadic tribes of Mongolia. It is round, about sixteen feet in diameter, and designed with a strong conical roof that could withstand the weight of several feet of snow. At the time, none of us had ever heard of such a thing, but we found it to be perfectly suited to the cold weather and heavy snowfall of the Idaho mountains. This one structure served as storage, lodging for extra crew, and as our winter kitchen and dining room.

Three tents for sleeping were scattered some distance apart for the sake of privacy. Each of these was supported by a wooden frame to withstand the heavy snow. Jake's idea was to place the tents and yurt on eight-inch raised platforms to reduce the impact on the land. The platforms allowed melting snow to run underneath the tents in the springtime and kept them above the frozen ground in the winter. A small woodstove stood in the middle of each tent, furnished with firewood from dead trees.

Near the yurt, we set up a large cook tent where Jake's wife, Patty, became the designated chef, specializing in what we called "haute-yurt" cuisine. The cook tent was the center of life during the warmer months. It was a large, airy, and wonderful place to spend a summer evening after filming, but when the weather got cold we dismantled it and transferred the essential elements to the smaller and sturdier yurt.

Throughout the project's six years, we continued to

make improvements and changes to the camp. Whenever we faced a problem that no one had experienced before, we improvised. Jake especially enjoyed inventing new and ingenious ways to provide creature comforts using the barest of essentials. I remember one morning he emerged from his tent looking bleary-eyed and bent over after a night sleeping on a foam pad on the tent floor. He rubbed his neck and said, "You know, I would have less trouble getting up if up weren't so far." By the end of the day, he had raised our sleeping mats eighteen inches off the floors, turning them into proper beds with storage space underneath. Eventually he added a dining table, cabinets, and writing desks. We rigged a funky shower tent with a lodgepole frame and canvas screen and hung solar-heated bags of water over a wooden grate. Jake even constructed a basin stand out of willow boughs for washing and shaving.

Patty was an accomplished warrior at garage sales and thrift shops and soon had the camp outfitted with colorful tablecloths, candlesticks fashioned from antique spools, metal dishes, old railroad lanterns, and all sorts of functional items. Everything she brought was rustic and whimsical, recycled or reworked to fit our needs. Of course not everything was an absolute necessity, but with her touch, camp began to take on a personality and spirit of fun.

Wolf camp eventually became so cozy that we received criticism for it, usually from young hard-core campers who sometimes worked with us as interns and were disappointed that we weren't "roughing it" more. It is a rather American concept, I think, that living out in nature loses its purity if one is not constantly picking bugs out of one's food, suffering from back pain, or caked in enough dirt to start an herb garden. Is it not as great an achievement to set up a comfortable existence from limited means?

I have traveled to Africa often and lived in many mobile camps there. In each one, I have marveled at the comforts they are able to provide with a little ingenuity and imagination. Nature in Africa presents many more dangers and discomforts than it does in North America—when you find an eight-foot black mamba in your tent, you know you're roughing it. The attention that African safari camps pay to safety and comfort comes across not as excess or luxury but as a celebration of life.

Our means at wolf camp were decidedly limited. Our heat came from firewood, our bathwater came from the creek or melted snow, and our light and cooking flame came from candles and propane. The luxuries we enjoyed came as a result of effort and inspiration: a table where the crew could eat together, a shower that made working in close quarters a great deal more pleasant, and comfortable beds—probably the most important thing of all when faced with a hard day of work ahead. What's more, a few added pounds in the pack or on the snowmobile from time to time meant real ground coffee, wine, and fresh produce. After spending three or four consecutive weeks at camp, such things certainly made a difference in morale. For a little extra labor at the outset, we created a pleasant environment for people as well as wolves.

Many years later, a sequence in *Wolves at Our Door* dared to show a bottle of wine in a scene. Some people were against including that shot because they thought it implied that we lived in too much luxury. I decided to keep the sequence in the film because I thought it depicted our lives truthfully. Afterward, I saw Jean-Michel Cousteau at the Emmy Awards ceremony and playfully asked him how he and his crew managed to be shown so frequently drinking wine on the *Calypso* without taking flack from editors and critics. His reply was, "We are French, of course."

Critics aside, I am very proud of the resourcefulness and ingenuity that went into the construction of our little camp. Every tool, every spare part, every blanket had its proper place, and operations were streamlined and practical; but where there was room for a dash of fun or a small human touch, we allowed our imaginations to go to work.

Above all, this was a film production that had some very practical needs. I required a clean space for working with precision equipment. I also knew that sometimes I would need to invite citified guests to spend the night there. Television executives or political figures who have the power to help the cause of wolves are not always accustomed to camping out in the mountains. Lastly, I envisioned an environment that was conducive to thinking creatively, a well-organized space that left the mind free to concentrate on the work at hand. In the end we achieved all these things, and everyone who passed any length of time in camp left some stamp of his or her personality there. What could have been a dreary collection of tents became a very special place, and my home for the better part of six years.

Jamie

JIM

The lush highlands of Kenya faded from view as the plane rose above Nairobi. My 16-year-old son, Garrick, and I were beginning the long trip back to the States from Africa.

We had been visiting my sister, Kathy, who operated a tented camp in a remote area of the Masai Mara. Her camp, providing a base from which she and her husband photographed and documented animal behavior, would later become the inspiration for my tented camp in the Sawtooth Mountains. But in this, the spring of 1987, I was not thinking of camps or of wolves. I was struggling to finish editing *A Rocky Mountain Beaver Pond* for National Geographic, my first commissioned film. Even more, I was struggling with the breakup of my marriage, my second, which had left me disillusioned and doubtful.

This trip would take me to Washington, D.C., where I would meet with Dennis Kane, then the head of National Geographic Television, before heading back home to

Idaho. I was relieved to have work in which to immerse myself, to keep my mind off my personal life. But first I would have to endure the endless flight from Nairobi and a tedious layover in London with little to do but think.

I sat in a sterile lounge in London's Heathrow Airport, waiting to be herded on to the next leg of the flight. Garrick managed to fall asleep in the torturous airport chairs and left me alone with my thoughts. I was too tired to read and too agitated to sleep, so I just sat and watched the people milling about and passing the time like me. One of the things that huge international airports do is bring together the most diverse and entertaining assortment of people imaginable. As the time ticked away, I watched them come and go: European students sitting on their backpacks, wealthy Arab businessmen standing in line behind an American family juggling children, soft drinks, and too much carry-on luggage.

I then noticed a woman, who looked to be in her mid-twenties, sitting quietly with a girlfriend a few yards away. She was dressed in Western clothing but somehow seemed very exotic with jet-black hair and dark eyes. A distinctive African beaded necklace shone against her deeply tanned skin. When her companion spoke to her, she smiled a broad, bright, wide-open smile.

Looking at her jewelry, I thought she must be returning to the States from Kenya and wondered what she had been doing there. I even toyed with the idea of walking over and talking to this stranger and began thinking up conversation starters like a teenager. It had been years since I had done such a thing and the mere thought of it brought waves of doubt. A moment later my flight was called, relieving me of the burden of a decision.

I boarded the plane and began placing my bags in the overhead, allowing myself to daydream about what we would have talked about and what she would have been like. When I looked up again, she was coming down the aisle toward me, a backpack thrown over one shoulder. I was so surprised at seeing her that I didn't have the chance to talk myself out of speaking up.

"Have you been in Africa?" I said. It was all I could think of.

"Yes, what gave it away?" Her response was tinged with good-natured sarcasm. Yes, she was American.

I mentioned her necklace and started to ask where she had been and what she had seen, but the queue was piling up behind her and she hurried along, leaving me with that same brilliant smile I had seen at the gate, and that was it.

I spent the first few hours of the flight trying to think of a way to resume our conversation. I began making little deals in my mind either to force myself into action or resign myself to the fact that fate was against me. I finally decided on a rule: If she was sitting in an aisle seat, I'd go back and speak to her again; if she was deeper within a row, I'd let it be. I turned around to survey the seats behind me, and sure enough, there she was, many rows back, sitting on the aisle. A deal was a deal, so back I went, not even bothering to think up an excuse.

She had been in Zimbabwe with her friend, visiting the country, touring the national parks and looking for wildlife. I told her about my sister's camp and the thrilling time I had spent photographing cheetahs as they hunted gazelles on the savanna. She was an amateur photographer as well and passionate about animals. This trip had been like a dream for her—a once-in-a-lifetime opportunity to see and photograph wildlife in a place she had only previously been able to imagine.

The longer I spoke to her, the more intrigued I became with our common interests. However, making small talk in a narrow aisle in front of three hundred people isn't the easiest thing to do, so, before overstaying my welcome, I returned to my seat, suddenly wishing we were on a slow-moving ocean liner instead of on a 747.

Sadder still, in the bustle of passengers pressing to get off the plane, she vanished. I looked for her in the shuttle, that plodding people-mover known to all who pass through Dulles Airport, but still she was nowhere to be seen. In desperation I made yet another deal with myself, swearing that if I saw her again I would go out on a limb and ask if I could contact her the next time I was in D.C. No sooner had I finished my private oath than she suddenly appeared at baggage claim, standing next to me. Fate, it seemed, was not going to let me off the hook.

Our conversation resumed easily, as if bumping into each other several times between Nairobi and Washington, D.C., was the most natural thing in the world. I began talking about my films and my current project on beavers. She confessed that she had always had a similar interest in wildlife. In fact, she was at that moment applying for a position at Washington's National Zoo, where she hoped to care for sick and injured animals in the hospital.

Finally I summoned my courage and told her that I would be back in town two weeks later and asked if I could give her a call. To my surprise, she gave me her number.

That spring and summer of 1987, I flew to Washington every month to meet with Dennis Kane and finish the beaver film. Each time I visited, Jamie and I met for dinner. Our conversations were lively and engaging, but I always felt that something was holding me back. I was still suffering from the sting of my recently failed marriage and was certain that I was not interested in trying that again. There was the issue of my two children and the age difference between Jamie and me. There was also Jamie's established East Coast life and her hopes for work at the National Zoo.

We never spoke about these things, not wanting to spoil the brief moments we had together. Still their shadows filled the pauses in our conversation and hung on our greetings and goodbyes—an intangible, indefinable feeling, like hopelessness.

One night in July, as I prepared to return to Idaho, Jamie suddenly turned tearful. She had always acted with the carefully maintained casualness that had been the rule of our relationship, but this time something was different, as though there was a desire to somehow express what we had chosen never to express before. Yet at the same time, I sensed a growing distance between us. Her farewell had the unspoken but unquestionable air of finality. Instead of goodbye, I repeated the first words I had ever said to her, "Have you been in Africa?" Jamie smiled sadly, understanding the sentiment.

Fate had plotted so carefully to bring us together that it seemed completely wrong to end up parting, but as I watched her car disappear that night, I was struck with an overwhelming hollowness, like I had just seen her for the last time.

I suppose, then, that it did not come as a surprise to me when Jamie called at the end of summer to say that she had become engaged. I listened to her words from two thousand miles away with the detachment of a condemned man. Every cell of my being told me that it was wrong, that I should say something—anything—to make her stop. But the pain of two failed marriages, the doubt, the uncertainty of it all seized my tongue and I said nothing.

Trust

JIM

As the pups Kamots, Lakota, Aipuyi, and Motaki grew throughout the summer of 1991, they began to take a real interest in their world. Their boundless energy required constant observation; not a minute would go by when they were not climbing, running, leaping, or chewing on something. Every new object held fascination for them, and the way they satisfied their curiosity was to chew on anything they could get a hold on. Shoes, watches, cameras, fingers, sizable clumps of hair, all were sacrificed at one time or another to the insatiable curiosity of the puppies. Even though I was well aware of the growth rate of young wolves, it was astounding to see just how fast they grew and how strong they became in a matter of weeks.

Wolf pups put on an average of three pounds a week for the first three months of their lives. In the wild, it is imperative that a young wolf achieve substantial size and strength by winter, otherwise it would not be able to keep up with the rest of the pack in deep snow. Although their soft puppy fur, curious demeanor, and unmistakable youthful countenances, give them away as juveniles for another year or more, they are nearly as large as the senior members of the pack after a mere six months.

By July of 1991, Kamots and the three other pups were like twenty-pound tempests with teeth. They were still living in a separate fenced area at camp while the adults, Akai and Makuyi, were acclimating to the main enclosure. Now it was time for the next stage of the project, to bring the pack together.

The slightest mention of the word "captivity" is distasteful for many people. However, audiences seldom realize that many of the animals they see in wildlife films are indeed captive. As I see it, this is perfectly fine as long as the film presents sound information. Often the only way to depict what happens in the wild is to enlist the help of nonwild animals. For example, a film may portray a bear digging up a rodent hole, then cut to the interior of the burrow as the rodent evades the bear paw threatening from above. The first shot in the sequence may be a real wild bear digging in the ground. The next shot, however, is a re-creation, a setup, perhaps filmed many miles away and many months after the wild bear was filmed digging in the ground. Because the burrow set is so well constructed, people often fail to understand that they are watching a mix of both wild and captive footage. In most cases these setups are done very sensitively and accurately. They are exceedingly valuable in helping the audience get a clear picture of the interaction between bear and rodent, while keeping the harassment of wild animals to a minimum. They also have the added benefit of assuring that the cameraman does not end up getting mauled by an angry bear.

In recent years, television audiences have become more sophisticated and more demanding. When there are a hundred channels to choose from, a shaky, distant image of a wild animal is no longer going to hold a viewer's attention. Audiences want to see seamless editing, better photography, and more interaction. The problem arises when these demands cannot be met by the pure form of wildlife filmmaking.

A thrilling scene of a cobra rearing up before the lens does not happen by chance. It is not the result of a cameraman haplessly stepping on one of the world's deadliest snakes and having the presence of mind to start filming instead of falling over backward in terror. Snakes, like wolves and most other animals, prefer to hide from people. A captive snake is therefore put in a natural-looking enclosure and given time to relax and acclimatize, then its behavior is recorded. Granted, this is a very basic example. A snake's behavior is more instinctive and less complex than that of large mammals, but the general idea is similar. I simply brought it to a much larger scale with beavers, cougars, and wolves.

The film I produced about beavers showed the animals harvesting food, building dams, even giving birth. Wildlife filmmakers may have a repertoire of tracking skills, inside information from biologists, and an arsenal of special equipment, but they cannot work magic. I could capture much of this behavior in the wild, but what I could not, I had to stage.

My beaver film contains a fifteen-second sequence of the animal snipping off an aspen branch, carrying it through the water to the lodge, and delivering it to its waiting offspring. This brief slice of behavior was pieced together from footage of three different beavers in three different locations over the span of an entire season. First, I filmed a wild beaver removing the lower branches of an aspen tree at the edge of his pond. Since I could not predict which tree the beavers would try to cut down, I decided to erect my own little aspen tree in their path, hoping that the new food source would catch the beavers' attention. Each night I brought the tree home with me so they would not harvest it in the dark, and each morning I replaced the tree, set up my camera, and waited. Finally the male beaver emerged. He chewed off a branch, dragged it to the water, and disappeared under the surface. This was the truly wild part of the sequence.

For the underwater shots, I trapped a beaver near my home in Ketchum and placed it in a different pond with especially clear water. I donned my wet suit and diving gear and filmed the beaver from many angles as it swam. Its strange webbed feet expanded and contracted effortlessly in front of my lens as I paddled furiously to keep up. At the end of the day, I let the beaver go where I had found it.

The den that Jake and I had constructed, and its resident pair of beavers, provided the final shot of the segment. Outside and below the lodge-set was a metal water tank in which we placed a daily supply of aspen branches. The interior of the den had a natural-looking mud entrance adjoining this tank. Following his instinct, the male beaver collected the branches we left for him and brought them inside.

In editing, we combined these independent shots to form seamless sequences of a beaver collecting food and bringing it to its waiting family. By gathering footage in many different situations, I was able to depict an event that definitely happens in the wild but would have been impossible to film there.

When next I proposed to make a film on cougars, I was enthusiastic and willing to try just about anything to get the chance to make another documentary for National Geographic and Dennis Kane. I asked Dr. Maurice Hornocker to be a part of the project, and he told me flat out that I would have to create an enclosure to get the kind of footage I wanted. An expert on big cats, he had only seen two of these elusive creatures in the wild without the aid of tracking dogs and radio telemetry. Obviously I wanted to film a relaxed cougar behaving naturally, so having a team of dogs chase one up a tree was out of the question.

We constructed an enclosure and located a cat to film there, but I was still worried about deceiving the audience. I didn't want to lie about the fact that I was using a captive animal, yet I didn't know how to explain the necessity of the enclosure within the context of the film. I voiced these concerns to Dennis on his first visit to our cougar camp, but where I saw a negative, he saw a positive. He was amazed by the project itself and by the dedication and work that we had put into it. He thought that the "behind the scenes" story was also worth telling. It was Dennis who suggested making the animal's captivity and our camp a part of the film, and he was right. Audiences had no problem dealing with the truth; in fact, they loved that human side of the story. It was a turning point in my career. I would use this technique two more times, with *Wolf: Return of a Legend* and *Wolves at Our Door*. As it turned out, audiences found the story of living with the pack just as compelling as the story of the pack itself.

Some filmmakers who use captive animals thought I was revealing too many "trade secrets," but I believe the truth does not reduce the entertainment and educational value of the work. In fact, it enhances it. On the other hand, there are those who are against the use of captive animals altogether, seeing it as a type of fakery that drains the work of any merit. I did have one distinct advantage in my work: I generally knew where the wolves were. But I wouldn't go so far as to say that this made things that much easier. What it did was raise the bar. There would be no excuse for failing to get breathtaking images and sounds of these animals. If I wanted to make people see all the depth and complexity of wolves, breathtaking is exactly what I'd need, each and every frame.

From a scientific standpoint, some people question the validity of any animal behavior documented in captivity. What they forget is that much of what we know about the social behavior of wolves has been recorded by biologists observing captive packs, usually in enclosures a fraction of the size of the one where the Sawtooth Pack lived. Renowned wolf expert David Mech gleaned extensive knowledge of wolf behavior from a captive colony of wolves. In *Wolves of the High Arctic,* he states, "If a person comes near their den, the wolves may move right out. If a wolf smells or hears or otherwise detects a human, it immediately runs away, before a human ever gets a chance to see it. . . . Putting radio collars on them and studying their movements via radio signal was the only way I could observe wolves up close anywhere . . . in the world, except by raising them in captivity and studying them in enclosures" (Knight, p. 15).

The fundamental problem, after all, is one of authenticity and integrity. Not all executive producers were as forward-thinking as Dennis Kane. Consequently, several years into the wolf project, I set off for Alaska's Denali National Park to gather footage of wild wolves that would augment footage of the captive pack. The great irony of that experience is that I felt far less in tune with nature in Denali than I did at my own wolf camp in the Sawtooths. For three weeks my crew and I scoured the park, by truck and on foot, looking for wolves. People often assume when they see images of a wild animal, that the cameraman has tracked the animal deep into the backcountry. In fact, the closest shots I managed to get of wild wolves were from the side of the road, where I stood with twenty other photographers next to a sputtering bus full of tourists. When I say the wolves were close, I mean that they were between fifty and a hundred yards away, which is actually very good for a wild wolf. Even so, the footage contained no interesting behavior. The wolves stopped and stared at us for a moment and then just moseyed on. It wasn't the sort of stuff that would make for an engaging film about these animals.

Every day for a week we hiked five miles over the tundra to observe a wolf den, under a special permit and accompanied by a biologist and a park ranger. We didn't want to disturb the residents, so we remained at a careful distance of half a mile away. The entrance to the den itself wasn't even visible at this distance, but we could see the wolves coming and going. We coined the term *"Canis lupus minisculus"* to describe the tiny wolf specks I was filming.

After our fifth day filming the den site, the biologist accompanying us said, "Well, you must have enough for your TV show by now." He was so enthusiastic that I didn't have the heart to tell him the truth. The distant and grainy images of wolves weighed down by huge radio collars were of absolutely no use to me. Although they were real wild wolves, nothing they did would convey the truth about real wolf behavior to a viewing audience.

The spectrum of wildlife documentary films ranges from the rigidly scientific to the unabashedly emotional. Films that are shot entirely in the wild can be extremely valuable and provide important information for scientific study. On the other hand, films that are intimate and emotional may do more to inspire conservation. Ultimately, I believe, all styles are valid, provided they honestly explain fundamental truths and serve to promote a better understanding of wildlife.

By August of 1991, the Sawtooth pups had reached the age where they had bonded sufficiently with us and were ready to be introduced to the adults. Following Dr. Zimmen's instructions, we went through the process slowly. On the first day, we brought the pups up to the fence and showed them to Akai and Makuyi.

Nothing holds more fascination for an adult wolf than a wolf pup. As I held little Kamots in my arms, Akai immediately approached the fence to inspect the stranger. In the short time I had known Akai, he had never been aggressive toward me, but I could see that protective instincts were taking hold of him. Having joined us at the age of four, he did not know me or anyone on my crew. He had not grown up with us and did not know that we could be trusted. He paced the fence, as if looking for a way to reach the pup and pull him through to safety. I was not overly concerned about this change in attitude. I was convinced that once the entire pack was together his aggression toward me would surely die down. Kamots squirmed in my arms, excited and eager to meet his new foster parents. Makuyi, though interested, held back. She seemed more bewildered than fascinated by the new faces.

As I fell asleep in my tent that night, I wondered what would happen when suddenly they were all together. I had planned and planned for this moment. Half a dozen experts had assured me that the adults would accept the new additions as their own. But there was no way to be absolutely sure.

Early the next morning, we gathered at the enclosure entrance. First, we placed the pups in the small lock-off section. Some days earlier we had reinforced the chain link with chicken wire to insure that the adults would not try to pull a pup through. In this way, all the wolves could become familiar with each other, getting used to new smells, sights, and sounds. I was relieved that Makuyi finally felt secure enough to approach the puppies, carefully sniffing each one.

My priority was to document this moment on film, so I readied my camera and stepped into the enclosure. I rolled the film and Janet swung open the gate that separated the adults from the pups. For an instant, nothing happened. Then the four pups charged into the enclosure toward Akai. To my great relief, they set upon him with licks and wagging tails, and Akai, happy to finally have the objects of his concern safely beside him, carefully looked them over, doling out copious grooming licks. The puppies recognized Akai as the dominant adult and one by one flipped over on their backs in a display of complete submission. Then, as if to show them their new home, Akai trotted off, keeping an eye on the pups, who eagerly followed behind him.

I was so thrilled to be filming this interaction between Akai and the puppies that I failed to notice Makuyi. When the gate was opened and the pups raced through, she had bolted. Now she was hiding somewhere among the willows, aspens, and pines. We did not see her for nearly three days.

I began to worry that Makuyi had somehow managed

to escape, though this was highly unlikely, given the amount of security we had built into the fence. In our search, we did find a surprisingly deep hole that she or Akai had dug not far from the fence line, but it looked less like an escape route and more like a hiding place. As I peered into the hole, half expecting to find Makuyi hiding there, Garrick spotted her crossing an upper meadow. She was alone, making no attempt to meet the newcomers. From the very beginning, the pups regarded her as a stranger.

Makuyi

JIM

Makuyi and Akai had been brought together by artificial means. When it was just the two of them living together, Makuyi actually seemed quite fond of Akai, but Akai merely tolerated her. Now with the new additions, Akai had even less patience with Makuyi. The pups regarded him as their leader and at five months old they began to chase Makuyi away from their territory. She had been such a sweet and playful wolf when I first met her in Montana. Why had she now become a frightened and solitary specter?

In the wild, a wolf's feeding schedule is dictated by the availability of food. After a kill, a wolf will gorge itself on a meal, consuming as much as thirty pounds of meat in a single feeding. The next few days are spent lounging and digesting the enormous meal before the search for food begins again. Wolves are also opportunistic, meaning that if they come across an old carcass, they will happily eat it, whether it has been ripening in the heat for many days or is frozen solid. I tried to mimic this natural pattern by bringing in road-killed deer and elk at random intervals between four and six days.

Akai and the pups, however, did not allow Makuyi to eat with them. Low-ranking members of a wolf society are commonly forced to wait until the others have finished eating, but Makuyi was not permitted to eat at all, essentially treated as a nonmember of the pack. She was far too afraid to assert herself and spent all her time at the most remote end of the enclosure, lurking in the thick evergreens and willows. Fearing that she would not get enough to eat by catching small game or scavenging what the others had left, I began smuggling chunks of deer and elk meat to her in secret. After the rest of the pack had gorged itself and was in no mood to do anything but lie around, I stuffed my backpack full of meat and hiked up the hillside, circling far away from the enclosure and entering by a different gate than usual. When I got to the clearing where I often saw her, I sat and waited, knowing that she was hiding somewhere just out of my sight, watching me, weighing her hunger and her fear. The first day she showed herself only at the fringe of a willow grove, not daring to approach the food until I left. Still, each week I persevered, determined to remain patient and gain her trust.

Something about the situation told me I needed to know more. If I could just get close enough to her I might be able to understand what was wrong. I was packing her food in on snowshoes by the time she mustered enough courage to approach me. She cautiously circled, creeping toward the hunk of venison that I had placed several feet away. I noticed a strange damp spot on her left flank and wondered if she had sat in tree sap. When she got closer, I realized it was blood. One of the other wolves had bitten her. Even scrawny and beaten, she was still a beautiful, gentle wolf. It was heartbreaking to see her in that condition. When she got to the food, she grabbed it and hauled it off into the forest as quickly as she could.

There was actually one occasion when Makuyi was able to feed on a carcass without being harassed. One of the neighboring ranchers gave us a steer that had died. However, when I brought it in for the wolves, they circled it with interest but did not attempt to eat it. I remembered Laurie Schmidt telling me that Akai never ate beef when he was under her care in Minnesota. He was unwilling to take a chance on the new food, and the younger wolves, following his lead, would not touch it either. Makuyi, on the other hand, had grown up eating everything from deer to chicken to beef. After the pack grew tired of examining the carcass and trotted off, Makuyi moved in and ate her fill.

Wolves seem reluctant to try meat they have not eaten before—or have not watched another wolf eat. I suspect that if they had been desperate and hungry, they would have been more apt to take a chance on an unfamiliar meal, but only five days since their last deer they didn't seem to feel the need to risk it. The implications of this are astounding to me. Perhaps wild packs are equally reluctant to kill a cow or sheep, unless they are desperate or had been taught to do it by another wolf.

After a day or two during which the pups and Akai had witnessed Makuyi picking at the carcass, they gave it a try. Once they discovered it was safe, the steer was gone in no time. Unfortunately this was the only time that Makuyi was well fed, and soon I was back to bringing meat to her hiding place. As the weeks progressed, I sat closer and closer to the food until one day I held a large piece in my outstretched hand. She seemed to be very dubious about this change, making several false starts toward the food, then backing off in fear. Eventually her hunger proved stronger than her fear and, in a burst, she grabbed the meat and ran for cover.

It was a breakthrough. After that moment she seemed to understand, at least to some degree, that I was a friend, and she quickly became more and more relaxed. Soon our visits no longer revolved around food. Every day I would spend time with Makuyi while the other wolves were distracted. In the blue-cold quiet of evening she would sit in front of me, a few feet away, enjoying the company of another being, even if it was not another wolf. I would talk to her softly, trying to soothe her apprehension. Once, she approached me timidly and gently licked my hand. It was heartbreaking to think that, even among her own kind, I was her only friend.

One afternoon in February, I was returning to camp after picking up food and supplies. Night comes early to the Sawtooths in winter, and the light was already fading when I parked the van in Stanley and prepared to head out on a snowmobile for camp. Still, I was sure I could beat nightfall, and the sky was crystal clear with no threat of storms. It was, however, bitterly cold, the coldest day of the winter so far, and the snowmobile refused to start. The engine oil had turned to glue in the cold, and it took all my strength just to pull the starter cable and get the flywheel to move.

After fifteen minutes of pulling, the cable snapped, sending me stumbling over backward with my own momentum. I sat in the snow, clutching the impotent pull starter and looking up at the darkening sky, trying to decide what to do next. My first thought was to hurry through Stanley in search of a repair shop that was still open, but it was too late in the day. Then I remembered that the little repair kit under the snowmobile seat was equipped with a sturdy spare cord for use in just such an emergency. I wound the cord around the flywheel and pulled. Nothing. After each pull the cord had to be rewound, ticking away another few minutes of precious daylight. On the fifth try, the wheel spun, the sparks fired, and the engine sputtered to life. For a second it chugged and faltered. I eased in the throttle and the engine hung on.

Darkness had already enveloped the camp when I finally pulled in and unloaded the cargo. I went to the fence to greet the pack, but, following our rules, I would not enter the enclosure after dark. It was too dangerous, especially with Akai's unpredictable nature, and it seemed appropriate to let night belong to the wolves.

When the pack had finished greeting me, I heard a faint sound in the distance. Makuyi had heard my approach and was howling alone in the forest, a long,

low, melancholy cry. The other wolves kept silent. They
did not even feel the need, as wolves often do, to howl
back to her. They already knew she was up there and,
since she was neither friend nor threat, they just ignored
her. She howled like this all through dinner and into the
night. There was nothing I could do but wait for morning. It broke my heart to hear her howl so.

It was impossible to comprehend the loneliness
Makuyi must have felt. The clichéd term "lone wolf" in
reality describes a situation that is merely temporary. In
the wild, a wolf may choose to separate from his or her
pack, usually for the purpose of finding a mate and starting a new pack, but it is doubtful that a wolf would ever
choose to be permanently alone. Next to human beings,
they are certainly the most social creatures in North
America. A wolf's identity is intertwined with that of the
group to such a degree that, in some ways, a solitary wolf
lacks much of what wolves are all about.

This was one of the first and in many ways the most
important lesson I learned about wolves. They are creatures that need, above all, to have a bond with each other.
It is not a mystery why the ancestors of our cherished
dogs took to domestication so well. A wolf's every
impulse tells it to be part of something larger, to have a
companion, to belong to a pack. In the relationship
between a captive wolf and a human being, this is the
deeper meaning of trust. It has very little to do with simple habituation, or bribery with food. Rather, it is a bond
that the wolf feels intensely and believes in completely. I
began to suspect that no matter how much time I spent

with Makuyi, or Akai, they would never completely trust me or bond with me. I had not raised them, nor had I been able to introduce myself to them slowly in the presence of a more trusted person. Makuyi was crying out for that bond. She desperately needed a relationship with the pack, or, if need be, with a human being, but she could have neither. The pack rejected her, and although we had achieved a level of trust, her own instinct kept her from completely bonding with me. Kamots and the other yearlings had known me from the moment they opened their eyes. Their trust was absolute and understood. I knew deep in my heart that the future of the Sawtooth Pack rested with them.

Nevertheless, months of slowly gaining Makuyi's confidence had paid off. She was at least comfortable enough with me to remain still at close range, finally allowing me to get a good look at her. I was immediately concerned with what I saw. On her rump and flanks there were an alarming number of bite wounds. I had often seen the female yearlings chasing her, but I didn't know the extent of the damage they had done. I also noticed that she had developed a routine that bordered on the obsessive. She could always be found hiding in the same few spots, and she followed her same worn trails over and over, never deviating or exploring. In moments of calm, I would frequently catch her looking up at the sky, as though searching for something. Most alarming were her eyes, the right one in particular, which was almost completely clouded over. I knew from the start that she had cataracts but they had obviously become much worse. She had been navigating by scent this whole time, following familiar trails around a familiar area. When she seemed to be gazing at the sky she was probably straining to see, perhaps through a clear spot at the bottom of her cornea. In fact, she was nearly blind.

I was at a complete loss for answers. Was there anything I could do to prevent Makuyi from succumbing to total blindness? Would correcting her vision help her integrate with the rest of the pack? I needed to talk to someone who had some medical experience with wolves. More than that, I needed to talk to a friend.

The only phone call I could think of making at that moment was the one I was most afraid of making. Jamie and I had all but lost touch since her engagement, speaking by phone only twice in two years. The last I heard from her she had fulfilled her ambition of working at the National Zoo Animal Hospital; so, despite the relative silence, our parallel careers had kept her in my thoughts. She was now caring for the same animals that were appearing in my films: beavers, big cats, and wolves, among many others. On one occasion she had given me valuable advice on administering vaccinations, mixing puppy formula, and keeping the wolves safe from domestic canine diseases. Several months later, she had called me in tears following the unexpected death of a kangaroo she had been caring for since its birth. I found myself incredibly moved by that phone call, not only because she cared so much for this animal but also because she had sought me out as someone who would understand how she felt. Now it was I who needed her understanding. I called her seeking professional advice, but more importantly I needed to hear her warm voice and her reassuring common sense.

Jamie explained how the National Zoo would stop at nothing to give the animals the best possible care. Often they relied on the outside help of specialists in veterinary or even human medicine. She knew that cataract surgery had already been performed on dogs, cats, and horses. If it was possible to correct a dog's vision, why not a wolf's? Neither Jamie nor anyone else could give a guarantee, but perhaps restoring Makuyi's eyesight would restore her confidence and the rest of the pack might finally accept her.

One of the most wonderful and terrifying aspects of being a documentary filmmaker is that I never know exactly what direction the story is going to take. During a lifetime of making documentaries, many filmmakers will at one time have to face the burden of intervention. Is it better to simply bear witness to events and document them in a truthful fashion, or are there times when it is necessary to get involved in the story and change the course of events?

I did not deliberate on the question for very long. I was not on the African plains, watching nature unfold in its own way. I had brought these wolves together and set up this enclosure. By my very creation of the project, I had already intervened. I had no choice but to try to help Makuyi regain her sight. If that was the direction the story was taking, then I would document it, wherever it went. As I became more involved in events, both emotionally and physically, I began to rely on the skill of my camera assistant, Bob Poole. He started filming me from a distance as I made my trips to the upper meadow to feed Makuyi and to try to gain her trust. It was Bob's debut as a cameraman, and as my role temporarily changed, from cinematographer to pack manager, he documented my work behind the scenes.

I had also been working with Randy Acker, a local veterinarian who provided medical supplies and advised me on the general health of the pack. Randy was a skilled vet, but a cataract operation was the domain of specialists. There was only one person he knew who had the skill and training to perform such a delicate procedure. Dr. Grant Mauer was a veterinary ophthalmologist in Portland, Oregon, who had operated on the eyes of domestic animals. He agreed to fly out to meet us and do what he could to help Makuyi.

I was a little concerned and wondered if the doctor understood what he was getting into when he sent a bottle of eyedrops with instructions to administer them to Makuyi twice a day as a preoperative procedure. This was no dog! Makuyi had only recently become comfortable enough to let me within ten feet of her. There was no way she was going to let me put something in her eyes. Drops were out of the question.

When Dr. Mauer arrived, he came with crates of medical equipment and a portable generator, transforming our little camp into something resembling an army field hospital. We didn't want to risk transporting Makuyi back to town on a snowmobile, so the only option was to set up a makeshift operating room in the yurt. With the information I had given him, Dr. Mauer concluded that it would be far less risky to operate on just one of her eyes rather than both. If we could restore vision to the completely blind right eye, she would at least be able to function normally again.

Like any other day, I hiked to the area where Makuyi hid out, but this time the food I carried was laced with a sedative. I knew that what I was doing was for her own good, but when she took the meat from my hand and devoured it by my side, I was overcome with a strange sadness. I could not help thinking of how long it had taken me to reach this minor degree of trust with her. To now be handing her drugged food felt like betrayal. I will never know if she connected the food with what was to come.

For three and a half hours, Makuyi lay in the operating tent. First Dr. Acker stitched up the flesh wounds that the other wolves had inflicted, then Dr. Mauer went to work on her right eye. He removed the damaged cornea and replaced it with a synthetic one, which he fastened in place with tiny sutures.

In addition to being cook and camera assistant, Patty Provonsha also happened to be trained as a nurse. Her presence completed the professional atmosphere as she worked with Dr. Mauer. The operation went without a hitch. By the end of the day, Makuyi was standing on wobbly legs, shaking off the effects of the anesthetic, no longer blind.

I thought it best to return Makuyi to the enclosure as quickly as possible. If a wolf is absent from its pack for a long period of time, there is an increased chance that the others will close ranks and not accept her; and in this case Makuyi was not even a true member of the pack. Before reintroducing her, I covered rags in antiseptic and Makuyi's blood and gave them to the other wolves to inspect. Wolves are so stimulated by any new sight or smell that I was concerned they would attack Makuyi just because she carried the scent of the operating room. In a few minutes, the entire pack had rolled in the rags and smelled identical to Makuyi.

I was hopeful that her new ability to navigate in her territory and to finally see her pack mates would make her relax and be less fearful. The pack, I hoped, would be whole again. I was about to learn another valuable and painful lesson in wolf behavior.

When we returned Makuyi to the pack, the response from the rest of the wolves was impossible to decipher. The yearlings completely ignored her, while Akai approached and inspected her. At least there was no aggression. Her vision was greatly improved; I thought she had no reason to be afraid anymore. With nothing else to do but wait, we settled down for the evening, hoping the rest of the pack would accept her.

When we entered the enclosure the next day, Makuyi, as usual, was nowhere to be found. It was certainly not the first time she had disappeared like this, but under these circumstances it was alarming. Immediately, we began to comb the enclosure for her. After an hour, we found Makuyi in her chosen hiding place, lying completely still among the willows. Around her, the blood of a dozen fresh wounds stained the snow. She had been savagely bitten by one or more of the other wolves. It was an attack so violent that, as I later learned, one of her lungs had been punctured. She hardly stirred as I carried her back out of the enclosure in my arms, through the same gate by which I had first brought her in, only eight months earlier. She had been a gentle, graceful wolf then. Now, in all probability she would not survive.

The rest of the pack was coaxed with food and held in the lock-off area as I left with Makuyi. The young wolves whimpered with interest at my burden. They seemed so playful and curious; it was nearly impossible to imagine that any one of them could have done this. But of course they had—probably one of the females. Female wolves see other females as a threat to their breeding rights and will seriously try to subdue the competition. Thus, fights between females are generally far more vicious than those between males.

I looked at Motaki and Aipuyi, the only other females in the Sawtooth Pack. Motaki was especially shy yet playful, always quick to back down when another member of the pack was displaying dominance. Aipuyi, on the other hand, was a much more complicated wolf. She had neither the calm dominance of Kamots nor the easy submission of Motaki. Despite being the ranking female, she was extremely nervous and had a quick and aggressive temper. I didn't draw any conclusions at the time, but years later, when Aipuyi's aggression became increasingly pronounced, I would come to assume that she was probably responsible for Makuyi's injuries.

If anything at all was working in Makuyi's favor, it was the timing of the attack. We had not even begun to dismantle the operating room in the yurt and were immediately ready to operate on her once again. The instant accessibility of two veterinarians and their equipment saved her life. But this time I knew there would be no returning her to the pack. Her eyesight was recovered but her status as an outsider had been decided many months earlier. Nothing would change it now.

As soon as her wounds were closed, we covered the sleeping Makuyi in blankets, placed her on a sled drawn behind a snowmobile, and carried her away from camp. As we dragged her across the snowy flats toward town, I vowed I would never let this happen to another wolf, no matter what the cost.

Several times along the way back to Stanley we stopped, thinking she had died. But, labored as it was, her breathing was steady. In Stanley we transferred her to my van and drove her back to Ketchum.

For the next two weeks, we put all filming on hold and moved back home with Makuyi. We set up a pen in my garage with soft bedding for her to lie on. I dressed her wounds and hand-fed her, but for days she was still too weak to even lift her head to eat. I felt so responsible for what had happened to her that I could not bear to leave her side. Each night I placed a camping pad on the concrete floor and lay down beside her to sleep, hoping the companionship would be of some comfort. One night I awoke in the darkness, sensing a presence beside me. As my vision cleared, a grizzled face came into focus staring at me from above. Makuyi was standing. She had been lying down for such a long time that I had nearly forgotten just how large this animal was. She looked like a horse looming over me in the dark.

From that moment, Makuyi began to improve rapidly and her personality reemerged. The next night I put my sleeping pad in with her and she instantly stood up and urinated on it, claiming it for her own. As annoying as this was, it was cause for celebration, for once again she was asserting herself as a healthy wolf should. I knew that she would quickly become too much for me to handle in my home but could never rejoin the rest of the pack. She lived for a time in a separate small enclosure back at camp. Later that summer, less than a year after I carried her into our enclosure in my arms, Janet delivered Makuyi back to Karin Rundquist's enclosure in Montana. Fortunately, since she had joined my project as an adult, she still had family there who recognized her. An old pack doesn't always welcome back a returning member, but to our relief Makuyi successfully rejoined her siblings.

Peace had been restored to the Sawtooth Pack, but it was an uneasy peace. I didn't feel that the pack had achieved real harmony; I had simply removed the object of their aggression. My worries now focused on Akai.

I can never be sure just what Akai thought of Kamots, Lakota, Aipuyi, and Motaki. My original assumption was that he would become the alpha of the pack with Makuyi as his mate, but he never really seemed to put much heart in the role. From the beginning, Akai did not rule with any kind of authority. His dominance over the others was based less on his leadership and more on the fact that he was the only adult wolf in the pack. At a very young age, Kamots began to assert himself and Akai did nothing to stand in his way.

Akai's tolerance did not extend to me, however. Initially I was not concerned, but little by little his threats got worse. It was as though he felt I was meddling in his affairs, trying to usurp his unstable position in the pack. Akai was protective of the young wolves and was simply following his instincts to keep any threat at bay. The yearlings were of course completely used to my presence and ran to greet me whenever I entered their territory. I could see that their open acceptance of me only served to further bewilder and enrage Akai as he tried to maintain order. He began to position himself physically between the young wolves and me, to prevent us from getting close to each other. Kamots, Lakota, and the others frustrated Akai with their disregard for his protection. They had come to know me as a foster parent and a friend and knew there was nothing to fear.

The situation was becoming increasingly dangerous. Earlier that year, Dennis Kane had flown out from Washington, D.C., to check on the project and Akai had greeted him by trying to bite him on the rear. It is very difficult to discuss a film project with an executive producer when he is being chased around by a wolf.

By the time I had taken Makuyi out of the enclosure, Akai had begun threatening me outright. Perhaps he thought I had injured Makuyi in some way. I will never know. Each time I approached the enclosure, he would follow me on the other side of the fence, snapping at the chain link and voicing his rage with a menacing growl.

The last time I entered the enclosure with Akai I was with my researcher, Karen McCall, taking still photographs of the pack. Akai followed us at a distance, a deep growl rumbling in his throat, trying to keep himself between us and the yearlings. The situation was just too dangerous and we began to head back out of the enclosure. When we turned our backs on Akai to open the gate, he attacked. I heard him approach from behind and swung around, crouching and holding my tripod in front of me as he jumped. The force of his blow nearly knocked me off my feet. His teeth missed the aluminum of the tripod and landed neatly on my forearm.

The bite of a wolf is twice as strong as that of a large dog, easily able to crush the bones of a moose. Fortunately, Akai was not attacking me with the same strength as he would attack a prey animal. He didn't want to hang on, he wanted to nip and get away. Even so, there was enough force in his bite to pierce my jacket and gouge my arm. After the initial charge, Akai fell back and we hurried through the gate. I did not enter again for twelve weeks.

Although he was initially more tolerant of women than men, Akai ultimately acted out his aggression on anyone within reach. For a time Karen was able to enter the enclosure, but Akai soon began to threaten her as well. One summer afternoon, he suddenly turned on Karen and pinned her against the fence, gnashing his teeth at her if she tried to move toward the exit. Worried that my entering the enclosure would be even more threatening to him and provoke a full attack, I approached the fence a short distance away to cause a distraction. Akai turned his aggression toward me, and Karen was able to creep through the gate.

As the gate closed behind her, it may as well have locked. Janet was now the only person he would allow inside. For reasons only Akai knew, he was less aggressive toward her, but even so, she was very cautious. Although Janet could continue to feed the pack, Akai had single-handedly shut down all other operations.

I realized with some disgust that I was living out the example of what Erik Zimmen had warned about socialization and the importance of having the complete trust of a wolf. With the pups I had done everything right—feeding them, nurturing them, and allowing them to bond with me. But in my hurry to get the project moving, I had cut a corner, trying to work with adults, failing to realize that they would not trust me. To Akai, I was a stranger. He was habituated to people in general, but not specifically to me or my crew. There was a very real and dangerous difference between habituation and trust, and I was staring it in the teeth.

There was nothing left to do but admit defeat. The project could not go on with Akai behaving as he was, so I began searching for a new home for him. Several weeks later we were dealt an incredible stroke of luck. Mission: Wolf, a wolf refuge in Colorado, called to say that they had adopted a lone female and were hoping to find a companion for her. An established pack would most likely not accept an interloper, but two lone wolves of opposite sex will generally get along well. We helped Mission:Wolf finance a new enclosure big enough for two wolves, and shortly thereafter Akai was flown to his new home in Colorado. He is still living there, successfully paired with his mate.

The wolf project was now a year old. The deep chill of winter was finally receding and the entire world seemed to be awakening, stretching, and coming to life. The small creek that trickled through our camp was growing into a babbling brook as each day brought a touch more sunlight and a touch more warmth.

Back in Ketchum, there was reason to be hopeful. Three brand-new pups were tearing up the mud room in my house, preparing to join the project in the summer. They were all male, born to the same parents as Kamots and Lakota, and were as different-looking as three brothers could be. One was nearly jet black. Another was an even-colored light brown, almost beige. The third had the markings of a "classic" gray wolf and promised to be a dead ringer for Kamots and Lakota when he got older. I looked forward to watching their personalities develop as differently as their coloring, optimistic that they would add a dynamic but stable dimension to the pack. The previous year had been a difficult one, but hopes now rested in Kamots and the other wolves I had raised from pups.

The problems I had faced thus far were all internal, originating within the pack itself. But the project did not exist in a vacuum; it was forever at the mercy of the wilderness that surrounded it, vulnerable to the whims of untamed and unpredictable nature. Two months later, the forest itself would deal the pack its most tragic blow and remind me just how little control I really had.

Motaki

JIM

A wolf pack is hierarchical in its social structure. As it has a top, so it has a bottom; where there is an alpha, there will also be an omega. However, whereas the alpha position is sought out and achieved by the most dominant male and female, the omega rank is thrust upon an individual by the rest of the pack. It must endure this position until it is able to assert itself over another wolf, generally a younger one, or until the rest of the pack decide to let the omega retire and turn their aggression elsewhere.

The omega's unfortunate status is largely beyond its control, but all the same, an omega, like an alpha, seems to be born with certain qualities that make it suited to the role. No other position in the pack requires as much talent for diplomacy and appeasement. The better an omega's ability to coax the others into setting aside the pack hierarchy for a while, the better its life will be. In the Sawtooth Pack the omega was clearly Motaki, a playful dark wolf with piercing yellow eyes.

Although she sometimes had to endure aggression from the rest of the pack, Motaki was not an outcast like Makuyi had been. She knew she was at the bottom of the pecking order, but there was never any doubt that she belonged. She howled with the rest of the pack and joined them at feeding time, although she was generally forced to wait until the others allowed her to eat. Most importantly, Motaki was the one who could work the pack into a playful mood and get a game of tag going. It was her role as omega, it seemed, to keep the mood of the pack light, and she took to it well. Still, there were times when the rest of the wolves would get a bit too aggressive with her and she would seek solitude. I learned not to be alarmed if Motaki disappeared from time to time.

The project had reached its second spring and we were celebrating the addition of Amani, Motomo, and Matsi. In a few months they would be integrated into the pack, but would remain somewhat free from the hierarchy for their first year or so. Initially, a pup holds something of a special status, indulged by the adults. Then it begins to assimilate gradually into the social structure, where it must compete for a position. When a pack has many adult wolves and a solidly established hierarchy, a young wolf can retain puppy status for two years, maybe longer. But with Akai as the only adult, and a weak leader at that, the younger wolves seemed to experience a quicker social maturation and began to establish a viable hierarchy of their own by the middle of their first year. I wondered if perhaps, in a year's time, one of the new pups would take over the omega position from Motaki.

I would never know. In June of 1992, the barrier that separated the Sawtooth Pack from the surrounding wilderness would prove insufficient.

It was a rainy spring evening. I had arranged for one of the crew to feed the wolves while I returned to Ketchum to spend the night with the new pups. I knew that Motaki had not been spending much time with the others, but such behavior was normal for her. No sooner had I arrived home than there came a call from the crew member, who was worried enough to have traveled to Stanley to use the phone.

Motaki had failed to show up for the feeding. Although she sometimes stayed out of sight, she never missed a meal. Her social position dictated that she would be last on the carcass, but she was never denied the right to feed with the others. I knew something was wrong, but it was already dark and too late to make the two-hour trip back. After a fitful night, I rose with the sun, left the puppies in the hands of a volunteer, and drove as fast as I could back to camp. There, with the rest of the crew, I began a search for Motaki.

The first thing we had to do was to keep the other wolves from following us on our search. If there was a hole in the fence, I didn't want to lead them to it. We placed some food in the lock-off area near the camp and made some noise to attract the pack's attention. Despite the fact that they had just enjoyed a full meal the day before, they eagerly rushed in for the bonus.

With the pack safely in the lock-off, Janet, Karen, Bob, and I began walking the fence line looking for a hole or a downed tree. Everything was as it should be; the fence was intact. The realization that Motaki had not escaped did not bring relief. If she was still in the enclosure, something had to be wrong to keep her from joining the others at a meal. Abandoning the fence line, we began to crisscross through the aspens, willows, and evergreens where she might be hiding.

I found her in an aspen grove at the southeast end of the enclosure, lying still and silent among half-fallen trees. The gentlest, most playful member of the Sawtooth Pack was dead.

In stunned silence, we stared down at her mutilated body. Motaki had fallen victim to something—but what? Whatever it was took advantage of the fact that she had been spending time alone and was temporarily vulnerable. Was it a wild animal or a human? Could the wolves themselves have done it? In a daze, we searched for any clues, tire tracks, footprints of man or animal, but we found nothing.

There is no question that wolves are capable of vicious attacks on one another; my experience with Makuyi was proof enough of that. But if the wolves had killed Motaki, they would have done so more or less by accident, as a result of their dominance going overboard. They would not have killed her for food. During the first year, I had never seen her enter into a violent confrontation with the rest of the pack. Even if she had, there would have been many injuries and scars resulting from a dominance fight, and there were none, just a horrible gash that tore into her belly.

This single wound was grizzly proof that something had indeed tried to eat her. Her belly had been opened and her insides were partly consumed. Having witnessed the way wolves eat, I couldn't imagine that they had done it. Wolves tear at a carcass, ripping sections off, competing for meat. Motaki's body was still intact.

As I lay in bed that night, I tried to put the pieces together, but it was a mystery with hardly any clues. I couldn't get my mind off that gash in her belly and who or what could have made it. I knew I'd seen a wound like that before.

In a flash, it dawned on me. Motaki's belly had been cleaned of fur around the wound. I remembered how the mountain lion I filmed in *Cougar: Ghost of the Rockies* would always lick at the bellies of the deer I left for her, methodically cleaning away the fur before beginning to eat her prey. When she ate, she always opened up the belly of the deer and consumed the internal organs first.

Having a better idea of what to look for, I began to search for signs of a mountain lion. In a partially toppled aspen tree, seven feet off the ground and only ten feet from where Motaki lay, I found black wolf fur. At the base of this tree, five feet off the ground, there were the dull claw marks of wolves, as if they had been trying to get at something up in the tree. Months earlier, they had made claw marks on another tree beneath a woodpecker's nest, trying to catch the bird. These new marks looked exactly the same. There were also needle-like scrapes higher up that could have been from a cougar claw, though it was difficult to tell.

A heavy rain had spoiled any paw prints or other clues that might have lingered, but finally I began to piece together a picture of what most likely happened. A mountain lion had climbed a tree close to the fence and jumped in over the electric wire. Mountain lions and wolves have been known to kill each other, competing for territory. It was possible that the lion had caught wind of the wolves and taken them as a threat.

The big cat had probably caught Motaki by herself, while the rest of the pack was far away. The kill was swift and silent. The single crew member at camp did not hear any commotion, but the wolves probably did and perhaps they ran to investigate. A single wolf has little chance against a cougar, but three healthy wolves would have forced the lion into the tree. Or the lion may have tried to drag Motaki into a tree, and was found there by the pack. In a mad dash to escape the wolves, the agile cat probably leapt to the ground dropping Motaki's lifeless body and dashed over the fence, shocking itself on the electric wire, but still moving forward in a panic.

As I pondered this possibility, another more frightening thought gripped me. The lion could still be in the enclosure. Again we scoured the area but found no trace of a lion's presence. There were no more footprints, no more claw marks in trees, and no impact to the fence.

The loss of Motaki was a serious blow to everyone who had come to know her. She was the epitome of an omega wolf—sweet-natured and playful. I'm not afraid to say that her death was clearly a blow to the pack as well, for their manner changed noticeably. For six weeks, they did not engage in any play, drifting around their home in a listless manner. Play is usually a daily activity for wolves, and in the case of our pack, it was often instigated by the omega. Without Motaki, they just lost the spirit.

I can think of no other word to describe their behavior than depression. Normally when the pack howled, they would gather together and sing enthusiastically as a group. The howl would be punctuated by excited yips and whines, as the rally reached a spirited frenzy. Following Motaki's death, their howling changed for a time. Instead of rallying together, each wolf remained still, apart from the others, often not even bothering to stand up. They sang alone in a slow, mournful cry.

Another indication of their mood appeared two weeks later. I was walking among the aspens with the pack following behind me through the area where we had found Motaki. As the wolves passed over the spot, they broke away from me and inspected the area, silently sniffing the ground, pinning their ears back and dropping their tails in a gesture that is normally reserved for submission.

I would have given anything to know what was going through their heads as they did this. Could they have known she was dead or did they fail to comprehend her absence? How deep was their understanding of death? Surely they had seen Motaki's body, but their howling really had a searching quality to it, as though they thought she might come back. Then again, is human behavior that different when faced with the loss of a loved one?

I can never be absolutely certain if the disruptive effect that Motaki's death had on the pack resulted from a change in their social structure or if they really did miss their companion. I can only speculate, and to me it appeared that they knew what had happened to her and were mourning her loss. I remember what a wolf biologist in Canada said about a wild pack that had suddenly lost one of its members. He described how the remaining pack wandered in a wide figure-eight pattern as if searching, and how they would howl long and mournfully, as if calling out to their vanished companion. To draw such a conclusion can be unsettling for some scientists, for it smacks of anthropomorphism. My interpretation is undeniably human, but I can find no other explanation for their change in behavior. Motaki was a wolf that inspired them to play. She accepted their dominance with grace, using her lowly status to ease tensions and bring harmony to the pack. She was a cherished member of their family, and I believe they truly missed her.

Over the course of six weeks, the pack's behavior gradually returned to normal, but there remained a deficit in its hierarchy. For a time there seemed to be no clear-cut omega, and squabbles amongst the wolves were more frequent than usual. Aipuyi may have felt that she was being set up to be the omega, and consequently she started to tangle with the other wolves, especially the young Motomo, in an alarming way.

Ultimately, however, the omega position settled on the head of Lakota. Although Lakota was as large as his brother, Kamots, he lacked his brother's self-esteem and confidence. Akai had always been especially hard on Lakota. Kamots, Aipuyi, and even the three new pups followed suit, cementing Lakota's status. It was difficult to watch this process take place, to see it gradually dawn on Lakota that he had been selected as the new scapegoat. Unpleasant as it was, it was necessary for the harmony of the pack as a whole.

As the year went by, I watched the new puppies—Matsi, Motomo, and Amani—grow to full size and begin to integrate into the pack. The older wolves did nothing to push any of these yearlings into the omega position. One by one, the young wolves found opportunities to dominate Lakota, thereby ensuring that they would not inherit the bottom spot. Lakota's status was firm and would not change for many years.

Eleven months after Motaki's death, spring was in the air again. When the first warm days came to the Sawtooths, it was like a great weight had been lifted off the world's shoulders. Everything was more difficult in the winter; just the mere act of living was harder. At 6,500 feet above sea level, the snow lasted six months. So when the color of daylight made a subtle shift from blue to gold and the wind carried the musty smell of wet earth, there was real cause for celebration. The once impenetrable snowpack melted to shallow patches here and there, and travel was no longer limited to a few well-worn trails. The urge to get out and explore was almost overwhelming.

It was one such beautiful morning that I decided to take a tape deck out into the surrounding forest and record the sounds of spring. The birds were rejoicing, the squirrels were chattering at one another in territorial disputes, the little brook was bubbling ferociously. It was a perfect spring day. I was about a half-mile from camp when I came to a patch of land that was more shaded and still had several inches of snow on the ground. When hiking, I always enjoy trying to find tracks in snow or mud and identify the animal that made them. In some ways, identifying tracks is especially difficult in spring because the snow melts so quickly that they soon become large undefined holes. On the other hand, it becomes possible to deduce how long ago the tracks were made based on the amount they have melted. Therefore I was more than a little startled when my eye caught a trail of enormous paw prints tracing a straight line across the snow. In the forest, these tracks were shielded from direct sunlight, but even so, the warm air would have melted them out in a day. These prints were crisp and sharply detailed, meaning they were fresh. I knew instantly what I was looking at. The lion was back.

Tracks of the cat family are unique and easily identifiable by the lack of claw marks. Moreover, there are not many animals out there whose feet make a four-inch-wide print. These were the tracks of a huge male from the looks of it, and they were pointing in the direction of our camp.

I hurried back toward the tents, following the path that the lion would have taken if he had walked a straight line. I scanned the camp for snow or mud that might bear a trace of the lion's passing. There was a small patch of snow shielded from the sun by one of the tents. To my horror, it revealed the same enormous fresh tracks. The lion had passed silently through our camp sometime during the previous night, even brushing against one of the tents.

There was little doubt as to what he was doing there. A large herd of elk had returned to its traditional calving and grazing range in the meadow just east of camp, where they took advantage of the newly sprouted grass. As the season progressed, the elk would move higher into the mountains, but for now there was still too much snow for them to graze there. Wherever elk go, a lion is sure to follow.

I made a hasty inspection of the territory, walking around the perimeter of the enclosure, making sure that no trees had fallen near the fence and that the solar-powered electric wire was still functioning. Everything was as it should be, and the wolves themselves seemed completely unconcerned. Still, I was uneasy. There were just too many trees to climb, too many places where the ten-foot fence could be breached by a predator that could jump and climb better than any other on the continent. Motaki's death was a haunting memory.

My concern for the safety of the pack was equaled by my concern for the safety of the crew, myself included. While there has never been a verified case of a healthy wild wolf attacking a person in North America, the same cannot be said of cougars.

Only a week later, I was returning from shuttling a visitor back to his car in Stanley. The trip had taken me much longer than expected and I found myself walking from the jeep trail back to camp in near darkness. By the dim light of a crescent moon, I could barely make out the tan flanks of the elk as they warily edged away from me and grunted softly to one another. It was a large herd, just the sort of thing that would attract the attention of a hungry cougar.

As I felt my way through the sagebrush, my heart begin to race. For a moment I truly had a taste of what it must feel like to be a prey animal in a vulnerable situation. I could feel the big cat waiting out there, surveying the herd, looking for one that was straggling or sickly, looking for any sign of weakness. It was not until I had walked to the middle of the field that it dawned on me just how stupid it was to be stumbling around in the darkness where a mountain lion was sure to be lurking, but I was already halfway to camp so there was no use turning back. Even if I did, someone else would surely venture out to look for me, putting themselves in the same danger. I just kept thinking, "Whatever you do, don't trip!" I didn't want to do anything that might imitate injured prey and attract attention.

Finally I saw the pale rectangles of tents take shape in the gloom and I felt a measure of relief. I never saw the cougar, never really knew if he was there or not, but that night at camp I could still feel the yellow eyes watching me from somewhere in the darkness.

As spring passed into summer, the elk moved to higher elevation and the lion that had come down to the valley in search of prey probably followed the herd, moving far away from camp. It was the last time I would see any trace of a mountain lion in our area, but every spring we could feel his presence, and we remembered Motaki.

Filming

JIM

To be inspired to save an animal, you have to see it first.
—Dr. Maurice Hornocker

When I began the Sawtooth Wolf Project, filming, as I knew it, had been about lenses and lighting and composition. I envisioned creating a setup similar to the one I had made for *Cougar: Ghost of the Rockies*. I couldn't have been more wrong.

It was certainly difficult work maintaining the cougar camp and working with an animal that could easily kill me, but in retrospect, the actual filming of the cougar was insanely simple. My two-person crew and I would enter the cat's enclosure, and simply wait. She would move through her territory, ignoring us completely, posing on rocky outcroppings as if on cue, and stalking squirrels and ducks that chanced to get into the enclosure. She always seemed to look beautiful no matter what she did. I was free to concentrate on cinematography and let her be herself.

To be sure, she was an unpredictable animal. We never ventured near her without big sticks to protect ourselves, but I always knew I could get the kind of shots I wanted. When I rolled film, her power and grace shone through.

In the summer of 1991, I let my camera roll for the first time on Akai resting in the grass, beautifully lit by the evening sun. This marked the official start of production of the film that would become *Wolf: Return of a Legend,* but when I looked at the footage, my heart sank. In his short summer coat, Akai looked like a big dog lounging in someone's backyard. There was never any question of mistaking the cougar for a housecat, but the qualities that separate a wolf from a domestic dog are more subtle. The first footage of the project was worthless.

To make matters worse, I was completely unprepared for how the wolves would react to my presence. Wolves, like their domestic relatives, are much more curious and social than their feline counterparts. The cougar usually ignored me, going about her business as though I were invisible, but not the wolves. I'd see the yearlings frolicking in the meadow and venture out with my camera to film their behavior. Immediately upon seeing me, they would stop whatever they were doing and stare with fascination at me and my camera. Much to my aggravation, they took a tireless interest in our activities.

I started to become genuinely concerned that I would not be able to film natural behavior in an enclosure.

Granted, anything that a wolf does in response to its environment is "natural," but I knew the difference between wolves acting naturally with each other and wolves merely reacting to people. Finding that balance between a controlled and a wild atmosphere would not be easy. It was something I would have to learn, degree by degree.

It was the first snow of the season in 1991. Huge wet flakes were tumbling out of the sky and collecting on the wolves' thick fur coats. The pack was ecstatic, bounding about and celebrating the arrival of winter with the excitement of children. Finally they were ignoring me, devoting all their attention to each other and their environment, or so I thought. I was intently trying to film their behavior, keeping my camera dry with a camouflage raincoat. While I focused on two other wolves, Kamots, nearly full size but still very much a youngster, watched me from the side. With my eye pressed to the camera's eyepiece, I was unaware of his presence until he made his first gentle tug on the raincoat, and by then it was too late.

He quickly ascertained that there was no danger and gave a swift pull. Instinctively I grabbed hold of the tripod to keep the camera from toppling over, but in doing so, sacrificed the raincoat, which became an instant toy. It was a twofold loss. Not only was a very nice rain jacket torn to shreds in minutes, but I had also lost a wonderful shooting opportunity. The light was perfect, the snow was beautiful, and the wolves were playing with a big man-made object—not what I would call natural behavior. Watching them in such a happy, playful mood was certainly endearing, but it was hardly conducive to filming a wildlife documentary.

I was amazed at the things they managed to steal when we weren't paying attention, things that I thought would be far too heavy or awkward for them to take. Nothing was safe. Once they managed to steal a sledge-hammer and had a marvelous time dragging it around the meadow, losing their grip, tripping over it and stealing it from one another. Another time Matsi pulled a massive red toolbox out of a cart, spilling its contents in a heap on the ground. The crash sent poor Matsi running and gave us a rare chance to retrieve our stolen items.

If an object really was too large or heavy for the wolves to pick up and chew, they sometimes chose to scent-mark it instead. When a wolf scent-marks something of yours, you wish he'd had the decency just to chew it up; the accepted means of scent-marking is to urinate or defecate on the object. We were treated to this charming bit of behavior very early in the project, when I had decided to rig a solar-powered electric wire on top of the fence to further alleviate our fears that a wolf might try to climb out of the enclosure. My son, Garrick, and I hauled a massive bale of wire inside the enclosure and set about slowly stringing it above the chain-link fence. At lunchtime, we carefully gathered tools, gloves, and other belongings to keep them safe from the wolves while we ate in the yurt, but we didn't bother removing the thirty-pound spool of wire. Upon returning to our work an hour later, we found the wire, still neatly coiled at the base of the fence, with three fresh wolf stools perched atop it like little trophies. The wolves, of course, were nowhere to be seen, though we couldn't help but imagine them off in the trees snickering to themselves. I have heard of this behavior occurring in the wild as well. Wolves reintroduced to Yellowstone were known for leaving similar little gifts on the doorsteps of ranger cabins, marking the territory.

We had no shortage of comic moments, living with these tirelessly curious and spirited creatures. In the project's third year, Ted Koch, a representative from the United States Fish and Wildlife Service, came to visit our camp. Although I was off in Washington, D.C., and could not be with him, I was overjoyed that my project could be discerned as an asset to the federal government. Ted was in charge of wolf recovery in Idaho, but since wolves were so scarce in the wild, he had never actually seen one. Visiting the Sawtooth Pack gave him the opportunity to get a close look at the animal he would be managing.

My assistant Val Asher took him into the enclosure and, as the story goes, warned him not to put any of his gear on the ground. Ted had brought a 35mm camera as well as a video camcorder and instantly began snapping photos of the pack. When the wolves approached him, Ted, in his enthusiasm, set his still camera beside him and began videotaping. A moment later, Kamots and Matsi were soon frolicking a short distance away, playing "keep away" with a small object. Ted was thrilled to be recording this sort of behavior. He looked up from his camcorder and innocently asked, "What is it they're doing?"

Val replied, as casually as possible, "They're eating your camera."

Within minutes they had reduced the camera to dust and scattered it far and wide. Ted was so enamored of the pack that he took it in stride. Weeks later, while walking through the meadow I found a small chunk of plastic, about the size of a half-dollar, with a few shredded wires dangling from it. I put it in an envelope with a note that read, "Dear Ted, Kamots enjoyed your camera; he's finished with it now."

Our bonding with these animals was necessary for their own safety and comfort as well as for the safety of the crew. We could not afford to work among wolves that were either too afraid or too aggressive. The pack needed to be completely assured that we would never harm them, for, as Akai demonstrated, a frightened wolf will often become a dangerous wolf.

Still, during the first year, it became clear that something had to be done to maintain the integrity of the project. The wolves' curiosity was not the real problem. Rather, I began to fear that our overtly affectionate reactions to them were beginning to encourage unwolflike behavior. We were walking a very fine line and no two people ever agreed on just where it should be drawn. I admit that it was difficult even for me. When a friendly doglike animal approaches you, it is hard to resist the urge to reach out and stroke its beautiful thick fur. But ultimately I knew that too much human attention would spell disaster for the filming.

I got a real sign that things were getting out of hand when I entered the enclosure with Jake and Garrick one morning and to my surprise found a crew member already inside, brushing one of the wolves with a doggy brush! With some regret, I decided that we needed to keep human and wolf interaction to a minimum. Four months into the project, I imposed the decree that no one was allowed to touch a wolf when we were filming or preparing to film. This was an unpopular law, especially among those who adored petting and scratching the wolves. No member of the crew would ever have dared enter the cougar enclosure alone for fear of being attacked. But the wolves were different, they seemed so friendly and predictable, and some people were simply unable to resist their magnetism.

I noticed this disturbing phenomenon right at the beginning and I have since witnessed it time and again: the profound and not always positive effect that wolves have on people. There is something about wolves—a combination of their intelligence, their similarity to dogs, their enshrinement in myth and lore, and their history of persecution—that absolutely captivates our hearts and minds. At the time of this writing, I have completed two films and a book of photography—all on the same subject—so I can well attest to the fact that wolves can indeed get under one's skin and into one's psyche.

I have since formed the opinion that, to certain people, being accepted by a wolf is a sort of validation of one's own sensitivity or spirituality. The thought process seems to be this: if a wolf gravitates toward me, it must be because the wolf's innate sensitivity allows it to perceive that I am kinder, wiser, and more in tune with nature than the average person. The truth, however, is much more straightforward. Wolves, being the complex animals that they are, have many reasons for preferring one human over another, none of which have anything to do with being able to peer into our souls. A person who is demonstrating subtle signs of fear may cause a captive wolf to shy away or to become aggressive. Some wolves simply feel more threatened by men than by women; conversely, some will display more aggression toward women, for no apparent reason. Like most habituated animals, wolves that have been raised by humans will gravitate toward the people with whom they are most familiar, people who have been close to them since birth and have consistently taken a role in their feeding and care.

Ultimately the limits I placed on our interaction with the wolves achieved their intended goal. It prevented the pack from developing the habit of soliciting affection from us. More than any other decision, this maintained the validity of our work.

Even without encouraging unnatural behavior, we still had to deal with the problem of the wolves coming across as "doglike" on film. When face to face with a wolf, there is no mistaking it for a dog. Not only is a wolf's fur much thicker, and its jaws and paws much larger, but a wolf has a certain mysterious and wild presence about it that one can sense instantly. Unfortunately, this "feeling" does not translate easily to film.

As the first winter approached, the wolves began to grow their heavy fur. This was an unexpected blessing. Kamots was nearly full size and looked beautiful in his regal bushy coat. A full-grown wolf looks much larger in winter than in summer and its markings are more defined. To this day, when I film or photograph wolves, I prefer to do so in cold weather when they appear their most "wolfish." Still, I needed something more, a way to make the wolf's dignity and grace come through on film.

Oddly enough, when I am in need of creative advice, I often turn to a chef for guidance—in this case, my old friend Johann Guschelbauer, who was born in Austria and is now the proprietor of a restaurant in the Cayman Islands. We met in 1970 when I was in the Caymans shooting my earlier underwater films. He became my dive partner and camera assistant and has since worked with me on every film I have made, if only for a few weeks at a time. Johann has an amazing knack for filmmaking and an understanding of what makes a compelling story. He also has a wonderful instinct for working with animals. Were he not such a superlative chef, I'd say he was in the wrong business.

Johann was with me at wolf camp during that first September and observed that the wolves lacked a high vantage point in their territory. In the previous project, the cougar had the benefit of a tall pile of boulders where she enjoyed standing and surveying the land. The rocks provided me with the advantage of shooting upward at the cougar from a low angle, accentuating her strength and beauty. Here, the Sawtooth Mountains made an impressive backdrop, but the land itself was a gentle uphill slope without any abrupt rise or rocky outcropping. Johann suggested that perhaps if the wolves had a hill where they could stand and howl, I could shoot up at them and better convey their majesty. Imagine Kamots howling into the evening sky, with the peaks of the Sawtooth Mountains behind him. It would be a marvelous image.

As the first snow fell, we purchased a supply of hay bales from a local rancher. In a corner of the wolves' meadow, Janet, Garrick, and I stacked them into a pile that resembled a six-foot-high Mayan temple. As night fell, we shoveled snow onto the hay, trying to give it an irregular and natural shape, then doused it with buckets of creek water so it would harden overnight. When more snow covered it naturally, it would look like a huge boulder covered with snow. During this entire process, the wolves watched us with great interest.

The next morning, we awoke and set out to put the finishing touches on our creation. When we arrived at the meadow, we let out a collective gasp. The hill was gone. In its place, a vast beige smear sullied the fresh snow. The wolves had waited for us to abandon our work for the night and then uncovered and untied each and every bale of hay that we had set out. In what must have been the most fun they had in months, they shredded, chewed, rolled in, and scattered the hay until it was nothing more than a dull little bump in the meadow.

It had been a great idea in theory, but it had failed to take the wolves' curiosity into consideration. Anything we touched, no matter how organic, was destined to be fully inspected—in other words, chewed up. Never again would we attempt such an ambitious alteration of the terrain. The little bump remained for two more years as it slowly rejoined the earth, but during the time it graced the landscape of wolf camp it was known affectionately as Mount Johann.

Not all of Johann's suggestions turned out to be such dismal failures. He and my camera assistant, Bob Poole, both helped to create the shooting style that took shape in *Wolf: Return of a Legend*. We spent many hours around the table in the cook tent discussing how to capture not just a wolf's image but also a sense of its power and mystery.

Because I had the luxury of getting closer to the animal than any cameraman could in the wild, I had been avoiding the use of telephoto lenses. After shooting several rolls of film, however, we decided that the standard-length lenses I was using might be making the wolves look ordinary. A telephoto lens imparts a particular look to an image, a certain compression of space that can give the viewer the sense of seeing something rare or hidden. Perhaps if I backed away from the wolves and used a long lens I could better convey the sense of an elusive animal.

It was a simple idea but it was a revelation. I was able to make the wolf stand out from its background, plus I could partly obscure the animal behind blurred branches or blades of grass, accentuating its secretive nature. Keeping my distance from the pack had the added bonus of making them less apt to turn their attention to my activities.

Still wanting to add another dimension, I decided to shoot the wolves in slightly slow motion. So much of a wolf's behavior goes by in the blink of an eye: a quick cock of the head, a flash of fangs, a lick. The language of wolves is very difficult to notice when it is happening in real time. By slowing things down ever so slightly, I thought I could draw attention to all the subtle interactions that were occurring moment by moment.

When we looked at the latest batch of footage, we instantly knew that we had hit the mark. Instead of manipulating the wolves or their terrain, we had altered our own approach to filming them and had finally succeeded in capturing not just their physical beauty but their very essence. Watching the images, I was aware that what I had filmed came close—closer than anything I'd seen before—to experiencing a wolf firsthand. As a cinematographer, that was the goal I had always been striving for—powerful images that would, both physically and emotionally, bring the audience face-to-face with a wolf.

Kamots

JIM

The behavior of young wolves is a fascinating tangle of contradiction. One moment they are as docile as lambs and the next they are viciously clashing over a bone. They can be intrepid one instant and suddenly tentative the next. Often something that momentarily frightens a wolf pup will become the subject of nearly obsessive fascination. A pup may initially shy away from an unfamiliar object, but he will remain fixated by it, moving closer inch by inch, sniffing it out, testing the limits of his knowledge.

Some pups naturally possess more of this curiosity and courage, some are more playful, some are more skittish. These personality differences are apparent at a very young age and form the foundation of what becomes the social hierarchy of a wolf pack. Of the first four pups that we raised during the summer of 1991, we noticed that the one we called Kamots was unfailingly the most alert, curious, and self-assured of the bunch. There is no more scientific way to describe his demeanor. He simply behaved with confidence.

On certain occasions when the pups were from two to four weeks of age, we would separate one pup or another from the litter to socialize them and help them feel safe around humans. When we removed Aipuyi from her littermates, she would become nervous, afraid to explore, anxious to get back among her siblings. It was not so much that she was afraid of me or my assistants; it seemed more that she feared the other pups might not accept her back. When she was returned, there would be several minutes of squabbling amongst the pups, as though Aipuyi were vying for her social position all over again.

Kamots, on the other hand, positively seemed to enjoy the chance to get out and explore. He would confidently inspect his human caretakers and investigate anything within reach of his inquisitive nose. He returned to his littermates calmly, free of doubt, his position assured.

As he grew, Kamots did not have to fight for the top spot; he did not have to knock a more dominant wolf out of the alpha position, as frequently happens. When he reached full size, he simply assumed the mantle. There was never any doubt in his mind or in the minds of the others that he should be anything other than the leader.

I had anticipated that Akai would be the alpha male of the pack before I fully understood what an alpha was. He had not been the alpha of a pack in Minnesota, where he was raised; rather, he had been a third wolf living with a mated pair. When he came to the Sawtooths, he was protective of Makuyi and the young puppies, but perhaps only in the sense that all adult wolves are protective of their own pack. As the sole adult male, it seemed natural that he would take on the alpha role, and while the other males were still puppies, Akai seemed to be comfortable as the leader. Yet day by day, I observed this young upstart Kamots blithely assume a higher and higher status with hardly a whimper from Akai. Social hierarchy among wolves was more complicated and mysterious than I had ever expected, and clearly not something that I could decide for the pack.

I had done considerable research on the social hierarchy of wolf packs, but had never experienced it firsthand. I did not realize at the time that Akai was not expressing the more subtle aspects of a true alpha—the alertness, the calm, the confidence. It was only after Kamots was fully established in that role that I saw how a natural-born alpha should behave. The alpha holds his tail and head high, he lifts his leg to urinate, while subordinate males usually do not. He is continually vigilant, not simply responding to obvious threats but maintaining a watchful eye at all times. Akai simply did not possess these qualities.

In some of the earlier photographs of the pack, Kamots, at less than a year old, is holding his head higher than Akai's during a howl. This would be considered a reckless challenge of dominance to a well-established alpha, but Akai let it pass. He seemed as willing as the others to allow Kamots his due. Ultimately, the position of alpha male had nothing to do with age, size, strength, or aggressiveness. It sprung from a source that we will never see and can barely hope to understand. It is a rule that the wolves themselves know, accept, and live by. There was no doubt in my mind that Kamots would have deposed Akai from the alpha position when he reached full adulthood, and that he would have done so without violent confrontation. I would never know, of course, as Akai was moved in 1992, leaving Kamots without any competition, the clear alpha of the Sawtooth Pack.

Kamots was a marvelous leader. The confidence he had shown as a pup blossomed into a calm benevolence that was a joy to witness. There was an alertness about him not present in the other wolves, and his face often bore an expression that, at least to people, registered as concern. When a new visitor arrived at the gate, Kamots was the first to inspect him. When a strange sound rang out in the surrounding forest, Kamots was the first to prick up his ears and trot off to investigate. Perhaps the rest of the pack did not behave this way because they knew they didn't need to. They knew Kamots would keep them safe.

Despite his benevolence, his rule was supreme, and he did not hesitate to make it known. His command over a deer carcass and his possessive displays were really quite terrifying to behold. The first time I saw Kamots distort his face in threat I was amazed. It was during a feeding. Lakota timidly attempted to approach the carcass and eat before his turn. Kamots raised his eyes from the meal and let out a loud growl, baring his teeth but keeping them fixed on the carcass. Despite the warning, Lakota pressed on. He seemed to think that if he could just make himself insignificant enough, he could sneak a bite or two before anyone noticed. In an instant, Kamots' features twisted into a mask of ferocity. He raised his lips high, exposing the full length of his teeth, his nose pulled back and his ears shot out to the sides like horns. His graceful muzzle became short and broad, making his jaws seem all the more powerful. With a savage snarl, he charged over the carcass at Lakota, who scurried a few paces before flipping over onto his back with a yelp of submission. The question of who would eat when was quickly settled.

Law in a wolf pack can certainly be tough, but I never saw Kamots behave with anything that resembled viciousness. In this particular encounter, Kamots' teeth never made any real contact with his brother; it was mostly show. Over the years, I have seen other wolves tear into a subordinate with an obvious intent to do physical harm. The abuse that one wolf can subject another to is often hard for human observers to witness. Kamots certainly removed many a tuft of hair and delivered many a stern bite, but once the order of things was restored, he quickly returned to his usual calm self.

All this responsibility and authority did not diminish his desire to play with the rest of the pack. In fact, he seemed to rejoice in temporarily abandoning his duties and indulging in a good frolic. He was just as apt to play with Lakota as to dominate him. At times his behavior was so benign, so puppyish, that it was impossible to imagine that this was the same creature who minutes earlier had displayed such ferocity over a meal. Holding a grudge, it seems, is not in a wolf's character. Yet even at play, there was something about Kamots that suggested that he was the leader. Sometimes he would not fully engage in the frolicking but would watch the others with a protective air. In games of tag, Kamots was usually the one doing the chasing, and, in general, he would win all battles of tug-of-war with sticks or bones.

Wolves of all ages love to play with objects, and we quickly learned that the wolves of the Sawtooth Pack had a special curiosity for objects that we had touched. As the boldest member of the pack, Kamots was always the first to steal an ill-placed glove, hammer, or lens cap. Once a wolf has something he wants in his jaws, it is almost impossible to get it back. I learned to keep an old shredded item of clothing with me for use as a trade. If Kamots stole something of value, I would, with much show, place the worthless object on the ground. I could see him weighing the value of the item he already possessed versus the new and possibly better prize. Eventually his limitless curiosity would get the better of him and he'd drop whatever he held in order to inspect the new object.

One of the items that interested him the most was my hat. Whenever I was focusing my attention on something else, peering through the eyepiece of my camera at another wolf, Kamots would quietly creep up behind me and try to snatch my hat from my head. I was always just a second too quick for him, pulling away just as he was about to grab the brim in his jaws. The wide-brimmed hat was already tattered and tired after years of service, so one day I decided that I would let Kamots win the prize.

When I saw him watching me, I pretended to be busy with my camera. I heard his soft approach from behind and felt his warm breath on the back of my neck. There was a powerful tug on the brim of my hat and off it flew. Kamots knew that victory was his and began to prance about, flipping the hat into the air. He quickly managed to get it over his face and began to charge around the meadow, completely unable to see where he was going but still determined to keep the hat from me and the other wolves. He tried to adjust its position and ended up tripping over a root, tumbling over and nearly losing possession of the sacred object. When he got to his feet again, the hat was back over his face and he was no better off than when he started. Finally he crashed through the willows with the pup Matsi in hot pursuit, and that was the last I ever saw of my hat. I never found even the tiniest shred of it.

It was while filming Kamots at play that I observed one of the first undeniable illustrations of the concern that wolves have for one another. It was a gesture of kindness that just bowled me over. Kamots was charging around the meadow, celebrating the first major snowfall of the year. Something about new snow thrilled the wolves to no end. After it was on the ground, they took it for granted, but while it was falling they greeted it like a gift from heaven. Even in late spring, by which time we were hurling curses at the sky for so much as another flake, the pack acted as if it were some fresh new surprise. As the snow began to accumulate on the frozen ground, Kamots led the festivities. He ran back and forth through the meadow, not playing tag or chasing another wolf, just darting about in unbridled jubilation. Amani, still under a year old and not full size, wasn't quite sure what to make of the alpha carrying on like that. He sat down in the meadow and watched Kamots run in circles and disappear into the willows.

Kamots burst from the bushes at full speed and in his exuberance barreled right over his young pack mate. Amani did a cartwheel and sat up, blinking and covered in powder, not sure what had just happened to him. Kamots' body language was unmistakable. He slammed on the brakes, turned, and hurried back to Amani, sniffing the little wolf up and down and giving him a few reassuring licks. I was profoundly touched by this display of concern; it was almost an apology.

Kamots secured his leadership and maintained it for nine years using a minimum of force and aggression. I believe it was his genuine regard for the pack that made him such a benevolent leader, and his confidence that made him such a secure one. From the time he reached adulthood, he knew he was the alpha, never imagining that things could be otherwise. He never showed evidence of feeling the least bit threatened, never felt the need to prove himself by bullying the others, and never seemed to doubt that the security of the pack should be left on his shoulders.

By 1993, three years into the project, so many things were going wrong. Motaki had been killed, Makuyi had been moved back to Montana, and Akai had become dangerous and had been relocated. Now Aipuyi, one of Kamots' littermates, was beginning to display a worrisome level of aggression. As she grew, she began to clash with the other wolves without any apparent provocation.

As if to mirror the dysfunctional wolf pack, relations among the crew were falling apart. The atmosphere alternated between uneasy silence and unpleasant bickering. The subject, as always, was who was getting the most "wolf time" and who should make decisions about pack management.

I had planned for everyone on the crew to take turns feeding, nurturing, and bonding with the pups. This way, when the wolves grew to adulthood, they would be trusting of all the people in their world, not just one or two. From the moment we picked them up in Montana, however, there were conflicts, even over something as silly as who got to sit next to the pups on the ride home. Since the pups were so adorable, I initially chalked this up to an overly enthusiastic concern for the helpless creatures. But as the pups grew, some members of the crew began complaining that another was taking on a proprietary attitude toward them, overseeing all caretaking and criticizing other people's efforts.

Finally, my good friend Jake Provonsha, who had worked with me so closely on the last two films, and who had always risen above petty disputes, announced that "Like an old wolf, I have lost my edge," and left the project. This was not simply losing a member of the crew. Jake and I had worked so many years together that he understood my mind and my process of filmmaking. His inventiveness had helped me surmount so many obstacles in the past that his departure left behind a deep void. This sad event turned out to be the tip of the iceberg, the start of a chain reaction that would resonate through the entire crew. I was grateful that his wife, Patty, had the tenacity to stay on a little bit longer.

Things went from bad to worse as the wolves grew older and as the new batch of pups—Matsi, Amani, and Motomo—were born and added to the pack. I frequently found myself caught in the middle, trying to keep the peace, but I was unable to accomplish this feat. As *Wolf: Return of a Legend* moved from filming to editing, and toward its broadcast, the crew departed one by one.

To this day, I know of no other animal that can evoke such a spectrum of emotions from human beings and create such conflict. Thankfully, I was not alone in this observation. Back in Washington, D.C., Jamie sympathized with my predicament, for she, too, was in a position to witness the often bizarre behavior of people toward animals. My calling her about Makuyi over a year earlier had rejuvenated our friendship, and that autumn she invited me to present the new film at the National Zoo. Over lunch, she entertained me with stories about her work and the strange and occasionally unpleasant methods people employ to get a closer visit with the animals there. The zoo's wolves, she told me, received more than their share of inappropriate human attention. Once, Jamie said, a woman had tried to scale the fence into the wolf exhibit. Fortunately, the barrier proved too much for her and she was found by security, her quest unfulfilled.

I found it hard to look at Jamie and not think of how it could have been. She could have contributed so much with her levelheadedness and enthusiasm. I imagined how much she would have loved Idaho and the wolves, if only I had asked her to join me years ago. But she was married now and seemed happy with her life, so I tried to put such thoughts behind me. I held on to her stories, though, for they helped me understand the problems I was facing.

Late that fall, I entered the enclosure in the Sawtooths alone, not to film or photograph, but just to sit and watch the wolves and think about where the project was going. Kamots approached me and licked my face, but instead of trotting off like he usually did after greeting me, he sat down on his haunches and looked at me quizzically. As I reflected back on the difficult times, I saw that I was not the one that truly held the project together. It was Kamots. In him I could see the strong leader that the project so desperately needed. I knew that he had the power and wisdom to guide the pack into a new stability, and I wanted to keep the project going so I could watch him do it. I could feel an understanding between us, a cooperation I had not experienced with Akai.

Then, in a gesture I'd never seen before, he raised his paw and stretched his foreleg toward me. I held my hand out to meet it and we sat there, palm to paw. At that moment, his strength and stillness were more reassuring than any kind words from another human being. If I could just hold up my end, he would hold up his.

Changes

JIM

The year that passed from the fall of 1992 to the fall of 1993 was one of transitions, for the pack and for ourselves. Kamots became a full-fledged adult and blossomed into a gentle leader. For me, the year marked the end of filming, the beginning of editing, the departure of the crew, and eventually the airing of the documentary *Wolf: Return of a Legend.* The project, as I had originally conceived it, was drawing to a close.

I had always known that the pack could not be set free. We had made a concerted effort to socialize them and reduce the innate fear of humans that is vital to a wild wolf's survival. In the West, the age-old hatred of the wolf is still commonplace in most areas. A wolf without fear of humans is a wolf under a death sentence. On top of this, releasing captive wolves into the wild is against the law.

My permit to keep wolves in the Sawtooth Mountains was temporary. I knew there would come a day when they would have to move. Thus, the search for a permanent home for the pack, a place where they could live out their lives in comfort and safety, began right from the start. I would not have gone forward with the project if I had not been confident that we could negotiate a good home for them somewhere close by.

Six months before the fence went up in the Sawtooths, I was approached by a wolf recovery organization from Boise that wanted to adopt the pack for an education center after my film was completed. This organization had access to a parcel of land in central Idaho where the wolves could live. We spent a year drawing up prospective plans. However, when the town organized a meeting where the local people could voice their opinions, I was shocked at the hatred that raged there. All those ancient myths persisted. One person described a scenario in which wild wolves, attracted by my pack, would come down from the hills and wait in ambush for innocent citizens.

Furthermore, Janet Kellam and I found the Boise organization to be too political, already doing battle with ranchers and hunters to get wolves back in the wild at all costs. The combination of an activist group managing a captive wolf pack in a violently anti-wolf area could only spell disaster.

My vision has always been to educate people about wolves, to shatter the perception of them as the enemy of man, but I wanted to achieve this goal without adding more fuel to an already raging political fire. Therefore, I decided the best course of action was to create a totally new nonprofit organization, one whose mission, as I conceived it, was to raise money for the pack and build a new enclosure in a place where the public was open-minded. Once that initial goal was achieved, the organization would focus on public education and noninvasive scientific research. I named the foundation the Wolf Education and Research Center, to stress that the focus should be on information and not politics.

The WERC, as it became known, borrowed its original staff from my film production company, but by the end of its first year, it was standing on its own as an independent entity. While I was happy to see the organization thriving, I could see that it, too, was moving in the direction of being a wolf advocacy group. Soon WERC and I began to have disagreements over the mission of the organization. I felt it was turning into the type of political organization I had wanted to avoid.

Like anyone who has come to appreciate wolves, I want nothing more than to see them return successfully to the wilderness, restoring balance to a system that has been awry since wolves were virtually exterminated so many years ago. But I have always been an advocate of natural recovery, letting them come back on their own to places where they can sustain themselves, leaving us to focus our energy on protecting them and the corridors of wilderness habitat that they need. The current wolf reintroduction process involves bringing them back artificially to places the wolves have not chosen. Perhaps I'm too sensitive to the plight of wolves, living with them as I have, seeing their intelligence and their social nature, but after witnessing how they care for one another, all this trapping, caging, and splitting up of families just to move them somewhere else seems needlessly cruel to me. Even after the wolves are moved, they must wear radio collars and be caught in leg-hold traps from time to time when the batteries run out. If they kill a cow or sheep, even on public land, the perpetrators are usually destroyed to appease angry ranchers.

I understand the mandate of the Endangered Species Act to do everything possible to preserve and bring back threatened and endangered animals. I also have the utmost respect for the individual biologists who are involved in the process and are caught in the middle of a no-win situation. But the hatred of wolves is still so strong that, for many of them, the price of reintroduction has been paid with their lives. Would it not be better to slow the process down, letting the animals return on their own, as they have been shown to do, protecting them with all the might of the Endangered Species Act and focusing our efforts on changing people's attitudes?

This vision was still in the forefront of WERC's mission for its first year or so. We put a proposal before the U.S. Forest Service to build a permanent home for the pack in the southern end of the Sawtooth National Recreation Area, just north of Ketchum. That area is, without a doubt, the most wolf-friendly in all of Idaho, and the nearby Sun Valley resort would bring in countless visitors. It could be a place where the public would be able to view these ambassador wolves from a distance, on a sensitively restricted schedule. From this experience, schoolchildren and adults alike could get a rare glimpse of this elusive animal and gain a better understanding of what wolves are all about.

For a time, the Forest Service seemed interested in providing land for the pack's permanent home, but, being a federal agency, it was in the difficult position of wanting to remain a neutral party between the environmentalists and the hunters and ranchers who were against the wolf's return. As WERC became more vocal in its support of wolf reintroduction, potentially polarizing advocates and opponents, I believe that the Forest Service representatives shied away from an association with us. There were, of course, other obstacles to this plan; providing a home for a captive pack of wolves was well beyond the mandate of a government agency. Still, I sometimes think that if we had been more politically centrist, the Sawtooth Pack might have found a permanent home in the land for which they were named.

To compound the problem, while this search for a home was going on, the pack was continuing to have conflicts. As Matsi, Motomo, and Amani reached adulthood something was changing. The female, Aipuyi, had always been the most skittish and unpredictable of the wolves I had raised from puppyhood, but as she grew, she had turned increasingly violent—not toward me, but toward the other wolves. Her behavior changed radically following the death of Motaki, as though she were afraid that she would be pushed into the omega position. She did not take her aggression out on Lakota, as might have been expected; instead she attacked the younger Motomo.

Aipuyi's aggression became more intense, and I began to have real fears for the safety of the pack. She and Motomo, the one-year-old black male, would regularly tear into one another in dominance fights. Motomo did not direct any unprovoked aggression toward her, but he was stubborn and would not back down when she tried to dominate him. This was especially confusing because females most often express aggression toward other females, with displays of dominance usually revolving around breeding rights. Conflicts between the sexes are much more rare. Knowing this added to my concern, for it made Aipuyi's behavior seem all the more bizarre.

In the winter of 1993, the battles became more and more bloody. I was faced with the terrifying realization that one of those wolves was going to die if I did not do something to stop them. Aipuyi's behavior was so violent that I was certain that if she killed Motomo she would then transfer her aggression to another wolf and then perhaps another. I had to take action.

I contacted Randy Acker, the veterinarian who had assisted in Makuyi's eye operation. It is well known that spaying a female dog can make her less aggressive, and the managers of other captive packs have used this measure with success in quelling cases of extreme aggression in some female wolves. Once again we went through the mammoth process of turning the yurt into a medical tent.

Her operation went smoothly, and in a matter of hours, she was back with the pack. While she immediately carried herself with an assertive air, there was no aggression. The next day, however, the peaceful silence was shattered by a burst of snarling and yelping. I didn't even need to look. I already knew what was happening.

Immediately, I began contacting other captive packs, like the one where Akai now lived, to see if a home could be found for her. The longer I waited, the greater the chance of Aipuyi seriously injuring Motomo or one of the others. I wanted so much to tell these pack managers that Aipuyi was a calm, gentle animal, but ultimately I knew that I could not saddle some other organization with my problem.

As with Akai, my only hope was to find a lone wolf of the opposite sex in another captive pack. If an organization had a single male, I could pay for a separate enclosure where he and Aipuyi could live together. I knew in my heart that it was a one-in-a-million chance, that I had been incredibly lucky with Akai. I waited as the violence escalated with each passing month, but no such organization could be found.

I had been warned by many experienced people that to isolate a wolf from its pack is tantamount to torture. The isolated wolf suffers daily at not being able to socialize with its family. If and when it is returned to the pack, the aggression usually gets worse. I still vividly recalled two years earlier, when I had tried temporarily removing Aipuyi and Motaki from the pack to give Makuyi a chance to heal before her eye operation. I was certain that it was one of the females who was attacking Makuyi, but I didn't know which one, so I removed them both. When I returned the two females to the pack, the aggression toward Makuyi resumed with more ferocity than before.

Thus I knew that removing Aipuyi again would only have delayed another attack, not prevented it, and it would cause her immeasurable torment in the process.

What I had been fearing happened one afternoon in late September. During a pack rally, Aipuyi began to challenge Motomo who, as always, refused to back down. In a fury, Aipuyi launched herself at him. He met her head-on and the two twisted into a blur of fangs and fur. I have never seen a fight between two wolves, before or since, that had this much ferocity and this much intent to do real harm. The other wolves, Kamots included, moved away, not intervening. I began to shout, hoping to distract Aipuyi, but she continued her assault. Trying to physically intervene would have almost guaranteed being bitten myself. I could only watch helplessly, praying that this would not be the end of one or the other of these wolves. Aipuyi flipped Motomo onto his back and bit deep into his flank. Motomo yelped in pain and flailed, trying to escape. Finally Aipuyi paused and Motomo was able to struggle to his feet and limp off into the willows.

What stuck in my mind most was the memory of Makuyi: the pain of having to sedate her and patch her together only to have her attacked again as soon as she was returned to the enclosure. I could not let this happen to another wolf. Wolves will always fight and sometimes draw blood, but these cases were different; they would have resulted in death. Motomo seemed to be unable to move one of his hind legs and I feared that Aipuyi had severed one of his tendons. Would I be forced to operate on him next?

Aipuyi was bleeding from Motomo's defensive bites though I could not determine how severe the injuries were. It didn't matter. I couldn't let this continue until one of them was killed. The next morning, I called Randy Acker and told him I had made the decision that we'd been discussing for months.

It was the most painful choice I had ever made and one that still reverberates to this day, both in my heart and in my relationship with the Wolf Education and Research Center. With the help of Randy and Karen McCall, I entered the enclosure and injected Aipuyi with a strong sedative. While Karen distracted the pack with food, I carried Aipuyi out to Randy's truck, where we quietly put her to sleep.

For the first time in months, there was no bloodshed during feedings. In complete contrast with their behavior when Motaki was killed, the wolves did not seem to mourn Aipuyi's absence, howl out to her, or even search for her the next morning. Rather, it seemed that a new calm and contentment settled over them. Perhaps, if the Sawtooth Pack had been wild, Aipuyi would have abandoned them to start a family of her own. Perhaps the others had been expecting her to leave for some time. Or, perhaps, they were just enjoying peace and quiet at last. As hard as that decision was to make, as painful and controversial as it has been over the years, there is no denying the positive effect it had on the pack. That is my one consolation.

While the euthanasia of Aipuyi created newfound harmony in the pack, it also created discord in the Wolf

Education and Research Center. My action put the WERC staff in the tough position of trying to promote the pack while simultaneously having to tell people that one of the wolves was vicious and had to be put to sleep, but I was thinking of the pack's safety, not of WERC's public relations. I have always felt that if the story were fully explained, everyone would understand why I had to do what I did, that I, as pack manager, had to deal with something that these wolves, being captive, could not. Euthanasia is an extreme and undesirable course of action, but sometimes it is necessary. Years later, when I criticized the organization, the story was twisted to imply that I had made a callous departure from proper management. Ultimately, the public was denied the knowledge that would have provided a real understanding of the issue. I think the wolves, the public, WERC, and I all paid a price for it.

It never ceases to amaze me how wolves can heal, and how they can continue normal lives with a wound that would land a human being in the emergency room. I thought that Motomo might have permanent damage to his leg, but over time the wound healed and soon there was hardly a scar left from the battle.

Best of all, the wolves were playing again, reminding me of their fundamentally temperate natures. The peace that permeated the pack was undeniable, and life at camp was wonderfully quiet during that autumn of 1993. The film was completely finished, and I gave Val, my remaining assistant, some much-deserved time off. For the first time, I lived in wolf camp without the pressure of filming, without having to leave to edit in Ketchum, and without deadlines. I was finally able just to enjoy the company of wolves. I sat among them for hours and together we listened to elk bugling deep in the forest and watched the aspen leaves drift into the still pond. Slowly autumn's brilliance disappeared under the pale gauze of winter.

Wolf: Return of a Legend aired on ABC Television's *World of Discovery* series and went on to be broadcast all over the world. Suddenly, hundreds of millions of people knew these wolves. The Sawtooth Pack had truly become ambassadors for their kind.

I was happy with the success the film achieved and I knew that it was very effective in de-vilifying the wolf, which is what we had set out to do. Secretly, however, I felt that it was somehow lacking, at least in comparison to what I was experiencing every day at camp. When I look at the film now, I can't help but see it as a catalogue of the catastrophes that plagued the early years of the project.

I had spent the better part of three years close to these animals. I had experienced amazing displays of pack unity and devotion to one another, yet I do not feel that the film really did the wolves justice in this regard. I was faced with the task of distilling three years into one hour, a painfully short allotment of time. There was just so much more to tell. The hard truth was that the project was just hitting its stride when it was supposed to be ending. Soon Matsi, Motomo, and Amani would mature and comprise the middle echelon of the pack's social hierarchy, submissive to Kamots and dominant over Lakota. How wonderful it would be just to watch them grow together.

In these final hours of autumn, spent in quiet solitary reflection, I was able to take a step back and see that I had created something truly magical there in the Sawtooths. The project, for all its problems, was a success, and the wolves were getting their message out over the airwaves. The future was uncertain, and I knew the next year would bring untold challenges. My permit for the land was about to expire and no new home for the pack had yet materialized. But, for the moment, as I watched the pack playing in an early snowfall, all the logistical troubles just melted away.

This newfound peace and calm seemed to attract a bit of good luck as well. While I lived alone at wolf camp, determined to take a break and enjoy myself, a delegation from the Nez Perce Tribe decided to pay the pack an unexpected visit. The tribe, which had been selected to manage the federal government's wolf reintroduction project in Idaho, thought that a wolf pack and education center on their land might provide a valuable connection. If the Nez Perce Tribal Council agreed, the tribe could lease a parcel of land to WERC. It would take many months to finalize any kind of agreement, but at the very least, it ended the year with a glimmer of hope.

Immediately, I applied for an extension to my Forest Service permit. It would buy some time for negotiations with the Nez Perce and allow WERC to continue raising money to build a new enclosure. I then booked a flight to

Washington to pitch the idea of a sequel to Dennis Kane.

Dennis was less than enthusiastic about another wolf film. He just didn't see how I could top the one I had already made. Jamie, on the other hand, thought it was a wonderful idea. We met for lunch in Georgetown and I told her all about how the pack was doing, and all the wonderful stories that I had been unable to put in a film as of yet. She had come to know the pack vicariously through conversations like this and thought that a more intimate film about their lives would be an obvious success. In telling me this, she expressed for the first time a desire to meet the wolves in person. She also let it slip that she and her husband were separating.

I took a deep breath and told Jamie that if I was going to make another film I would need help. My head spinning, I asked if she would be willing to come to Idaho, on a temporary basis, of course, and work with me. Coincidentally, I, too, had just ended a rocky relationship several months earlier. Feelings that had been denied for years suddenly burst forth, moving so fast that my brain was racing to catch up.

Jamie and I regarded each other for a moment, making sure we both knew what it was we really were talking about. Then she smiled, that same broad smile that had shone through the Heathrow crowds, and said yes.

I could have floated all the way back to Idaho. Suddenly everything around me was charged with new momentum and direction. As I looked around camp, I imagined Jamie seeing everything for the first time and how she would gradually infuse the place with her spirit, bringing her special touch to life there. Most of all, I couldn't wait for her to meet the pack and to watch them get to know and trust her.

Strangely, it seemed as though my old friends who had worked as my crew could sense a new beginning and began to trickle back. The first to return were my children. My daughter, Christina, had just finished college and agreed to join me as my camera assistant and still photographer. Although Garrick would soon be heading off to school, he returned to spend Christmas at wolf camp.

I noticed that Lakota was exceptionally affectionate toward Garrick, approaching him and licking his face. Normally the omega was very afraid, never allowing strangers, especially men, to come near him. Garrick, however, had bottle-fed him as a puppy. Although two years had passed, Lakota must have remembered my son's kindness.

Normally there was an unspoken rule that there would be no radios or other music at camp since it might disturb the wolves and spoil the wonderful sounds of nature. But in the spirit of the occasion, we brought in a small tape player and some Christmas music. We decorated the yurt with candles and built a cozy fire in the woodstove. In the warm glow, we settled down to a dinner of roasted lamb, a thoughtful surprise that Christina had brought. Outside, the wolves gathered, attracted to the new sound of carols. Before long all five were howling away like a ghostly madrigal choir.

Jake and Patty Provonsha soon returned as well, and their renewed enthusiasm was an inspiration to continue what we had started. Just before the New Year, I picked Jamie up at the airport and in a few days she, too, came to live in a tent in the mountains. I had no contract for another film, and no company was even showing interest in funding one. Nor did I have any scripted story in mind. But in my heart, I knew that if I kept on living with the pack they would tell me a story of their own. It was the beginning of the best years of the project.

Arrival

JAMIE

> He had left me a word, tossed me a key to a door I never
> knew was there and had still to find. A word grows to a
> thought—a thought to an idea—an idea to an act.
>
> —Beryl Markham, *West with the Night*

We all have moments in our lives that, in hindsight, we realize were milestones. It is curious how, when looking back and seeing how perfectly events have lined up, how all the cards fell into place, it is impossible to imagine things happening any other way. So it is for me when I look back on my life in the years before I uprooted myself and moved to Idaho.

I was stopped by a man in the aisle of an airplane in 1987, a brief and pleasant meeting that would turn my life upside down six years later. This handsome gentleman asked if I had been in Africa. Knowing I was sporting a dark suntan and an elaborate necklace of coral and warthog tusk, neither of which are very easy to come by in London, I said, "Yes, what gave it away?" That was the beginning.

He had a sweet smile and his blue eyes sparkled when he laughed. We had three conversations on our way back home, exchanged names, and spoke about Africa—mainly about all the different animals we had seen there. Like me, he was quite a wildlife enthusiast. The conversation turned from where we had been to the homes we were returning to.

I have to admit I was surprised to learn that he lived in Idaho. Although I had just been to Africa, I had never actually been west of the Mississippi. Like most Easterners, all I knew of Idaho was that potatoes came from there and that it was not Iowa. I don't think I had given Idaho a single thought since the second grade, when I had to learn to spell the names of all the states. It was not a place I expected a soft-spoken, worldly gentleman to call home, and certainly not a place that *I* ever expected to call home.

After college, I had consigned my love of animals to being just a childhood fancy, something to cast aside in favor of a responsible life and a career. Yet, years later, all it took was a trip to Africa, and meeting a man who had turned his passion for wildlife into a career, for those smoldering dreams to begin to spark and flicker once more. Of course, it didn't happen in a flash of revelation. It took another year or so before I was willing to really listen to my heart and take a position at the National Zoo. In many ways, I feel Jim gave me the strength to make that career change. In him, I saw the possibilities of a life

I deeply wanted to live, but there was too much that kept us apart. Idaho was such a distant place, and there were so many unknowns. Jim was just getting over a divorce and was so unsure of relationships then. I could not conceive of making such a complete change, giving up everything I had ever known for something that was so uncertain. Instead, I made one last attempt to embrace what was familiar and secure and do what I thought was expected of me—I got married, literally to the boy next door.

When I told Jim of my plans, he said he understood. He congratulated me and said nothing more. All it would have taken was one word from him and I would have dropped everything, but the word never came.

After my wedding, my relationship with Jim dwindled to two or three phone calls a year. Initially our conversations were brief and maintained a professional air. Jim called me with questions about raising infant animals, asking how best to substitute for a mother's care or how to supplement a lion cub's or wolf pup's nutritional needs. Slowly, however, we began to share stories of our lives and to talk more frequently as friends. I was excited to tell him of all the animals I cared for at the zoo—of the joy I experienced raising a tiny kangaroo in a pouch I had made from a flannel pillowcase. When it died unexpectedly, I was devastated, and Jim was the one I wanted to call. Another time, it was he who needed support, over a wolf named Makuyi. His voice trembled when he spoke about her, as I could hear the anguish and the affection he felt for those animals. It was a feeling I experienced in my own work, a feeling that I knew Jim shared and understood. It seemed that we always reached out to each other at our most trying and emotional times, moments when there wasn't another person in the world who could sympathize. After these conversations, I found myself picturing him filming animals and living in his camp in the wilderness. I wondered if I might be living the wrong life, but no, it was all too foreign, too far beyond my reach.

Over the next five years, the spirit of our friendship endured despite the distance between us. In fact, our lives were evolving quite similarly since we'd met, moving along the same course, unconnected but on parallel tracks. On the opposite side of the country, I followed his career as it moved from beavers to cougars to the first wolf film, watching when his specials appeared on television and saving the *National Geographic* articles where his photographs appeared. I was even taking care of the very animals that were the subject of his films. The few times he came to Washington, we had lunch and talked about our work.

In hindsight, it was probably telling that the one topic Jim and I never discussed was our separate relationships. I suppose it would have meant admitting our dissatisfaction with things as they were. For me, it would have meant confronting the reality that I had married a good man, but for the wrong reasons. Somehow I knew that if I fully embraced the new direction my life was taking, that my soul was demanding, my marriage would not survive.

With each passing year, my life was turning further

toward interests I had had when I was much younger—the outdoors, wildlife, even riding—passions that my husband did not share. Try as I might, I was unable to pack these things away like a chest of old keepsakes. My husband and I struggled to reconcile our differences, but we could not. Ultimately, I knew I had to leave behind the comfortable and known life I had so carefully created.

When Jim came to town to meet with his executive producer, we got together for lunch and he told me about his plans to make a second wolf film. For the first time in five years, I mentioned my personal life to him. I told him my husband and I were separating. Jim admitted that he, too, had ended a long relationship only a few months earlier. Before seeing him this time, the future had been a completely blank page. Now it all seemed to make sense. The path that we, in our fear and uncertainty, had lost years ago was suddenly shining right in front of us. Jim needed help on the new film, and for the first time he asked if I would be interested in joining him in Idaho. Finally, here was a chance to pick up where we had left off years before. We didn't know where it would lead but we knew at least we had to try. Three weeks later I was on a plane heading for Idaho and the unknown.

No sooner had I arrived in this strange new place than I found myself on my way to a tented camp on the edge of the wilderness. The road from Ketchum to Stanley wound over a mountain pass and then plunged into a valley to run beside a string of jagged peaks. The land was remote and unfamiliar, but what views, what scenery—the wide-open valley, the river, the snow-capped mountains!

I stared out the car window onto the early winter land-scape, just taking it all in. Every strange new sight brought home the dramatic transformation that my life had suddenly undergone. From time to time, I caught myself wondering why I wasn't more terrified. A few days ago, home was a comfortable house in the Maryland suburbs. Tonight it would be a tent without plumbing, water, or electricity. I had abandoned everything I knew, everything that was cozy and familiar, and yet I never felt safer than I did sitting beside Jim as we made our way toward wolf camp.

I was especially excited to meet the wolves. Jim had spoken about them with such unabashed affection and in such detail that I almost felt I knew them already. My old childhood fantasy about befriending a black bear was resurfacing, only this time it was about to come true. What a shock it was to realize that I was suddenly closer to the person I had been at the age of seven than to who I was at 32.

Although it was the end of December when I arrived in Idaho, there was not much snow yet. There was enough to keep us from driving all the way to wolf camp, but not enough to allow passage by snowmobile. We walked the final mile into camp with our gear strapped to our backs. The change in terrain and plant life was amazing as we moved from the valley toward the mountains. We began walking through scrubby sagebrush that stuck out of the thin snow, but in half a mile the landscape changed from a dry sage prairie to a forested alpine glen with babbling brooks and stands of pine and aspen. I had never even seen lodgepole pines before. A single lodgepole is hardly impressive in terms of height or mass. But looking out over thousands, millions of them as far as the eye could see, all arrow-straight and neatly spaced by the hand of nature, I was mesmerized. All the while the mountains loomed huge, gray, and cold in front of me. In the middle of this picturesque setting, I saw a cluster of white tents and knew we had arrived.

Jim told me that whenever he returned to camp after being away for a few days or more, he liked to announce himself to the pack. He stopped and cupped his hands to his mouth and howled. For a moment the air was still, then a strange sound began to rise and echo off the mountains. At first I thought it was a person calling back to Jim from a distance, but other voices quickly joined in. It actually took me a few seconds to realize that it was indeed the wolves howling in response. It literally stopped me in my tracks. It was an otherworldly sound, at once joyous, mournful, calming, and exhilarating, not at all like the clichéd wolf howls of the movies. Years later I remain equally thrilled by it and equally unable to describe it.

At a distance, the sound seemed to come from everywhere, floating on the air. Had I not known there were only five wolves present, I would have guessed that the number was closer to fifteen. I later learned that they purposefully avoid singing in unison. Each wolf varies its pitch to achieve a perfect dissonance, perhaps to make their numbers sound greater, or perhaps because they enjoy the effect. All I knew then was that it was the most beautiful sound I had ever heard.

When we reached our destination I dropped my bags, not bothering to unpack or acquaint myself with camp just yet. Before anything I had to meet the wolves. I found myself suddenly nervous. Would they like me? Would I be worthy of their trust?

The reception they gave me put my fears to rest. They were waiting for us, huge mounds of fur, whining in expectation, eager to greet their friend Jim and this stranger he brought with him. We entered through a double gate, and the wolves began to gather around me excitedly. Jim suggested I crouch down so I wouldn't get knocked over.

There are many different words I could use to describe that first greeting, none of which would really do it justice. Imagine being engulfed by a soft, fluffy tornado—with tongues. Each one of the wolves wanted to meet me at once, and the way they meet someone is to lick absolutely every inch of the person's face. I very quickly learned to keep my mouth closed during these greetings, which was extremely difficult to do because the urge to burst into a smile was overwhelming. One of the wolves—I don't remember which one—actually managed to get his lower canine tooth stuck up my nose! Now that is an odd sensation.

In addition to all the licking, there was an emphatic conversation going on. All the wolves were whining in excitement but, above that, they were issuing serious growls and snarls. It was a bit disconcerting at first to have all of this going on inches from my face, but Jim explained that it was not directed at me. The higher-ranking wolves were telling the lower-ranking ones to "back off" and let them inspect the stranger first. Despite the growling and the flashing of fangs, I really felt quite safe. The only wolf I did not see was the one called Lakota. Jim assured me that I would meet this shy and special member of the pack when he was ready.

After the enthusiastic greeting, the wolves turned and trotted off into the brush. For a moment I was almost insulted. In human culture, we'd never think of meeting someone, then turning our backs and walking off. We would at least feign interest for a little while and ask a few polite questions. Wolves, however, are unburdened by such rules of etiquette. They had made their greeting; each one had introduced himself to me and had taken his turn inspecting me. As far as they were concerned, the exchange was complete.

Having met the pack, it was time to familiarize myself with camp, which was amazing to say the least. It was as if an elaborate African safari camp had been dropped in the middle of the Idaho mountains. Three tents were spaced among the aspens, all equipped with beds, tables, chairs, and woodstoves. The tents were supported by internal wooden frames to withstand snow and wind.

Nearby stood a larger cook tent that had an entire kitchen, complete with propane stoves and a dishwashing area, a large dining table, storage space, and a sitting area that could be converted into an extra sleeping space. It was far homier and more spacious than I ever imagined. Jim explained that this tent was too large and airy to keep warm during the winter months, nor could it handle the weight of a heavy snowpack. He had left it up a little longer since, so far, it had been a low snow year, but soon we would have to dismantle it and move the kitchen. He pointed to a round tent called a yurt that was currently empty but would soon become the cooking and dining tent for the winter months, as well as sleeping quarters for extra crew members.

Far beyond the yurt, too far—way too far—was the outhouse. I stood there imagining making my way toward the tiny tent in pitch darkness, during a January blizzard, or in July, weaving my way among the snakes and bears that would undoubtedly be waiting for me to make the journey. But for the time being, I cast this concern aside.

That night Jim cooked cheese fondue over a small propane stove and we sat by candlelight in the cook tent, drinking wine that he had packed in for the occasion. It was really our first chance to relax for a moment and catch up on each other's lives. Jim had no shortage of stories about the wolves, all of which made me wish I had been there from the beginning. At the same time, I was overcome with excitement, thinking about what lay ahead. One moment our conversation got a bit too raucous and the wolves started to howl, excited by our laughter. We let our dialogue drop and just shut our eyes and listened to them sing in the darkness.

As we dined, a large pot of water heated on the woodstove. After our meal, we divided the hot water into two plastic tubs. Into one we mixed a sparing amount of biodegradable soap for washing, and the other we used for rinsing. After cleaning the dishes, we poured the used water into a hole filled with small rocks to leech into the ground. I was impressed with how thoughtfully everything was planned and carried out and how comfortable it all was without any of the modern conveniences to which I was accustomed. When everything was cleaned and put away, we shared some more wine and talked on into the night.

Finally it was time for bed. As I pushed the cook tent flap aside and stepped out, a blast of cold air hit me like a sledgehammer. Sitting beside the woodstove in the coziness of the cook tent, I had all but forgotten that it was December in the high mountains. The sharp cold on my face shocked me into recalling just how far I was from family and friends and the only home I knew. Not once had I ever imagined my life in such a frigid, landlocked, unpopulated place. For the first time, I felt a wave of apprehension. Would I ever adapt to life in this place? Had I made a terrible mistake?

We hurried through the cold to the sleep tent. An hour earlier, Jim had lighted a fire in the small stove and already it was warm and inviting. Old Navajo blankets covered the walls, and on a small handmade desk, candles flickered and cast a warm glow. The bed, though nothing more than a pine frame and foam mattress, was quite comfortable. Jim had fitted it with thick flannel sheets and a large overstuffed comforter. Best of all, there were pillows—real pillows. All my apprehension, all the intense and conflicting emotions that had battled inside me all day long, drifted off like candle smoke as I sank into bed.

The next morning I awoke to glorious sunshine. The

first thing I noticed was how the ceiling of the tent was beautifully dappled with the silhouettes of fallen aspen leaves. The next thing I noticed was the cold. The fire had died during the night and the tent was definitely frostier than it had been when we had climbed into bed. But Jim was already stoking the fire again and the tent soon began to warm up. It was going to be a busy day, for today we would finish preparing the camp for winter—a project that Jim had started a month earlier. The last order of business was to dismantle the large cook tent and move a scaled-down version of the kitchen into the yurt.

First, however, it was time to experience the camp "amenities." I bundled up for a trip to the outhouse, which was actually rather attractive. It was a tiny white tent with red trim and a half moon cut in the back. Best of all, it had been situated behind a grove of willows, with the entrance facing away from the camp, providing plenty of privacy without sacrificing the nice view of the mountains. As I sat there, I wondered what my parents must be thinking. My mother, of course, could not understand why her child would want to live in a tent in the middle of nowhere and, God forbid, use an outhouse! My grandmother was so bewildered by the whole affair that I decided to wait until the project was over before telling her that we did not, as she believed, stay in a hotel every night. She would have loved to hear about the bath I took that evening.

For warm weather, there was a shower tent with bags of water that were hung up to heat in the sun. But due to the short summers in the mountains, this luxury only lasted for about three months a year. It was way too cold to use the shower tent now. For winter bathing, the middle of our sleep tent had a small trap door cut into the wooden floor. Lifting the door revealed a wooden grate over the ground. I heated a large pot of creek water on the woodstove, crouched over the grate, and ladled the water over me. It was a rather respectable bath.

Time and again, I was amazed at how well organized camp life was. Jim and his crew had placed sticks and rocks along the trail to keep us on the proper path and avoid impacting more of the ground than necessary. When we took apart the cook tent, I saw how the essentials fit very neatly into the smaller yurt. The stoves, the pots, the table, the dishwashing tubs—everything had a specific space where it fit perfectly. Baskets and mesh bags hung on the walls, providing storage for winter gear where air could circulate and allow for drying pants, gloves, and hats. A bench doubled as an extra bed, tucked nicely against the wall. As we transferred everything, the yurt went from being a cold and empty shell to a snug little dwelling. Although I would cherish the long summer evenings in the spacious cook tent, this cozy, efficient little yurt that was the center of life for most of the year is what I remember most fondly as home.

Lakota

JAMIE

O n that initial day at wolf camp, when I prepared to
meet the pack for the first time, Jim explained that
I should expect the wolves to rush up and greet me, all
except Lakota. I should not expect a greeting from him;
he rarely greeted anyone.

Kamots was first to step out of the group, snarling lest
one of the others dare to approach me before he had
given me the initial going-over. Once he had checked me
out to his satisfaction, Matsi, Amani, and Motomo
rushed up. As suddenly as it began, it was over. Despite
what Jim had said, I still found myself waiting for the fifth
greeting. But not only did Lakota neglect to greet me, he
was nowhere to be seen.

Jim explained that Lakota had been forced into the
omega position by the other wolves following the death of
Motaki, the pack's original omega. When the omega
died, the social order was thrust into a state of chaos
while the pack sorted out the ranks of its individual mem-

bers. This resulted in a series of dominance fights in which it was established once and for all that Lakota was the new lowest-ranking member of the pack. He was just beginning to accept his lot in life as the scapegoat, the focus of the pack's aggression. It was an unenviable status that he would endure for the next four and a half years.

Jim explained that Lakota's unwillingness to greet me was not only due to his shyness around strangers—something that was just part of his personality and contributed to his being selected as omega—but also because Lakota knew that the arrival of a new face would get the other wolves excited. It was best for him to keep his distance until things calmed down.

The social hierarchy of a pack is what maintains order, dictating who makes decisions, who mates with whom, who eats first, and who eats last. This order is constantly reinforced by displays of dominance and submission. Unfortunately, the omega bears the brunt of this behavior. One or many of the wolves will assert themselves over the omega, who can be expected to flip over onto his back, whimpering in surrender. Generally this is a bloodless exchange, but at times, especially during the breeding season, it can get vicious and extremely difficult to watch.

In more complex wolf packs, there will be an alpha male and female and frequently an omega male and female. In wolf hierarchy, the males tend to dominate other males and the females dominate other females so that there is generally a low-ranking member of each sex. The alpha pair would never allow the omega male and female to mate; therefore the omegas are not pair-bonded to each other like the alphas. When I joined the project, the Sawtooth Pack was small, consisting only of five males. So Lakota held the omega position alone.

The following morning, we still had not seen Lakota, and Jim began to get a bit uneasy. The previous spring he had seen cougar tracks in camp. We began walking together through the dusting of snow, searching among the dense willows and fallen lodgepole pines.

On one occasion, I chanced to look back over my shoulder and was quite startled to find the pack following close behind me. It was my second day at wolf camp, and I was still getting used to the sudden appearance of large predators. Kamots led the way, followed by Matsi, Motomo, and Amani, lined up in single file, not making a sound, behaving like perfect schoolchildren on a field trip. When we stopped to look around, they would all halt and wait patiently for us to resume walking. I was amazed at how completely silent and graceful they were. Our movements were inefficient and downright clumsy compared to their purposeful glide. I wondered how on earth we could ever find Lakota in all this space if he didn't want to be found.

We continued to search the enclosure for over an hour and found no trace of poor Lakota. By the time Jim and I returned to the spot where we had started, our little band of followers had grown bored with our walkabout. Kamots glanced around with a kind of air that implied he had better things to do and moseyed off to chase squirrels. Matsi, Amani, and Motomo dutifully followed him.

As soon as they were out of sight, we heard a rustling

in the bushes and out crept Lakota. He had been shad-
owing us the entire time! It seemed he didn't want to
miss our little walk but thought it best to keep out of sight
lest the other four members of the pack decided to pick
on him. A wolf can disappear into its surroundings with
an almost magical ability—there one second, gone the
next—and they can move with amazing silence. Here was
a 125-pound dark-gray beast moving silently only a few
feet away from us, completely undetected in a field of
blazing red willows and fresh white snow.

One of the first things I noticed about him was his posture. He kept his tail tucked, his shoulders hunched, and
his head lowered as he moved uncertainly toward me. It
wasn't until he reached me that I realized he was a huge
wolf, larger than the three other mid-ranking wolves and
possibly even larger than his brother, Kamots, the alpha,
although his submissive posture made it difficult to tell.
His paws were definitely bigger. Obviously there was more
to social rank in a wolf pack than mere size and strength.

Lakota reached me and timidly licked my face. I ran my
hand down his back through his new winter coat. His skin
was riddled with small bumps and scabs where the other
wolves had nipped him, and there were small scars on his
muzzle where the fur would not grow back. In dominance
displays, a dominant wolf will frequently grab the muzzle of
the submissive wolf, as a mother might do to discipline her
pups. Lakota's face bore the marks from such encounters.
As I sat with him, he began to relax a little, beginning to
trust that I wasn't going to hurt him. Then he took his paw,
gently placed it on my shoulder, and gazed at me with his

sweet, wise, amber eyes. We sat that way for quite a while. From that moment, I was captivated by him and would forever hold a special place for him in my heart.

Over the years, Lakota and I continued to have this special bond. Sometimes I would purposefully sneak away from the rest of the pack to carry on this clandestine friendship with the beleaguered omega. We were careful not to show any interest in each other when the rest of the pack was nearby; both of us were concerned that he would call attention to himself and risk being disciplined by one of the mid-ranking wolves. Instead, I would join him at times when he was by himself, and we would sit together, his paw on my shoulder, as we had done when we first met.

It may sound odd, but he became a wonderful omega. In some ways, the omega is like the court jester. He must suffer terrible abuse at the hands of the king and court, but he is undeniably loved. Like a jester, the omega is often the one to instigate play and act the fool.

During a period when the pack's mood was calm and relaxed, I watched Lakota approach his brother Kamots. The omega suddenly crouched into a play stance with his head low, front legs splayed wide, rump and wagging tail in the air. Kamots sprang into action, darting and snapping playfully. Soon they were tearing through the meadow, Lakota only inches ahead of Kamots' jaws. The knowledge that this chase was not a dangerous dominance display was written all over Lakota's body. He zigzagged through the grass with his mouth agape and his lips pulled back as if in a smile, nearly allowing himself to be caught, then leaping ahead. Eventually Lakota was caught, or let himself be caught. He flipped over onto his back in surrender, bestowing on Kamots the full victory. Kamots straddled his brother, snarling and snapping in mock aggression. Lakota gently licked the muzzle of the victor, the wolf equivalent of saying "uncle," and the game was over.

On another occasion, I again saw Kamots and Lakota racing through the meadow in a game of chase. The two brothers are extremely similar in appearance—large with very typical black and gray markings—so it took me a while before I realized to my amazement that this time Lakota was chasing Kamots. I couldn't imagine how this role reversal could be happening. In an amazing variation of their standard game, Kamots was allowing himself to be the victim!

As I grew to know these wolves, I realized that this was a regular occurrence, one that bears no scientific explanation other than the fact that sometimes it is fun to be the one getting chased. To me, it implies that there is a lot more going on in the inner lives of wolves than we can imagine. In human relationships, an older, stronger brother might let a younger brother pin him in a mock wrestling match, feigning defeat and letting his younger sibling celebrate victory. Both know who the dominant one is, but it is fun to reverse the roles. Many a scientist would gasp at the thought of ascribing emotions to an animal, but since I'm not a scientist, I can allow myself the indulgence. Witnessing scenes like this, the only interpretation I could make was that

Kamots and Lakota genuinely cared for each other.

Some years later, while scouting for wolves along the Yukon River with Jim, I watched from a small airplane as a pack played a game of tag in the deep snow. Though it was too far to make out, I could imagine their expressions of joy as they took turns running after each other and nipping at one another's tails. I knew that one of the wolves below me was the omega, inciting the others into chasing him and keeping the game going.

Sadly, there were times when Lakota's playful attitude would backfire. The attention he would draw to himself could sometimes result in a full-on mobbing. As he'd run, we could see him realize that the pursuit was not a game this time. It was painful to watch his hopeful expectations dissolve, fear spring into his eyes, and his entire posture change. Quickly he'd flip over onto his back and yelp in submission while each mid-ranking member of the pack got his digs in. Amazingly enough, he would return time after time, inviting the pack to join in a game of chase, or tug-of-war, eternally brave and eternally hopeful.

Group rallies were another risky time for Lakota. Often the pack gathered together and howled, as if to celebrate its solidarity. The real reason for this ritual is unknown. Sometimes it appeared that Kamots would purposefully start to howl, apparently calling the pack together to remind everyone of his leadership. Other times the rallies seemed more impromptu, a spontaneous howl bubbling up inside one of the wolves, then bursting forth uncontrollably.

When one wolf began to howl, the others would quickly join in and assemble around Kamots. As the rally grew in intensity, the wolves often displayed their dominance, sparring, growling, and pinning each other to the ground. These were dangerous times for the omega. Regardless of the bickering that went on between the mid-ranking wolves, Amani and Motomo, most of the aggression was ultimately transferred to Lakota. All the same, he would often be there, lending his voice to the group howl.

When I began recording the sounds that would later be used for the soundtrack of *Wolves at Our Door,* I made an effort to record each wolf's individual voice as cleanly as possible. I would try to find an occasion when a wolf was howling more or less by himself, rather than right in the middle of the group. This was easier with Lakota because he often stood on the fringe, howling but trying to keep a low profile. With the eight-foot boom microphone in front of me, I'd slowly and quietly approach him in a crawl, careful not to disturb his singing.

When I first recorded his howl, I was amazed at what was coming through my headphones. Lakota, eyes shut and head thrown back, was just pouring his heart out. His rich, mournful voice soared into the evening and hung in the air for what seemed like forever. I actually found myself welling up at the sheer beauty and expressiveness of his song. I felt as though I were listening to him sing the blues, giving voice to all the loneliness and pain that his low status brought him. Even when new pups were added to the pack in later years, no member of the Sawtooth Pack ever voiced a howl that came close to Lakota's in its beauty and sadness.

To experience a pack of wolves howling together is to bear witness to one of the most mysterious and awe-inspiring events in nature. It almost seems that the wolves themselves have no choice but to join in when the alpha howls. Lakota could never be certain if his participation would get him into trouble, yet he could not help but be a part of it. He would slink from wolf to wolf and pay his respects, his tail tucked and his head nearly scraping the ground. But as Kamots continued to howl, you could see Lakota's voice welling up inside him, and, after a few tentative mumbles, he was howling away, trying to keep off to the side, but wanting to be involved.

His participation was regarded as offensive by some of the mid-ranking wolves, as if he were overstepping his bounds. Amani seemed especially determined to put Lakota in his place, and during pack rallies he would frequently rush at Lakota, snarling and flashing his teeth. It often looked as though Amani had knocked Lakota off his feet, but in reality Lakota was just flipping over in surrender. There would follow a chorus of growls and yips while the other wolves got into the action. Although Lakota was rarely hurt in these displays, his cries were agonizing to hear. Amani would stand triumphantly over Lakota, making the omega beg to be let up. Once he was satisfied with his own display, Amani would relent and Lakota would slink away quietly, through with howling for a while.

I had grown accustomed to being extra careful when giving attention to Lakota, but there were times when our surreptitious meetings would be discovered. Any human activity always drew intense interest from the pack. If Motomo or Amani spotted Lakota and me sitting together, they would hurry over to investigate and to find out why Lakota was getting attention and they were not.

In some ways they reminded me of children. If one wolf had something—a bone, a stick, or the attention of a person—all the others wanted it. I was most concerned at these moments that my display of affection would become an occasion for Lakota to get pummeled, so I quickly learned to turn my attention to the other wolves when they approached. This seemed to satisfy them and keep the peace. Lakota knew the rules all too well and would discreetly walk away from me, unharmed but always the underdog.

Moving Camp

JIM

The quickest way to learn the language of a species is to do so as a social partner.

—Konrad Lorenz

When Jamie joined me at wolf camp that winter, it was like the entire world breathed a huge sigh of relief. Both wolves and people were experiencing a new-found calm. It was wonderful to see everyone—Jake, Patty, Christina, and the wolves—take to Jamie so well. She brought with her from the National Zoo a gentleness and confidence with animals, tempered by a professionalism that did not allow her strong love of wolves to dissolve into fantasy. From the moment she met them, she instinctively knew that everything was to be on their terms. She never tried to approach them when they were not in a social mood and she never treated them as pets. Working with her by my side, I knew she shared my vision and I finally felt complete.

Immediately upon her arrival, Jamie took a great interest in filmmaking. She was already an accomplished photographer and immediately began taking photos for a picture book that we would call *The Sawtooth Wolves*. Although she did not have experience with filmmaking, she had watched my films and other wildlife documentaries over the years and had actually developed a keen sense for how they were put together. She made me see the wolves through fresh eyes, full of wonder and amazement. With Jake, and sometimes Johann, Jamie and I began to develop ideas for a new documentary.

Jamie also began training to operate the sound recording and mixing equipment and took to it naturally. Sound recording became her passion, her obsession. With contagious enthusiasm, she set herself to record not only the "live sounds" that would correspond to the film I shot but to build an entire library of wolf vocalization. She captured all the different sounds that made up wolf communication, in every context and every mood: the haunting dissonance of a far-off howl, the excited conversation of a pack rally, even the faint little whines they make to one another almost constantly. Soon Jamie was able to identify each wolf by voice alone. Although I had been with these wolves for three years, I hadn't developed such a skill. It didn't take long before I was asking her which howl belonged to which wolf.

With the renewed vitality that Jamie and Christina brought, I decided that it was time to change our approach to filming. Although I was happy with *Wolf: Return of a Legend,* I always thought it could have gone deeper into the private life of wolves. What I had most hoped for was to get as close to life inside a wolf pack as a human being could, and to bring the audience along with me. The politics, the history, the reintroduction of an endangered animal—these were all fascinating topics, but what I really wanted to share was the essence of the wolf, the feeling one gets just from being in their company.

We needed to live closer to the animals than before. The calm that the pack was demonstrating and their trust in us made it possible. I decided in the spring of 1994 to move our camp inside the wolves' territory.

The old system and the old camp had always had shortcomings. No matter how I tried to disguise it, the enclosure was a barrier between the wolves and me. The time I spent inside was temporary. The wolves could hear us at camp but could not see what we were up to. When we entered the enclosure, they always heard our approach and never failed to come to investigate. After all, the sound of the gate opening sometimes meant the arrival of food and, at the very least, it meant the arrival of people and an interesting diversion from business as usual. Although they were completely used to human presence, they were so intelligent and curious that they always felt compelled to greet us when we entered their territory. Granted, after a while they would lose interest in us and go about their business, but by that time our arrival often would have disrupted the very behavior I had set out to film. More and more, I began to wonder what would happen if we were already living inside their territory instead of coming and going each day. What if we became a part of their lives, like furniture, virtually ignored?

There were also more practical reasons for wanting to move our tents. Every summer the cattle from a nearby ranch would wander from their neighboring range up into the national forest and into our camp. In Idaho, people put up fences to keep cattle out, not in. They are pretty much free to roam where they please, and this bunch decided that our cool meadow setting with its tender grass was the perfect place. Consequently, every summer we'd find ourselves rebuilding trampled tents and dancing around the minefield of cow-pies that seemed to be everywhere. It was exasperating that all our efforts to stay on the narrow paths, to avoid tearing up creek beds or trampling the wildflowers, were rendered irrelevant when these half-ton beasts ambled through.

One might think that a pack of five wolves would be an adequate deterrent to wandering bovines, but the cattle seemed oblivious to the threat. The wolves really did not know what to make of the slow, dull-witted creatures. I remember entering the enclosure one summer day and being surprised and a bit concerned that the pack did not come to investigate as usual. After twenty minutes of searching, I found them at the southern perimeter, tails wagging, gazing at a group of four or five cows on the other side of the barrier. Far from behaving like fierce predators, they carried themselves in the same manner they did when they played, looking as if they had just made some new friends. The cows, too, seemed strangely intrigued.

We had to wait until the snow melted completely before beginning the process of moving camp, but as soon as the ground was dry, we set to work. With Jake back on the crew, the new plan began to take shape. The camp would be simplified, comprising only the yurt and a sleeping tent for Jamie and myself. The other tents, the shower, and the outhouse remained outside. The yurt became the center of life, the place where everyone gathered for meals, to work on equipment, and to discuss the production.

Jake and I decided that the best way to make a livable camp in the smallest area possible would be to construct a platform eight feet high on which the yurt would stand. The platform would be wrapped in chain link so that gear, firewood, and tools could be stored underneath it. At one end of the platform, the fence would be extended to enclose our sleeping tent at ground level.

Our first job was to erect the support posts, cut from dead lodgepole pines, and then lay down planking to form the deck. All this activity provided endless fascination for the wolves, who couldn't get enough of stealing tools and lumber. Believing that wolves would not try to climb our steep staircase—more of a ladder than actual steps—we began setting up the yurt on top of the platform before installing the fence. Jamie and I were setting up the kitchen inside the yurt when a huge shadow on the canvas, like something out of Little Red Riding Hood's worst nightmare, made us both jump. Kamots, always the most brazen, had scaled the eight-foot staircase and was exploring the foreign structure. Before sacrificing too many tools to the pack's inquisitive spirit, we decided to add the chain link as soon as possible.

When the move was completed, we had created a tiny enclosure for people inside a huge enclosure for wolves. Our presence quickly became commonplace. Daily activities such as chopping wood or repairing gear were now performed, in full view of the pack, inside this little compound. When we passed through the single gate from our world into theirs, it was a nonevent. Almost immediately, we began to see subtleties of body language and behavior that we had failed to notice earlier.

It was my daughter, Christina, who put our technique of observation in the plainest language. She made the analogy, "Dad, if you were to move into a glass house and knew you were being watched, your lifestyle would probably change. You would at least stop singing in the shower. But if you had always lived in a glass house, you would do what comes naturally." That was it—having grown up with observers, the Sawtooth Pack could behave more "naturally" than wild wolves would with people in such close proximity. Moving our camp was the culmination of this philosophy, and it made an incredible difference.

Filming wild wolves in Alaska and Yellowstone, I had learned that I could never observe the same rich social interaction in the wild that I could among the Sawtooth Pack. First of all, I could never get truly close; the animals are just too wary of humans. Furthermore, the process of filming wild wolves, the mere presence of an observer, intimidates the animals and changes their behavior. In general, observations of wild wolves have been conducted from afar, using radio telemetry and spotting scopes. Most of what we know of a wolf pack's social structure comes from observations of captive packs in enclosures much smaller and less natural than ours. Some of what Jamie and I were to observe in the years to come had simply never been seen before.

One of the first revelations, and one that I had not anticipated, was the pack's behavior as they awoke each morning. With the camp outside the fence, we had never been able to see them perform this ritual. Even if I had tried to enter the enclosure before dawn, the noise would have quickly roused them. The very first morning in the new camp, Jamie and I silently slipped from our tent, climbed the platform, and watched the pack greet the day.

Surprisingly, the pack slept separately, many yards from one another, even in winter, when I assumed they would huddle together for warmth. In spite of this, they seemed to all begin stirring at exactly the same moment, as though their minds were connected by some subconscious thread. This particular morning Motomo, the black wolf, was first to his feet. He stretched luxuriously and let go a contented yawn, genuinely appearing to enjoy finding himself in the conscious world again.

The first thing Motomo did was to walk directly over to Kamots, and the two wolves touched noses. Motomo endeavored to hold his head lower than Kamots' in a gesture of deference. This was not easy since the alpha was still lying down, and Motomo had to rest his head on the ground in order to be appropriately submissive. As Kamots rose to his feet, Motomo gently licked his leader's face and whimpered, much like a pup would do.

One by one, the other wolves from Matsi to Lakota did exactly the same thing, licking Kamots' face to acknowledge his rule, then turning to bestow a quick good-morning lick on one another, all the while vocalizing intently back and forth. We began to realize how important these greetings were to the pack, since they conducted the same ritual every morning without fail. It seemed to be a sort of morning reaffirmation of their bond. Occasionally the greeting would escalate into a full-blown pack rally, but more often than not, it was a quiet affair, lacking a rally's frenzy and dominance displays.

After watching this for several weeks, I realized that the pack greeted Jamie and me in much the same way they greeted one another. Franz Camenzind, a friend and cameraman who had taken over for Bob Poole, wanted to get a shot of the wolves greeting me in the morning. After I had been out among them for a few minutes, he asked if I could return to my tent and repeat the process so he could film it. When I repeated my actions a second time, the wolves completely ignored me. Their attitude seemed to be, "Oh, it's you. We already said hello to you today." To them, I suppose my actions were as pointless as arriving at a dinner party and shaking the host's hand, then returning to the door fifteen minutes later and trying to do it again. It made no sense to them at all. Having the pack respond to me this way was actually quite a relief. Although we wanted to get this shot, their response meant that moving our camp was having the desired effect. They were reacting less and less to our presence.

The raised platform of the yurt provided a wonderful vantage point from which to film and observe the pack unobtrusively. From there, I was able to film a long sequence of the wolves playing in the meadow without them even noticing me. They had come together for a late afternoon game of tag and as they took turns pulling one another's tails and leaping from the willows in ambush, I got the feeling that I was seeing truly wild behavior. The bird's-eye view of their game became one of my favorite segments in *Wolves at Our Door.*

There were some wonderful surprises as well. One day early that July, I was sitting on the yurt platform, watching the pack as they slowly milled around the flowering meadow, apparently looking for something. For a moment, I honestly thought they were smelling the flowers. The wolves always sniffed anything that smelled remotely interesting, but they moved on once their curiosity had been satisfied. As full of interesting behavior as these animals were, I nonetheless would have found it hard to believe that they were lounging in the meadow, like Ferdinand the Bull, smelling the new summer blossoms.

Not wanting to approach them and possibly disturb their behavior, I retrieved my binoculars from the tent and focused in on Motomo. Rather than sniffing, he was contentedly chewing on something. Had they found an early bunch of grasshoppers or a nest of pocket mice? I turned my attention to Matsi just in time to see him snip the blossom off a wildflower, chew, and swallow it. Amazingly enough, these ferocious carnivores were having a little salad.

It took Jamie and me several days of watching them to realize that they were methodically seeking out and eating only one particular flower—the shooting star, a member of the primrose family with bright magenta and yellow blossoms. Jamie sampled a flower or two and reported them "rather bland," but I have since read that the indigenous people here sometimes roasted the leaves and roots for food. Whatever the reason, the wolves appeared to enjoy this, and only this, flower. We never saw them touch another variety, but every year they would graze on this plant.

Although these vegetarian moments did not make it into the final cut of *Wolves at Our Door,* another unexpected revelation became one of the film's highlights. In the film's opening, there is a night feeding scene in which the wolves run toward the camera, their eyes glowing, pulsating green, red, blue, and gold in the darkness. Without a doubt, the new camp setup gave me the inspiration, albeit inadvertently, for what is probably the most recognized sequence in the film.

The circumstances that inspired this sequence were purely accidental. The only disadvantage to living inside the wolves' territory was that the outhouse was now on the other side of two locked gates, making the unanticipated midnight trip a great deal more complicated than it had once been. It was now an ordeal of stumbling through the darkness, trying to negotiate the double gate and padlock through the fog of sleep, while trying to avoid tripping over any wolves. Instead of carrying flashlights, we took to wearing headlamps for the undertaking, freeing our hands to work the gate. The sound of the rattling fence would often attract the pack's interest. When I returned from my trip, Matsi, Motomo, and Amani came trotting in my direction.

What I saw woke me from my half-sleep. Out of the absolute darkness, six glowing circles danced. The effect was dazzling! Three pairs of disembodied eyes, reflecting the light of my headlamp, bounced as the three young wolves ran toward me. Not until they were nearly in front of me did their soft forms emerge from the darkness.

I had often witnessed how their eyes reflected light, but until now it had always been the beam of a hand-held flashlight, which I carried at waist level. With the light now shining from my forehead, the wolves' eyes reflected directly back into mine, and I was dazzled by their unearthly radiance.

Jamie and I both knew that it would be an amazing scene if we could re-create it for the film. And we were right; to this day, the night hunting sequence is the one that receives the most praise, and from what I have heard, is probably responsible for the film winning an Emmy Award for Cinematography. I usually don't have the heart to tell people that their favorite shot was inspired by a midnight trip to the loo, but inspiration often strikes at strange times.

People often assume that I used some elaborate technical wizardry to create the effect of glowing eyes. In fact, it was achieved by taping a flashlight to the top of my camera and narrowing the beam with a cardboard paper-towel roll. I then rolled the camera at a very slow speed, allowing more light to reach the film and making the image a bit blurry, exactly like taking a still photograph at a very slow shutter speed. The result was that the wolves appeared as streaking trails of light, emerging from the darkness like devils. It worked perfectly for the segment that presented the wolf as "beasts of our dreams and nightmares."

Moving the camp had all sorts of other unanticipated side effects. I was finally relieved of the annoyance of having to drag my camera equipment with me every time I left, a process that was hard on the gear. I could now leave everything at camp, behind a locked gate, surrounded by five of the best guards anyone could ask for, confident that no one would risk trying to steal it.

On the other hand, after the move, we suddenly began seeing a growing number of field mice in our tents. Having lived for three years in a 25-acre death zone, the rodents quickly learned that there was now a little island sanctuary where they could hide out. The word spread like wildfire among the mouse population and our camp was nearly overrun. Releasing trapped mice back into the meadow became just another part of the daily routine.

When I look back on the day that we moved ourselves inside the wolves' territory, I see it as the moment when the human world and the wolf world merged. It was the true fulfillment of my vision that had been developing since my work with beavers. We were no longer living close to the animals; we were living among them. From that point forward, every second of film we shot, every still photograph, every observation we made was richer and more intimate. I don't know if I would have opted to make this move if it hadn't been for Jamie, for when she joined me at camp, she made it fun again. Her enthusiasm revitalized the project, sparked new creative energy, and inspired me to tell the story of our lives with the Sawtooth Pack.

New Additions

JAMIE

Wolf: Return of a Legend brought the Sawtooth Pack a certain celebrity status throughout the country. Best of all, it had succeeded in attracting the attention of some influential neighbors to the north. Shortly before my arrival, the Nez Perce Tribe sent delegates to visit the pack. Jim met with Tribal Chairman Charles Hayes to discuss the possibility of providing land for the pack's future home. After some lobbying by Chairman Hayes, the Nez Perce Tribe agreed to lease WERC a parcel of land where an enclosure could be built. We had made that first step in providing a new home for the pack, finding a place where they would be safe when the filming was completed. It was a huge relief.

For the next several months Jim, Jake, Patty, and I made periodic journeys up to Winchester, Idaho, to inspect the land during different seasons and stake off an area equal in size to the wolves' current territory. Each trip we made reassured us even more that the pack's future was secure. WERC was raising money to build an enclosure and visitor center and assured us that the facility would be ready by the summer of 1995.

In the years that followed, Carla Higheagle, a representative of the Nez Perce Tribe, visited the pack and stayed overnight in our camp. Initially, she seemed a little bit intimidated by the wolves. On her first visit, she wore quite a bit of makeup, probably because she knew that Jim would be filming her. Since neither I nor any of the women on the crew ever wore makeup at camp, I don't imagine the wolves had ever encountered it before. Apparently they found it to be irresistibly delicious. Poor Carla crouched in the snow, struggling to maintain some semblance of dignity for the camera, while the wolves just mobbed her. Carla managed a nervous smile with her lips glued shut, while Kamots, Matsi, Motomo, and Amani endeavored to remove every trace of makeup from her face. After that introduction, she began to relax around them and grew to enjoy her visits.

Thinking the situation was well in hand, Jim allowed himself to be talked into resigning from WERC's board of directors. The board felt that his filmmaking business created a conflict of interest unsuitable for a nonprofit organization, and, in truth, that was a legitimate concern. We were told that his departure was merely a technicality and that he would be needed as an advisor. Sadly, that promise proved hollow in the end. Ultimately, it meant that Jim relinquished any real influence over WERC's actions from that point forward. It was a mistake that would plague us for years to come.

At wolf camp, however, the bureaucracy of WERC seemed far away. When we focused on the job of making a second film and caring for the pack, life was never better. The work was difficult, but the job at hand was clear. In our relationship with the wolves, there were no such things as duplicity and façade. While we were in their world, we were free from the hidden agendas that can plague human relationships.

Everything was running so smoothly with the pack that when Jim's old friend Karin Rundquist phoned to say that two pairs of her adult wolves had bred, Jim and I agreed that if there was ever a time to add more wolves to the small pack, this was it. The one element obviously missing from the Sawtooth Pack was the presence of female wolves. It was a crucial factor in creating a situation that really mirrored the behavior of a wild pack. We knew we wanted to make a second film that would delve deeper into the inner mechanics of wolf society than any film had done before. There was so much that we wanted to observe and share: the way young wolves integrate into an adult pack, the emergence of an alpha female, perhaps even the birth of pups.

Karin runs a small wolf education center of her own, allowing school groups to come and experience wolves. Neither of the two litters were large and she needed to keep most of them for her own pack, but she was willing to part with two or three pups. As we drove north along the Salmon River and over the Bitterroot Range into Montana, I squirmed in my seat with all the anticipation and concern of a mother on her way to pick up an adopted child. The spectacular scenery of my first road trip out West only added to my excitement. At Karin's place, three ten-day-old puppies were waiting for us in a cardboard box—three of the tiniest balls of fur imaginable, all curled up together.

Two of the pups were nearly identical, a gray male and female from the same litter. The third pup was a black female, born a few days earlier to a different set of parents. Initially, Jim was reluctant to take more than two pups, but the black female's parents had been the parents of Motaki, one of Jim's favorite wolves—and the one who had been killed by a mountain lion.

After a quick trip to the veterinarian, we set out for home, a journey that was doubly long because we had to continually stop to feed and clean up after the pups. I had prepared a formula to simulate a mother's milk, and the little things couldn't get enough of it. After eating, they would fall asleep in a clump and all would be quiet for a time, but soon one of them would begin to stir and incite the others to play. They seemed so wobbly and weak on their tiny legs, but in an instant the trio could transform into a single snarling fuzz-ball that ricocheted around the cardboard box in the back of the van. Their attention never strayed too far from their stomachs, and after a half-hour of play they would settle in to another round of feeding. Then they dozed off and started the process all over again.

Such tiny pups need their mother's body to keep them warm on chilly spring nights. Since they didn't have the benefit of a mother, we elected to keep them inside in climate-controlled comfort for the first couple of weeks. So, like the rest of the Sawtooth Pack before them, these three spent their early days of life in a pen in the mud room. The cardboard box that was once their home now served as a makeshift den where they could huddle together and sleep. Hot-water bottles wrapped in soft towels helped to substitute for a mother's body heat.

When the older five males were born, Jim's crew gave them names taken from the Lakota Sioux and Blackfoot languages. Knowing now that one day the Nez Perce would be providing a home for the pack, I decided to give the new wolves Nez Perce names. With the help of a tribal historian, I tried to pick out words that described personality traits that a wolf might have and that just sounded nice.

The gray male received the name Wahots, the Nez Perce word for "howls a lot" or "likes to howl." Of course we had no way of knowing what kind of personality Wahots would grow up to have, but it seemed like an appropriate name for a wolf. Oddly enough, he did end up being one of the most vocal members of the pack. To Wahots' nearly identical sister we gave the name Wyakin. Wyakin is a guardian spirit said to come to Nez Perce children during vigils, revealing truths about life and teaching special songs.

The little black female was a bit more difficult. Jake began calling her "Black Lassie." It was not the kind of name that stirred the imagination, but I did my best to accommodate him. Because colors in the Nez Perce language are repeated, their word for black is "chemukh-

chemukh"; and "ayet" is the Nez Perce word for girl. Thus Chemukh-Chemukh Ayet was the closest thing to Black Lassie I could come up with. After about five minutes, her name was simplified to Chemukh.

I remember Nez Perce Elder Horace Axtell laughing when he heard the name, since in the Nez Perce language it made absolutely no sense. These were not real names, just stray terms plucked from a dictionary, so of course, to a member of the Nez Perce Tribe all our choices sounded a bit ridiculous, like naming a child Olive Dip, or Fax Machine.

Feeding took place every four hours, though it seemed like the pups were hungry all the time. We warmed the formula to make it more appealing, while the pups scampered around the mud room in anticipation. It was important that we hold the puppies as we fed them so they would associate human contact with food, comfort, and security, helping them to develop a bond with us. The little things tore into the bottles so voraciously that the rubber nipples had to be replaced every few days. I could only imagine what a mother wolf goes through, especially after the pups' needle-sharp baby teeth begin to grow in. Maybe that's why she weans them so quickly.

After feeding, we spent more time handling the pups, talking softly to them, and allowing them to play. We did not roughhouse as one might be tempted to do with a domestic dog puppy. These animals were programmed by instinct to know that the stakes were high, that one day they would have to compete for a place in the pack. While play was certainly enjoyable, it definitely had its serious side. One day after feeding, Wyakin got hold of a rag that I had been using to gently clean her. When I tried to reclaim it, she let go a snarl that was vicious beyond her years. It was amazing that such a tiny little thing would challenge me so. In her way, she was simply playing a game of tug-of-war with me, but at the same time she was asserting herself in earnest. I couldn't let her keep and possibly swallow the rag, so, just as an adult wolf would have done, I flipped her onto her back and growled in disapproval. Wyakin understood that she had crossed the line and relinquished the rag.

Having gone through the process of raising these pups, it is beyond me how anyone would try to keep a wolf as a pet. I can't conceive of how a person could enter into this kind of responsibility as casually as if they were raising a domestic dog. Imagine the most rambunctious and unruly dog possible. Now multiply that by one hundred. That is a wolf pup. Few people would ever think of raising a cougar as if it were a house cat, yet the resemblance between wolves and dogs lures people into believing that there is no difference in their behavior. While it is true that there are numerous similarities between the two animals, the wolf takes every one of its doglike traits to the extreme. Wolves, for example, are highly territorial and possessive of their food. Think of the display little Wyakin made toward me over a rag that she wanted to play with. Now imagine that the wolf is two years old, weighs eighty pounds, and is standing on your kitchen table claiming the pot roast for herself. Suddenly you've got a dangerous situation on your hands.

Wolves are also extremely protective of what they identify as their immediate family and are usually wary of strangers. While this may seem like a positive quality, your pet wolf may decide that its immediate family includes you but not your spouse or your children or your friends.

When it reaches an age of two or three years, a pet wolf often begins to assert itself, just as its relatives do in the wild when integrating into the pack hierarchy. A strong and confident wolf tries to enter the pecking order somewhere in the middle, seeking to displace older established wolves. This frequently results in skirmishes until the social order is sorted out. Normally these battles are not bloody by wolf standards, although the warning bite that would be shrugged off by a fellow wolf, with its bushy coat and thick hide, would send a person to the emergency room.

Even if a pet wolf is calm, well behaved, and has never shown any signs of aggression, its hunting instinct can surface at any time. The sight of a child falling, crying, and struggling to get up can trigger what biologists call a "prey response" in which the wolf instinctively attacks something that is behaving like a wounded animal. The wolf is not acting out of meanness or aggression; it is not bad-tempered or crazy. It is acting exactly as a wild wolf should, following an instinct that has helped wolves and other wild predators survive for thousands of years. Reports, in fact, indicate that this is the most frequent scenario in which a pet wolf injures or even kills a person, usually a child.

Many people believe that the way around these instinctive traits is to acquire a wolf-dog, or wolf hybrid. Since there are no laws controlling breeding, there is no way of knowing what percentage a hybrid is. Guessing at percentages is, in any event, a useless method of predicting an animal's temperament. The conflict that rages within wolf-dogs can result in them being even more unpredictable than pure wolves. Instinctive behaviors such as the prey response might have been bred out of a hybrid. Then again, they might not.

Owners of wolves and wolf hybrids often opt to keep the wolf or hybrid out of the house, tying it to a stake in the backyard or keeping it behind a fence, hoping the kid from next door doesn't wander into the yard to retrieve his baseball. With tragic regularity, an innocent animal pays with its life for the owner's foolishness, and in this way are age-old myths about the wolf's savagery and cruelty perpetuated.

Every year, Jim and I receive phone calls from people with problem pet wolves or hybrids. I try to be helpful and provide the names of some rescue organizations, but such shelters are usually filled to capacity. Above all, I stress that they should not let the animal "go free." While putting a wolf to sleep may seem extreme, the practice of releasing the animal usually results in a worse fate for the animal—a slow death by starvation. If a released wolf does manage to survive without hunting skills or fear of people, it generally does so by rummaging through garbage or by killing livestock and family pets. In the nearby town of Bellevue, Idaho, a fury erupted when a prize-winning sheep fell victim to an unseen predator. The town was up in arms, blaming the killing on wolves that had been reintroduced to the north. A few days later, the culprit was revealed to be someone's pet wolf-dog that had either escaped or been set free. It is unknown how often this scenario repeats itself, but hybrid and pet wolf owners (who are often great fans of wolves) are probably indirectly responsible for more livestock depredation than they could ever imagine. Even more disastrous is the possibility that the animal could survive long enough to meet up with wild wolves. A wild pack may kill it, or they could follow it onto farms and ranches, where easy prey can be found. In the case of hybrids, the animal could even mate with a wild wolf, corrupting the genes of an entire species.

We never for a minute thought of the Sawtooth Pack as pets and never would have entered into this project had we not had a filmmaking mission, twenty-five acres of land where they could be wild, and a crew working around the clock. Even so, it was an exhausting and nerve-wracking experience, requiring every ounce of our time and energy. Luckily we had no shortage of volunteers to assist in feeding and caretaking. We were very careful to warn all visitors to wear long pants and long-sleeved shirts and to tie back long hair and remove jewelry. Those who did not heed our warning frequently left with bloody arms and legs. This is not to say that we let the puppies run rampant and do whatever they pleased. In wild packs, an adult wolf's patience is finite, just as ours was. A mother wolf, or any adult in the pack, is quick to discipline a rowdy pup. If one of the pups became too rambunctious, biting a person or tearing clothes, we did our best to imitate an irritated mother wolf, as I had done with Wyakin.

Although they were still very young, the pups' personalities had already begun to take shape. Wyakin, despite being the smallest of the lot, was the most aggressive and feisty. Wahots, her brother, was more watchful, curious, and clever. Chemukh was by far the most timid and often played by herself. Wahots and Wyakin took turns climbing on each other's backs, already playing at dominance, and sometimes the two of them ganged up on little Chemukh. Their own private hierarchy was already being established.

In a few weeks, the three pups were large enough to move from the mud room to a pen in the backyard. The pen was equipped with a mesh roof and a wooden "den" to provide shelter. We also began to introduce them to meat. Initially, we used finely ground chicken mixed with formula and heated slightly to simulate regurgitated food. To us it was downright nauseating but to rapidly maturing wolf pups it was like filet mignon.

After a mother has weaned her pups, she will resume hunting with the pack and leave the pups behind at a secure rendezvous site with another pack member, probably a less experienced hunter, acting as a caretaker. After joining the pack to make a kill, the mother will gorge herself and return to the waiting pups who instinctively rush to her and lick her mouth, begging for food. This action stimulates the adult to regurgitate a portion of her meal in a warm, easily digestible stew, the wolf equivalent of baby food. Sometimes the mother chooses to stay with her pups instead of hunting. In this case one or more pack members will return to the rendezvous site and regurgitate for the pups. Several wolves in the pack may, at one time or another, take on the role of baby-sitter or sacrifice a meal for the pups. It is one of the most amazing ways that wolves demonstrate pack unity and devotion to their family.

While the adult wolves selflessly surrender food to their young, the pups are only in it for themselves and are all about consuming as much as is physically possible. As Wahots, Wyakin, and Chemukh developed their baby teeth, we started them in on raw chicken parts. The ferocity with which they would tear into the food was unbelievable. During one feeding, I watched Wyakin swallow an entire chicken thigh nearly as big as her head. Like a horrifying cartoon, the huge chunk of meat and bone protruded from her throat while she bucked madly, trying to get it down. After a remarkably brief effort, the piece was consumed and she immediately dived in for more.

This sort of behavior is natural for a wolf, for in the wild, mealtime occurs whenever the pack succeeds in making a kill. This is why wolves developed the ability to gorge, consuming as much as thirty pounds in a sitting. It was almost frightening how much their stomachs could stretch. All three puppies would consume enormous amounts, but none would expand to such grotesque proportions as Wyakin. She was like a little tick.

What the pups couldn't consume in a feeding, they would often try to stockpile for later. Wyakin, always out to get more than she could hold, would pick up large chunks of meat, carry them into the wooden den, stash them under a blanket, and then stroll out proudly to continue eating. Wahots, however, caught on to her little scheme and would hide behind the den and wait for Wyakin to emerge. Then he would casually amble into the den as if he were heading for a nap and quietly feast on Wyakin's cache. Poor Wyakin could never figure out what happened to her stash of food and would wander around the pen, looking under blankets and leaf piles, trying to find her leftovers.

By mid-June of 1994, we decided to start bringing the pups with us on our trips to camp to introduce them slowly to their new extended family. Early one morning, we configured a small pen to fit in the back of the van so the pups could stay together for the one-hour trip north. Domestic dog puppies are known for taking automobile trips in stride—even enthusiastically. I assumed that five-week-old wolf pups would be much the same. After all, they had been fine on their first trip down from Montana, but Jim warned me that this time would be different.

We were barely out of the driveway when Wahots started to vomit, then Chemukh and Wyakin, one by one, like exploding bottles in a bootleg brewery. No sooner would one finish than the next one would begin, and when they all had finished, the first one started again.

The mixture of raw chicken and puppy formula, neither of which were that pleasing to the nose to begin with, now flowed in a homogenized state across the newspapered floor of the pen, changing course with the vehicle's movements and spilling through the wire mesh as we twisted and turned our way over the mountain pass. As I scrambled to contain the mess, I was at least thankful that I had had the foresight to cover the back of the van with a plastic tarp. The pups didn't seem to mind at all, though I was on the verge of being sick myself. I bent over the walls of the pen and hung upside down with my face inches above a jiggling pool of puppy vomit, trying as best I could to clean up. Whenever I reached in with a handful of newspaper, Wahots and Wyakin grabbed it and tore it to shreds, just having a marvelous time. When we arrived at camp they were happy and ready for action. I needed to lie down.

These continued to be exciting but exhausting weeks as Jim and I split our attention between the adult pack, the job of moving camp, and the extra needs of the puppies. Time spent with the more sedate adult wolves was a much-needed break where we could just sit and watch them without having them pounce on us. As for the pups, we still worried about the danger of predation from great horned owls and thought it best that we keep them inside at night for a few weeks more. While we slept in our tent inside the enclosure with the adult wolves, the pups slept in a pen in the old cook tent, which was soon to be dismantled permanently, now that the yurt was serving as the full-time kitchen. The last feeding of the day occurred at about ten o'clock at night. After that, poor Christina was left with the night shift. Not only did she have to keep the fire going all night long for the pups' comfort, but they had a habit of erupting into a chorus of growling, yipping, and crying every hour or so. Needless to say, she was a little less than bubbly in the morning.

We had to make four trips to and from camp during the next month, returning to Ketchum to ship film to the lab, and to pick up supplies for the new camp. Both for safety and to continue the bonding process, we brought the pups with us and let them stay in the backyard pen for a few nights. Each time we drove with them, we tried a different feeding regimen, in hopes that we would stumble on one that would keep them from vomiting during the trip. We tried withholding their food the day of the trip, and even the night before, but no matter what we did, the ride always resulted in a vomit festival. On June 21, 1994, the pups made their last trip north, traveling to wolf camp for good. For some reason, on this trip they finally managed to keep their breakfasts down.

At this stage, Wahots, Wyakin, and Chemukh moved into the half-acre auxiliary enclosure where Makuyi had lived during her recovery. The little area was near the main enclosure but not adjacent to it, thus avoiding the possibility of an adult trying to pull a puppy through the fence. All the same, Kamots, Lakota, Matsi, Amani, and Motomo could all see their soon-to-be pack mates and were totally enraptured by their arrival. The adults spent a considerable amount of time gazing at the pups and whining in excitement. They howled more than ever with the pups nearby, and when they did, Wahots, Wyakin, and Chemukh tried their best to howl back. Howling, it seems, is a skill that develops over time. The little pups threw their heads back and put all their hearts into it, but all that came out were a few high-pitched yodels.

Part of the purpose of the slow introduction to the rest of the pack was to give both adults and puppies the chance to get used to one another's presence before being thrust together. Often we would carry the young pups from their enclosure up to the main fence to meet the adults face-to-face. At these times, Wahots and Wyakin were quite bold and probably would have loved for us to open the gate that very second. Chemukh, on the other hand, was much more wary, keeping back from the fence and holding herself in a decidedly submissive posture. We hoped that meeting the adults like this several times would alleviate her fear.

Chemukh's personality had become evident several weeks earlier in her interactions with her two step-siblings. Wahots and Wyakin would gang up and make a game out of tormenting her. We were fairly convinced at this time that Wyakin was destined to become the alpha female of the pack, and wondered if Chemukh was so submissive that she would take over the omega female role and relieve Lakota of some of the burden.

In August, when the pups were twelve weeks old, we could begin to answer these questions. It was finally time for the merging of the adults and puppies. We lured the pack with food into the lock-off and carried the 35-pound pups inside to our little fenced-in human camp. We let them stay there for most of the day so the adults and pups could get used to one another for a final time. The adults were so excited about the pups that they brought them presents of bones and leftover deer hide and pushed these gifts through the fence. Deep in my heart I was certain that everything would be fine, but I couldn't help worrying about little Chemukh. She was so timid. Would the others accept her?

The golden light of the summer afternoon was beautiful as Jim readied his camera and I set up my microphone and recording equipment. At about five P.M. our new assistant, Megan Parker, who had taken over from Val Asher, opened the gate and we let the wolves do the rest. I had expected the pups, at least Wahots and Wyakin, to charge out to greet their new family, but to my surprise they became quite apprehensive. With a gentleness one would never expect from a fearsome predator, Kamots walked calmly over to them and softly licked all three, introducing himself. This immediately bolstered Wyakin's courage. She cautiously crept through the gate and made her way toward Matsi, who was whining in encouragement. As they got acquainted, Wyakin tumbled over onto her back, exposing her belly in submission.

As I recorded their sounds, I noticed a continuous high-pitched whining going back and forth between pups and adults. Watching their body language, I really felt that they were conversing. Although I have no way of knowing, I imagine the adults were reassuring the pups and welcoming them into the group. Wahots immediately found his sister and began to play with her and Matsi. If the play got too rough, Matsi would discipline one pup or the other by rolling it over and gently pinning it for a moment.

As I had feared, however, Chemukh was not so brave. She crept away, seeking the shelter of nearby willows. With deep concern, Jim recounted the story of Makuyi's behavior when she was rejected by the pack. It was impossible to tell if Chemukh could somehow sense that she was not completely welcome, or if it was all in her own mind. Whatever the cause, there was nothing we could do to change her social position. Whatever happened now was up to the wolves.

After an hour of hiding, Chemukh emerged from the willows and hesitantly joined the others. As we watched her very tentatively begin to play with Wahots and Wyakin, we breathed a collective sigh of relief.

So much of a wolf's social position depends on the confidence it displays right from the start. If a human child presents himself on the playground in a meek and timid manner, often the other children will instinctively pick on that child. As in human beings, fear in a young wolf is, sadly, destined to become something of a self-fulfilling prophecy. Wahots and Wyakin played by the rules. They were quick to flip over onto their backs and submit to the adults, but Chemukh was just too afraid. Instead of submitting, she kept running away—in effect, breaking the social code. When the adults finally caught up with her, she would submit in a panic, but by that time the adults would be in a lather and discipline her strictly. It almost seemed that Chemukh was to be given a harsh initiation until she figured out the rules.

When things settled down, we began to put away our film equipment, letting the adults and puppies continue to get acquainted. As I was stowing my sound gear in the tent, I heard some faint whining that I assumed was coming from the other side of the fence. A moment later, I began to get the uneasy feeling that I was being watched. I turned and there was little Wahots, poking his head through the tent flap. He was so small that he must have come back through the gate when our attention was on something else. There was so much wolf traffic back and forth that we failed to notice that he had been left behind. He was now looking at me with an expression that said, "Where is everyone? Where am I supposed to be?" As I coaxed him back through the gate, I couldn't help feeling like a mother bringing her frightened child to school on the first day. Although Wahots was excited to be with his own kind, I could tell that he also found those big wolves a bit scary. Maybe he needed just a little more reassurance from his surrogate human parents. As I led him through the gate a second time, gentle Matsi was waiting there to take over.

Jim, Christina, Jake, Patty, Megan, and I spent the last hours of the long summer evening sitting on the deck outside the yurt, watching the five adults introduce the pups to their new home. Wahots and Wyakin stuck to Matsi like glue and followed him wherever he went. Chemukh trailed several steps behind, wanting to be a part of the action but held back by her shyness. It would be a difficult road for Chemukh, yet there was no doubt that the pack had at least accepted her as one of their own.

The permissiveness that the adult wolves demonstrated toward the pups was astounding and never more apparent than at feeding time. When we set out a deer carcass for them, Wahots and Wyakin would pounce on it with ravenous abandon. Kamots still enforced the adult hierarchy; Lakota was still obligated to wait his turn. Wahots and Wyakin, on the other hand, were permitted to gorge to their hearts' content, and even timid Chemukh was allowed to eat without waiting, at least for the first few weeks. Matsi stood guard over the pups while they ate, joining in the feast at their side. If Amani, Motomo, or Lakota dared get too close, Matsi would growl protectively, not allowing anything to prevent the pups from getting their absolute fill.

As the pups got a little older, we were amused to see Wahots and Wyakin's old comedy routine reappear. Toward the end of the meal, Wyakin would begin collecting chunks of meat and carrying them off into the bushes. In her greed, she kept trying to carry more than she could possibly hold in her mouth. She would drop a deer bone halfway there, and in trying to recover it, she would invariably drop another. She looked like a caricature of some chubby laundry lady as she waddled off toward the willows. It was hard to keep my mind on my work with this comedy of errors being played out a few yards away.

Wahots, as always, watched his sister intently, very much aware that she was up to her old tricks. He had learned early in life that if he sat back and waited, Wyakin would do all the work for him and amass a bountiful supply of leftovers in a secret place where he could eat in private. When she began to hoard food, he took a step back and watched where she went, shifting his attention between Wyakin and the rest of the pack, lest anyone else catch on. When she returned to the carcass for more, he tiptoed (if a wolf can tiptoe) off along her trail, only to return a few moments later with a casual air. As became her pattern, Wyakin spent the next hour checking under logs and bushes in absolute bewilderment. The siblings played out this scenario time and time again and Wyakin never did catch on.

Well fed, the pups grew rapidly and were practically full size by winter. In a year or so, we would be able to see how they integrated into the pack, how Wahots would fit in among the other males, and how Wyakin and Chemukh would sort out their breeding rights. But for now, their lives still revolved around play and learning how to function within the pack. Kamots handled most of the discipline and the establishment of rules. The gentler and more subtle job of educating, caretaking, and confidence-building fell upon the shoulders of a single wolf—Matsi.

Matsi

JIM

A wolf pack is an exceedingly complex social unit, an extended family of parents, siblings, aunts, and uncles. There are old wolves that need to be cared for, pups that need to be educated, and young adults that are beginning to assert themselves—all altering the dynamics of the pack. Thus, when we introduced three pups, one male and two females, to the existing pack of five adult males, we knew we were creating a much more complicated society, and one that more accurately mirrored a wild pack. Previously unseen personality traits surfaced as each wolf responded to the new pups in his own special way. The most dramatic of these was to be seen in Matsi.

Matsi was the littermate of Motomo and Amani, born in 1992 to the same parents that had given birth to Kamots and Lakota a year earlier. In a perfect example of how variable wolf markings can be, these three siblings ranged from Motomo's coal black coat, to Amani's traditional gray and black, to Matsi's uniform beige coloration and complete lack of darker facial markings. Because of his sunny appearance we named him the Blackfoot word for "sweet and brave." Throughout his entire life, Matsi lived up to that name.

Around the time that Lakota was forced into the omega spot, we could see Matsi emerging as the pack's beta wolf. Not much is written about betas, and their role in the pack structure is unclear when compared with the well-defined positions of alpha and omega. In the very simplest of terms, the beta male is the second in command, dominant over all but the alpha. While the positions of mid-ranking wolves are somewhat fluid, the beta generally enjoys a more stable existence. Since there are more or less separate hierarchies for males and females, there will generally be a beta female as well as a beta male.

Scientists suggest that the beta male will assume command of the pack if the current alpha is killed or injured. For this reason, a beta may have to perform the most delicate balancing act of any wolf in the society. Matsi was certainly the gentlest wolf in the Sawtooth Pack, both with me and with his pack mates. It could well be that his kindness was a way of garnering support in case his time ever came to be the alpha. In my observations, however, Matsi seemed completely uninterested in social rank. While Amani and Motomo jostled for position, Matsi conducted himself in a fashion similar to that of Kamots.

Back when he was a yearling, things had been somewhat different. Matsi had been fairly aggressive and seemed intent on asserting himself, especially over his brothers. When he was barely a year old, Matsi helped to solidify Lakota's omega status. It seemed as though he set out to prove himself to his elders and to secure a dominant role in the pack early on. Once his beta position was firmly established, Matsi relaxed, becoming one of the least aggressive wolves in the pack. He seemed to know which rank suited him.

Matsi possessed an intangible quality that I still find difficult to describe. In all affairs, he conducted himself with an air of calm dignity. He never seemed too concerned with what we humans were up to, though he did seem to enjoy our company. Often he sat quietly by my side, never expecting anything, never trying to solicit attention, just spending time with me as a friend, an equal, and I respected him for that.

There are two occasions when the social structure of a wolf pack is most apparent. The most volatile time is during the breeding season when the dominant males and females aggressively demonstrate their status. We had thus far been unable to witness this scenario, but with the pack soon to contain adults of both sexes, we were expecting it to happen in the next year.

The other time that brings out the fiercest demonstrations of social rank is feeding. Much of the footage of dominance and submission that went into my films was shot on or around a deer or elk carcass. As I had learned to do earlier, I shot a great deal of this footage in slow motion so it would better reveal subtle nuances of the wolves' behavior.

Kamots' favor seemed to shift regularly. Some days he would let some of his pack eat immediately, some days he would make them wait. But one factor remained constant: Matsi was always allowed to eat with Kamots. This is not to say that he was not cautious. Like the other subordinate wolves, he selected a spot far away from the alpha and kept his eyes on him as he ate, but he never doubted his place at a kill.

It was during feeding that Matsi's reputation as a peacemaker was born. As the meal progressed and more and more of the deer disappeared, Motomo and Amani would become increasingly agitated. Frequently they would work out their frustration on the unfortunate Lakota, who was always waiting in the wings, torn between the desire to snatch a bite of food and the fear of drawing attention to himself.

Once as I was filming, I watched Lakota give in to his hunger and try to pick up a morsel that had been flung aside. Upholding the pecking order, Matsi growled and chased Lakota several feet away from the kill and then returned to his meal. Amani, still waiting for his turn to feed, and eager to make a show of prowess, took over where Matsi had left off. He turned toward Lakota with a growl and tackled the confused omega, flipping him onto his back and straddling him as he often did. To our surprise, and perhaps even Lakota's, Matsi again left the kill but this time he rushed at Amani, knocking him off Lakota. Matsi was disciplining Amani for disciplining Lakota.

We thought at the time that this was a fluke, that Matsi was simply displaying an excess of dominance that day. The more we screened our slow-motion footage, the more we realized that there was a pattern. Matsi was continually sticking up for Lakota. One particular roll of film that I had shot of a pack rally was the first to bring our attention to Matsi's peacekeeping ability. The rally was especially energetic and had turned sour on Lakota. Perhaps he had joined in the howl too enthusiastically or howled too well. Or perhaps one of the mid-ranking wolves just felt the need to assert his dominance. Whatever the reason, the pack had formed a mob around the hapless omega, blocking his escape. Even the yearlings— Wahots, Wyakin, and Chemukh—were old enough by this time to get involved in the action, not really harassing Lakota, but nevertheless adding to the mayhem. As always, Amani was the main perpetrator of any aggression aimed at Lakota. He closed in on the omega, climbing on his back and nipping at his flanks while Lakota sunk to the ground and tried to worm-crawl his way out of the ring.

A moment later, Matsi charged into the fray as well. When I filmed this action, I assumed that Matsi was simply abusing Lakota along with the others. It was Jamie who observed during the third or fourth screening of the footage what we had failed to see in the blur of fangs and fur. Matsi was not digging into Lakota; rather, he was forcibly inserting himself between Lakota and his tormentors. In effect, he was body-checking Amani out of the way, giving Lakota the opportunity to make a dash for cover.

We were never able to explain the special bond that Matsi developed with Lakota. If we had tried to look at it with a purely scientific eye, it would have been very hard to see what Matsi got out of it. Their relationship was especially surprising because Matsi had played such a huge role in forcing Lakota into the omega position to begin with. Once the ranks were established, however, Matsi was extremely gentle with the omega.

While the rest of the pack was spread out, these two often slept side by side, and when Matsi went exploring, Lakota often joined him. At the very least, Lakota knew Matsi to be the one wolf who would not pick on him and might even offer him some protection, but there seemed to be more to it than that. Matsi genuinely seemed to enjoy Lakota's company. With Matsi, Lakota was free to do things he wouldn't dare do around the others. He would never have jumped on Amani or Motomo's back to instigate play. No wolf, not even benevolent Kamots, would have stood for that sort of audacity from an omega. Matsi, on the other hand, let it pass. He actually appeared to enjoy it, since he nearly always took the bait and launched into a mock fight or game of chase with Lakota. One of the happiest sights I witnessed in my time with the pack was these two frolicking together and the look of joy on Lakota's face, freed for a moment from his burdens.

Could it be that Matsi was simply showing his care for Lakota, understanding how the omega suffered and offering a moment of relief? Though it is difficult to observe such subtle behavior in the wild, evidence for this kind of care does exist. While we were on location in Fairbanks, Alaska, a biologist showed us the skull of an average-size male wolf. Examination of the skull revealed, unmistakably, that the wolf had suffered a broken jaw in his lifetime, probably the result of a kick delivered by a moose or caribou. Such an injury would have rendered the wolf unable to hunt or even tear hunks of meat from a kill. Yet the skull indicated that the bone had mended and the wolf had continued to live for several years. The only way he could have survived is for the other wolves of his pack to have fed him. They would have had to bring food to him from a kill, possibly even regurgitating for him, nurturing him as they would a pup.

Observing Matsi's behavior, I genuinely believed that if one of the Sawtooth Pack were injured, he would be the one to take charge of the nursing and care. The survival of the pack seemed that important to him. Of course, this also meant that the rules of society were important to him as well. Although Matsi was more than willing to let the social order bend, he was by no means willing to let it break. I don't recall seeing Lakota behave as freely with Matsi when they were in the company of Kamots and the others. Perhaps Lakota didn't want to attract attention to himself, or it may have been that Matsi would not tolerate the same liberties "in public." Matsi certainly wasn't going to budge an inch when it came to food. If Lakota overstepped his bounds at mealtime, Matsi was quick to make his displeasure known.

One day, as I was photographing the pack, I noticed Lakota cowering under a tree. He was tucked into a deep crouch with his ears plastered back, looking as if he were trying to be absorbed into the ground and disappear. As I watched him and wondered what he had done, Matsi walked up to Lakota, lifted his leg, and urinated all over

the unfortunate wolf's back. I had missed whatever earlier development—an altercation?—had provoked this
extreme demonstration of dominance, but it was clear
that Matsi felt the need to put Lakota severely in his
place. I was so shocked by this behavior that I was too
dumbfounded to squeeze off a photo. That afternoon,
however, I spied the two playing together by the pond,
and that night they slept side by side.

Matsi's protective nature blossomed in full the
moment he set eyes on the pups, Wahots, Wyakin, and
Chemukh. While all the adults were captivated by them,
Matsi's attention was of a more serious sort. Before the
pups were placed with the adults, we brought them into
our small, fenced-in camp so Randy Acker, our veterinarian, could inspect them, weigh them, and tattoo them for
identification, as required by the Idaho Department of
Fish and Game. Unfortunately, the pups had to be mildly
sedated for this process.

Thinking my presence would have a calming effect on
the pack as they witnessed the procedure, I decided to sit
outside among them while this was taking place and let
Jamie, Randy, and Megan do the job. In hindsight, we
should have conducted the procedure in one of the tents,
rather than outside, for the sight was just too much for
Matsi to bear. He paced back and forth, whimpering in
agitation, as Randy, an unfamiliar person, placed the
seemingly lifeless bodies onto a blanket on the ground.

I was sitting in the grass next to Matsi, observing the
procedure, when he turned to me and snapped his jaws
an inch from my face. The impression was powerful and

unmistakable, like a heavy encyclopedia being slammed shut in front of my eyes. It left me in shock for a moment. He had always been so gentle with me and all people, yet of all the wolves I raised from puppyhood, he is the only one ever to threaten me in that way. Even then, I knew that this was not really aggression so much as desperation. It was his way of telling me, "Don't let this happen." I understood how he felt. I didn't like watching the pups get sedated any more than he did.

My first act was to move slowly away from him and get myself behind the safety of the fence. Then I began speaking to him softly, trying to reassure him that all was well. It was not until the pups had awakened and I presented them to him, unharmed and frisky as ever, that he finally relaxed. Fortunately, such a demonstration never happened again with Matsi or any other wolf, but it remained a healthy reminder that everything was, and should be, on the wolf's terms. Matsi's threat did not make me more wary around him. Rather, his show of concern for those pups, who were not even his own offspring, made me feel all the more respectful, and closer to him than before.

When the hour finally came for the pups to cross the threshold into their new lives, Matsi took charge of the situation from the very beginning. Kamots, exercising his authority as alpha, was the first to inspect the new pack members, but Matsi was close behind. Kamots' main concern seemed to be to make the pups submit and to let them know that he was in charge. When he had assured himself that all was well, he backed off, leaving them in Matsi's care, yet still watching their every move.

Matsi seemed to want to herd the pups together so that he could watch over all of them at the same time. Wahots and Wyakin were so interested in exploring that he had a difficult time keeping up with them. When he finally got the two gray pups to follow him, he would try to lead them to Chemukh, but she was so skittish that she kept running away from him. He was visibly distressed that Chemukh couldn't get her head around the notion that he was her friend. For many days, Matsi exhausted himself keeping track of all the pups and slowly gaining Chemukh's trust. By the end of the first week, she was stuck to him like glue.

Matsi's parental instincts were most profound at feeding time. The two gray pups, Wahots and Wyakin, might have been a bit wary of the large adult wolves but they were far too hungry to resist bellying up next to Matsi at the kill. Motomo and Amani were quibbling on the sidelines as usual. When Motomo finally made the decision to move in for a bite, he chose a spot too close to Wyakin. Looking like an alpha himself, Matsi froze in his position and fixed his eyes on Motomo. He let out a low growl and pulled back his lips to bare his fangs. This was enough to get the point across and Motomo moved away from Wyakin.

After Chemukh's first few weeks with the pack, Kamots decreed that she would not have a place at the kill and that she should wait with Lakota. In my observations over the years, I saw that pups usually live in a somewhat blissful state outside the adult hierarchy, but this time the alpha singled out young Chemukh as being somehow less deserving than the others. It may well have been that if she had aggressively leapt on the kill as her step-siblings did, Kamots would have let her eat. As it was, when she skittishly approached the carcass in a crouch, ears back, tail tucked, taking two steps forward and one step back, Kamots wouldn't stand for it.

When I watched Kamots, sometimes I felt as if he was acting like a drill sergeant, trying to toughen her up and make her more assertive. It could well have been that he sensed her aloofness and timidity and was sending her a message. It is in the best interest of a wolf pack to have all its members working together as a cohesive unit; a wolf that can't work with the others is a liability. Perhaps Kamots' treatment of Chemukh was his way of making sure she would grow up to be a team player and an asset to the pack.

Matsi was not about to go against the ruling of the alpha, but he didn't exactly enforce Kamots' rules, either. If Chemukh wanted to sneak a bite of food, Matsi would let her, but he wouldn't defend her if Kamots chased her off. Together they set up a good cop/bad cop system in their treatment of Chemukh.

When most of the deer was consumed, Matsi turned toward Wahots and Wyakin, his belly distended from his huge meal. Instinctively knowing what he was about to do, the gray pups leapt to their feet, ran to him, and began whining and licking his mouth. Matsi trotted to a partially hidden place among the willows with Wahots and Wyakin close at his heels. His whole body convulsed and in an instant he brought forth a huge pile of partially digested deer meat. Although the pups were allowed on the carcass from the beginning, their small size meant that they sometimes had trouble consuming enough food with five larger adults tearing off huge mouthfuls in every bite. Matsi was making sure they were well fed. Due to his protective nature he never regurgitated for the pups in plain view. I don't know if the larger wolves would have eaten the puppy food, but he seemed to be concerned about that possibility. As a frustrating consequence of his stealth, I was never able to catch this behavior on film.

Chemukh knew a good opportunity when she saw one and followed closely behind her step-siblings. She was too timid to actually lick Matsi's mouth and solicit the regurgitation response, even though I have no doubt that Matsi would have happily provided food for her. As it was, she didn't need to. Wahots and Wyakin begged for the food, and Chemukh was allowed to share in the meal. By the grace of Matsi's tolerance, Chemukh was always able to eat her fill.

Matsi was so protective of the pups that we really felt honored that he allowed us near them. He certainly would have challenged anyone he didn't trust. One September evening, I photographed Jamie as she walked among the pups with Matsi close by. She sat down in the meadow and the pups immediately rushed to her, tugging at her jacket and crawling onto her lap. Seeing that the pups were in good hands, Matsi settled down in the grass next to Jamie, crossed his paws and allowed his eyelids to droop. It was a beautiful picture of trust.

Earlier that spring, when the pups had just been born, I had taken Jamie to a place of great significance to us:

the pond where I had filmed the family of beavers seven years earlier. I had been completing that project when Jamie and I met, thus we felt strangely indebted to the beavers and to National Geographic's office in Washington, D.C., for bringing us together. The setting was a crystal-clear pond, teeming with brook trout, glittering at the base of a sweeping mountain peak. There, in front of the long-abandoned beaver lodge, I did what I should have done so many years before. I asked Jamie to marry me.

Now, I stood watching the woman who was about to become my wife. The evening light glowed around her as she unselfconsciously played with the pups, reaffirming their bond. How gentle she was. How easily she had gained the respect of Matsi and the others. How lucky I felt.

I have often said that Kamots' confidence is what made him such a superb leader. Although Matsi did not have the drive to lead the pack, he did seem to possess some of that same confidence. One of the reasons Motomo and Amani were quick to pick on Lakota was because they themselves were insecure in their status and felt they had to make a show of dominance. Matsi just didn't feel the need. He knew exactly where he stood.

As I look back on my years with the Sawtooth Pack, I see Matsi as the embodiment of all that was magical about them. He was a wolf that gave everything of himself for the benefit of the pack. He patrolled their territory, took care of the pups, maintained peace and order—and throughout all this, he seemed completely content not to rule. Matsi taught me that the workings of a wolf society are deeper and more complex than I will ever know. Although competition is prevalent and the drive to become the alpha can burn fiercely in the hearts of certain wolves, the good of the pack, the family, is more important than anything.

Scientists are continually debating rival theories of the emotional life of animals and only lately has real consideration been given to the possibility that a creature such as a wolf could be capable of so complex an emotion as compassion. If we can't use the word "compassion" to describe a wolf, then what word should we use? What word would a wolf choose to describe protecting the omega from aggression, or when (as has been observed in Alaska) it brings food to an injured pack mate? When a worried mother brings her sick child to the doctor, no one would suggest that it is because she knows the child carries her genes, or that she wants the child to care for her when she is older. The claim that we human beings hold a monopoly on elevated feelings is impossible to support.

This insight is the gift that Matsi gave to me. It has been an underlying theme in my films and the single most important message about wolves that I can share. They possess something beyond their more obvious attributes of beauty, strength, and intelligence. These animals, who have been maligned for centuries, despised as the embodiment of all that is cowardly, savage, and cruel, clearly care about one another and show signs of what I would call nothing less than empathy and compassion.

Motomo and Amani

JAMIE

As in any society, the majority of wolves that comprise a pack are neither leader nor underdog. Most are mid-ranking wolves, filling the vague area below the beta and above the omega. The social position of these wolves is more difficult to determine through observation because it appears to be rather fluid. All the same, within the middle echelons, no two wolves have exactly the same status, and their rank may change from week to week.

It is extremely difficult for a mid-ranking wolf to depose a well-established alpha or beta. However, there is always the hope of moving up a peg or two in the pecking order and of improving one's lot ever so slightly. For this reason, much of the squabbling in the Sawtooth Pack occurred within the middle ranks.

Over the years, the pack grew in size and the middle echelons became more complex, but the two older wolves who epitomized this nebulous and volatile group were Motomo and Amani. Their brother Matsi had solidly established himself as the beta wolf, effectively sealing off their hopes for social climbing. The only other option left to them was to descend in rank, and it was easy to see that neither of them was about to do that. Consequently, they jockeyed for position with each other, each trying to assert himself as the more dominant of the two. When that got old, they resorted to displaying dominance over Lakota, just to remind the rest of the pack that they were definitely not omega material. During my years with the pack, I would only have been able to guess at which of these two was really dominant and which was subordinate on any given day, but I'm quite sure that they knew.

Motomo was the darkest wolf of the pack, jet black with a white patch on his chest. Jim's first crew had named him the Blackfoot word for "he who goes first." Of all the wolves, he seemed to take the greatest interest in the activities of people. It wasn't so much that he craved direct contact with us, he was just incredibly curious and loved to observe us. Long after the rest of the pack had moved on to other business, Motomo would stay close by. When we walked the perimeter of the enclosure to check for fallen trees or other potential threats to the fence, Motomo usually followed us the entire way, as if supervising.

One of Jim's photographs that became a successful poster is a head-on shot of Motomo in which he is lying in the snow and staring directly into the camera with his deep yellow eyes. That is exactly the way I remember him—sitting completely still and scrutinizing us intently from a few yards away as we set up our camera gear, split wood, or shoveled snow. At times, he really appeared to be trying to figure out what on earth these strange primates were up to, always scurrying about, always busy.

There was something wonderfully dignified about Motomo. He enjoyed our company but kept his cards close to his chest. He wasn't going to lower himself to the point of actually soliciting our attention. His brother Amani couldn't have been more different.

In both appearance and demeanor, Amani was a near opposite of Motomo. He had the perfect markings of a classic gray wolf: mottled gray fur with a black mask, a pale muzzle and throat, and rich caramel eyes. His name was the Blackfoot word for "speaks the truth," a name that was not particularly fitting. Where Motomo was dark, mysterious, and rather reserved, Amani was all flash and showmanship. He was a little like the class clown, the kid at school who would do anything for attention. I recall him sitting calmly in the grass one day, and as I walked by, he suddenly fell over on his side with a thud. I swear he was just acting silly to attract attention. He would perform goofy tricks like this all the time.

All this foolish behavior earned Amani the nickname "the sheep in wolf's clothing," but in truth that was only half the story. When it came to social status he was dead serious and could be a downright bully. As he did when he played the clown, Amani approached social competition with great flair, making sure that he had an audience. Oddly enough, when Amani was a yearling, he was the shyest of his siblings. Perhaps this fear lingered throughout his life and he continually felt the need to prove himself.

Unfortunately, the wolf that was almost always on the receiving end of Amani's posturing was Lakota. Amani would use any available opportunity to demonstrate his dominance, sometimes even pouncing on Lakota out of the blue when all was otherwise quiet. During pack rallies when displays of dominance were common, Amani could be counted on to lay into Lakota with special zeal. Once he started, Motomo, Chemukh, Wahots, and Wyakin would often get involved, making the situation all the more miserable for the omega.

Amani also seemed to dominate his brother most of the time, making a show of climbing on Motomo's back and growling. Motomo didn't seem to mind the fact that he was being pushed into a submissive role most days. A man of few words, Motomo decided to save his energy for when it really counted—mealtime. As calm and docile as he was, Motomo's personality transformed once a deer carcass appeared on the scene. It was here that we could really see who was on top when the chips were down. With his black coat and yellow eyes, he looked utterly sinister as he bared his fangs and tore into the deer or elk. Hair from the animal would get stuck in his mouth and the ensuing spitting and snorting to get rid of it made the image all the more frightening.

When Motomo moved toward the carcass to eat, he met with less resistance from the more dominant wolves than did Amani, a probable indication of their rank in the eyes of the pack. Once Motomo was savoring the kill, he made a point of trying to keep Amani off. It was much more important to him than it was to Kamots or Matsi.

He would snarl and chase his brother away in what seemed like payback for all the previous days' dominance. Sometimes Amani was left circling the carcass for quite a while, jockeying for position and taking out his frustration on Lakota.

There were rare occasions when Motomo and Amani set their competition aside and joined forces for their mutual benefit; at least this seemed to be the case. There was one particular feeding that stands out in my mind as a time when the two mid-ranking wolves actually appeared to be cooperating so that they both could eat. One crisp October morning, we brought the pack a young deer that had been killed on the highway a few days earlier. They had recently eaten, but since the deer suddenly became available, we brought it to them. Wolves in the wild are used to eating this way, bringing down kills of different size at irregular intervals. Still, this unusually small meal heightened competition over the carcass. The only ones really to get their fill were Kamots, Matsi, and the pups Wahots and Wyakin. Lakota and Chemukh were going hungry on the sidelines and Motomo and Amani were frantically sniffing around the scene, snatching up any scraps that had been inadvertently cast aside.

I heard them vocalizing to each other in an exchange of frustrated whines, and then they turned toward Kamots, who was towering over the carcass. The small deer had been torn to shreds and nearly consumed. All that remained were two disembodied hind legs and a portion of the torso, and Kamots appeared to be intent on finishing it all. As the two mid-ranking wolves faced Kamots he uttered his warning growl, telling them not to even think of approaching the deer. They whined back to him, or to each other, appearing to be begging for food.

The scene that followed occurred with such incredible speed that it stunned us as much as it did Kamots. Looking as if he had been shot from a cannon, Motomo dashed directly at the carcass and grabbed a small chunk of fur and meat that was lying off to the side. Kamots took the bait and chased after him for a few feet, momentarily leaving the carcass unattended. Capitalizing on the tiny window of opportunity, Amani rushed in and snatched one of the remaining deer legs. Recognizing his mistake, Kamots turned, but not fast enough. Amani clung to his prize and made a beeline for the willows, Kamots now close on his tail. What was most fascinating was that, instead of continuing to eat his small chunk of meat, Motomo dropped the morsel (much to the pleasure of Lakota) and turned back to the carcass. He grabbed the other hind leg without breaking stride and veered off in the opposite direction. This final maneuver bewildered Kamots so completely that he broke off his pursuit of Amani and returned to stand guard over what was left of his deer.

This interaction was the subject of ongoing debate and discussion among us in the days that followed. It could well have been that what we had witnessed was a spontaneous "every wolf for himself" situation, in which both Motomo and Amani were able to capitalize on the chaos. However, it all appeared so perfectly timed and adeptly executed that mere chance and opportunism didn't seem to account for what had transpired. The way they approached Kamots together, the unusual vocalizations they made to one another, the way Motomo dropped his "decoy" piece of meat the instant Kamots turned his attention toward Amani: these factors indicated to me that they had actually hatched a scheme and deftly pulled it off.

It is hardly far-fetched to suggest that Motomo and Amani had worked together. After all, a wolf's strong cooperative nature is perhaps its greatest survival skill. A solitary predator like a cougar is physically far better equipped for hunting than a wolf is. With its sharp claws, a cougar can grasp its prey long enough to deliver a suffocating bite to the throat; its forelegs are powerful enough to snap the neck of large elk. Wolves lack a cougar's power, stealth, and weaponry, but they do possess one great advantage—each other.

Had they been part of a wild pack, Motomo and Amani's cooperative efforts would have served them well in the hunt. They would have been the grunt labor, in the thick of the hunt, getting the job done. But these two also taught us that being a mid-ranking wolf bears no similarity to being a foot soldier, part of a large force of equal "worker bees." In a wolf pack there are no equals. Someone always has the slightly upper hand, even if it changes from day to day, and there is always the chance of moving up the ladder a rung or two. It is in this nebulous middle rank where one sees the true and fascinating paradox of life in a wolf pack, the incredible balance of competition and cooperation.

Kamots at ten weeks old

Aipuyi, Akai, Kamots (head held highest), and Motaki

Jamie with Lakota

Jim nurses the pup Amani

Lakota, the omega

Jamie observes the Sawtooth Pack

Matsi and Wyakin

Matsi as a pup

Wahots investigates Jamie's hat

Wahots and Wyakin were inseparable playmates to the end

The Sawtooth Mountains rose 4,000 vertical feet
above the pack's territory

Chemukh's pups explore just outside the den

Wyakin in the willows, just after a rain

In a role reversal during play, Lakota chases Kamots

The new camp inside the enclosure:
the yurt on the platform and sleeping tent below

Changing film inside the yurt

Patty Provonsha prepares dinner

Christina Dutcher with Wahots

An all-important task—clearing the path to the outhouse

Kamots

Lakota

Matsi

Motomo

Amani

Wahots

Chemukh

Wyakin

Makuyi

Kamots presides over a carcass

Jim photographs Kamots

Lakota heads for his hiding place at the top of the enclosure

Lakota and Motaki at five months old

The pond added to the diverse ecosystem and
was a favorite spot to explore

Jim holding the pup Kamots

Piyip mimics his father Kamots, on one of
our last happy visits with the pack

We were honored to have earned their trust

The Pack

JIM

As Jamie and I grew to know each of these wolves, we marveled at their individual personalities. Even brothers like Lakota and Kamots, who looked so similar, were so incredibly different from one another. It was such an honor to get to know them as individuals; however, as our understanding of them matured it was not their individuality that impressed us but their solidarity. I had always thought a wolf pack to be a group of individuals who stuck together for mutual benefit. It is in reality so very much more. A wolf pack is a wholly devoted extended family. It is bound together by a common purpose and, at times, it seems, a common mind.

Before I understood what a pack really was, I had been terribly afraid that one of the wolves might try to climb the fence and run away. A bold wolf, I thought, would find the call of the wilderness beyond the chain link impossible to resist. Over time, I found that the exact opposite was true. Not a single member of the Sawtooth Pack ever tried to get out or even paced the perimeter. True, their spacious territory was an ideal place to live, but the environment was not the reason for their contentment. The reason was each other. Each wolf knew that it belonged with the pack, with the family. Even Lakota, who had to endure abuse from every member of the pack, and who occasionally sought relief in solitude, never showed any indication of wanting to get too far away. When times were difficult for him, he'd move off a short distance, but his attention was always fixed on the pack. Wherever they went, he went, even if a little behind.

Watching the way they interacted with one another, it was easy to see why so many early human cultures revered wolves. Hunting societies especially admired and even imitated the wolf's skill, for as predators people and wolves have similar limitations and must employ similar techniques. It is in the hunt that wolves' near-telepathic cooperation is most apparent. A wolf pack may trail a herd of elk, caribou, or other large prey for days before making its move. During this time, they are already hunting, assessing the herd, looking for an animal that displays any sign of weakness, and this is just the beginning. Wolves must also factor in other conditions that will affect the hunt; weather and terrain can tip the scales in favor of predator or prey. For example, a wide-open plain favors the ungulates, who, if full-grown and healthy, can outrun the fastest wolf. On the other hand, crusty snow or ice favors the wolves, whose wide round paws have evolved to perform like snowshoes and carry them effortlessly over the surface. An experienced wolf is well aware that hoofed animals break through the crust and can become bogged down in deep snow.

Wolves have learned to use these conditions to their advantage. A biologist friend told me of a particular pack in Alaska that he had observed following a herd of caribou on a narrow packed trail through deep snow. The wolves know that their mere presence, following close behind, will eventually panic the caribou. When the rearmost caribou spooks, leaving the hard trail and attempting to run to the middle of the herd, it founders in the snow drifts. And when that happens, it is all over. In warm weather, this same pack of wolves changes its tactics, herding the caribou into a dry riverbed where many of the ungulates will stumble on the round stones.

A wolf pack, therefore, weighs multiple factors when selecting its target and, as circumstances change during the hunt, the target may change as well. Initially they may be pursuing a calf, but if a big healthy bull stumbles unexpectedly, they all know to go after the bigger meal. Conversely, if too many factors seem to be in favor of the prey, they may choose to wait. Sometimes it is better to stay a bit hungry until the odds improve rather than expend precious energy on a fruitless chase.

Other observers of wild wolves have reported that often fewer than half of the wolves on a hunt are actually involved with physically bringing down the prey. The youngest wolves frequently do nothing more than observe and learn from the sidelines. Each of the other pack members contributes according to its particular experience and ability. Speedy, lightly built females often take on herding roles, darting back and forth in front of prey, causing confusion and preventing escape. Slower but more powerful males are able to take down a large animal more aggressively and quickly (Bomford, p. 73).

Some of the wolf's bad reputation stems from the apparent mob scene that ensues when the prey begins to falter. Wolves are not equipped to dispatch their victims quickly; prey usually die of shock, muscle damage, or blood loss. If it can, one of the stronger wolves will seize the prey by the nose and hold on tight, helping to bring about a more expeditious end, but the animal can still take many minutes to succumb. Equipped only with feet for running and jaws for biting, wolves make the best of their assets. A wolf pack's ferocity and apparent brutality is really a defensive measure. It is not rare for a wolf to be seriously injured by flailing hooves and slashing antlers. A well-placed kick could break a wolf's jaw, rendering it unable to feed itself. It is much safer to harass the prey and let it tire before moving in close. Far from being a mob scene, a hunt is a masterfully coordinated group effort, well deserving of our admiration.

Although the alpha male is usually in the thick of the hunt, it would be an exaggeration to say that he is leading it. The alpha may select the animal to be pursued, or he may chose to break off the hunt if it is going poorly. But he is not barking out orders to his subordinates like a general on the battlefield. The wolves just seem to know what to do, and they do it as one.

In my youth, I spent countless hours diving off the Florida coast with my friend John Jolley. Together, we explored deep reefs and shipwrecks and experimented with early underwater cameras. Beneath the sea, communication is limited to a few basic visual signals—a real handicap when quick cooperation is imperative. We occasionally found ourselves in tight situations—huge tiger sharks or hammerheads could appear at any moment, rising out of the darkness—and we had to resist the temptation to panic. But after diving together for years, John and I instinctively knew how to work together. Even in that dark and unpredictable world, our knowledge of our joint and individual capabilities made us stronger as a team. We were so in tune with each other that we didn't even notice the lack of verbal communication.

I imagine that wolves on a hunt are operating in much the same way. The young wolves watch the behavior of the older ones and see how the game is played. They witness how the adults change their strategy according to conditions and type of prey. They learn how the hunters handle each different situation: what to do when the prey dashes for open ground, or jumps into a river, or turns to defend itself.

When juvenile wolves finally join in the hunt, they imitate the more experienced wolves and practice the skills of herding and tackling. By the time they are full-grown adults, they have become part of a well-oiled machine. Even if they were able to communicate verbally with each other during the hunt, it would be unnecessary. They know exactly what to expect from the others and what is expected of them. It is almost eerie how a pack can appear to be of a single mind.

Our project, by its very nature, had its limitations. The animal's prowess as a hunter was one aspect of wolves that we were unable to feature. Nor were we able to show certain other qualities, such as the great distances they can travel, or the way packs defend their territory. These limitations were balanced by our ability to examine their personal relationships with one another, and it was here that the more subtle signs of pack unity revealed themselves. Rarely did two wolves pass each other without playfully rubbing shoulders together or exchanging a brief lick. So often Jamie and I would see two wolves relaxing together, curled up beside each other, the head of one draped over the neck of the other in a gesture that was both assertive and affectionate. Wahots and Wyakin lounged together like this every day and were nearly inseparable. Wyakin would inevitably get a little feisty and grab at a clump of Wahots' fur. This would spark a friendly bout of jaw sparring, a game akin to thumb wrestling in which each wolf tries to clamp down on the jaws of the other. All the while, they would be carrying on a spirited conversation that sounded more like Chewbacca from *Star Wars* than anything else I could compare it to. Everything about this interaction reassured each of them of their closeness, as siblings and as pack mates. More than hunting or travel, this is the behavior I hoped to reveal in my films, because it is the side of wolves that people understand the least.

After observing this pack for so long, I have come to believe that the bond a wolf has to its pack is certainly as strong as the bond a human being has to his or her family. One would hope that this similarity would give us an instinctive sympathy for wolves, but we stubbornly resist granting another species qualities that we cherish as singularly human. How would our management of these animals change if we imagined ourselves in their place?

A clue can be found in the story of another highly social mammal a continent away. Game wardens in parts of Africa continually struggle to manage "problem" elephants that destroy fences and ravage crops. For many years, the solution was to cull the adults of a herd, and relocate the orphans to a different area. Far from achieving the desired goal, however, this type of management often resulted in even greater problems. The young elephants that were moved became known as "delinquents" and were frequently violent and unpredictable. Occasionally the remnants of the herd roamed together as an unruly mob, at times even attacking other animals with whom they traditionally coexist. And why would anyone expect otherwise? They have been robbed of their family and their home. They have lost the sense of security that comes from being nurtured by their own kind. Equally tragic, they have lost their history. Traditional routes of travel, the best places to forage and find water, what to do during a flood or drought—all this knowledge has vanished with the adults. What is left is no longer a herd, but a loose collection of desperate and depressed animals that lack both the mental tools and the emotional stability to live as they should.

Because wolves are similar to elephants in both their intelligence and strong social bonds, it is legitimate to wonder if this country is creating "delinquent" wolves. Adult wolves, especially the alpha male and female, hold the knowledge of the pack. When we trap a few members of a Canadian pack, often the young or inexperienced, then relocate them to selected parts of the United States, what happens to that knowledge? How well do these new wolf packs cope with the demands of hunting and raising young? These are certainly questions worth asking.

Winter

JAMIE

The Salmon River is famous for being one of the longest free-flowing rivers in the lower 48 states. It first appears as a thin ribbon of silver, shimmering on the valley floor below Galena Summit. As it makes its way northward, it doesn't meander casually like the lazy rivers of the Midwest, it flows straight, strong, and icy cold. Along the first leg of its journey, a mere thirty miles from its source to the town of Stanley, Idaho, the Salmon is joined by one creek after another as melting snow tumbles out of the Sawtooth and White Cloud mountains. The river's volume grows so much in this short trip that Stanley does a brisk business in outfitting kayakers and white-water rafters.

When I first saw Stanley, it looked to me the way I had imagined a remote Alaskan town to look, like something out of *Northern Exposure*. The main street, with its two saloons, post office, and laundromat, remains unpaved. The improved state road that runs to one side of

town features the familiar modern establishments that
provide food, fuel, and accommodations to people on
their way to somewhere else. During the height of the
summer tourist season, the town's population peaks at
about 120 residents. Stanley's rough-and-ready attitude
can be summed up by a bumper sticker I once spotted
there—an advertisement for a local bar. It read: WE
DON'T HAVE A TOWN DRUNK, WE ALL TAKE TURNS.

The town of Stanley is surrounded by the Sawtooth
National Recreation Area (managed by the U.S. Forest
Service) and by a variety of privately owned ranches. Stanley's
small population generally falls into one or the other corresponding lifestyle: cattle and sheep or backpacking and river
rafting. So when a pack of wolves moved into the Sawtooths,
some local residents were elated and others incensed.

Whenever Jim and I introduced ourselves to someone, we could expect about a sixty percent chance of getting the cold shoulder. At the same time, those who
approved of what we were doing greeted us with unbridled generosity. One family let us park our sleds and
snowmobiles on their property, saving us from hauling
them back and forth from Ketchum on a trailer over the
icy mountain pass. Residents also alerted us when someone had accidentally killed a deer or elk on the highway,
and the sheriff allowed us to collect it for wolf food.

Few people have had the pleasure of picking up road-
kill. It just isn't something that comes up that often in
everyday life. I learned two important facts about dead
deer my very first time out: they are heavy and they smell
bad. Wolves would just as soon eat carrion as hunt, as it

requires far less effort and is quite a bit safer. Their powerful jaws can tear through a carcass that has frozen rock-
hard in the winter. Similarly, their resilient stomachs have
no problem digesting meat that has gone very ripe in the
sun. What smells delectable to a wolf is enough to make a
person turn green and, believe me, there is no way to get
a 400-pound dead elk into the back of a pickup truck
without getting up close and personal.

I was thankful for the years I had spent working at the
National Zoo. One of my duties there had been to assist
in necropsies on animals who had died, so I had long
since lost any squeamishness around such grizzly scenes.
The goal was straightforward: get the thing off the road
and onto the bed of the truck. The techniques for achieving this goal were various but always involved brute force.
Animals like mule deer and pronghorn antelope could
simply be rolled onto a tarp and hoisted into the truck,
but even a small ungulate is a lot of dead weight.

Jake and I spent an entire afternoon dealing with six
pronghorn that a single driver had managed to hit at once
as they crossed the highway. As we grunted and stumbled, lifting the unfortunate creatures into the truck bed,
we discussed how we really ought to get a winch for this
job (though we never did). Getting them in the truck was
only half the battle. With the truck fully loaded, we drove
north to the local fish hatchery, where the manager gen-
erously allowed us to use part of a large walk-in freezer to
store food. There we repeated the entire process in
reverse, with the added chore of schlepping the antelope
into the freezer and neatly stacking them.

Larger animals like elk were just too heavy to lift and therefore required a bit more creativity. By creativity, I mean a chainsaw. If that experience didn't turn me into a vegetarian, I don't believe anything ever will. Keith Marshall, Megan's assistant, who went on to become the primary caretaker of the pack, spent the very first day of his career hacking up an elk carcass with a chainsaw. Keith arrived from the East Coast fresh from college with a brand-new Carhartt jacket, little beatnik glasses, and a wonderfully enthusiastic attitude. All of these probably contributed to Megan's decision to take him out for road-kill collection on his first day.

Megan's friend and our former assistant, Val, opted to come along for the fun. Val is a very intelligent woman and continues to work for wolf recovery, but she can be a little rough around the edges when she chooses to be. She emerged from a cabin in Stanley holding a beer bottle in each hand. As she took swigs from one, she alternately spit tobacco juice into the other. Val broke the ice by backing her truck into Keith's little economy sedan. As Keith watched the trail of steam rise from beneath his hood, Val informed him that she had no insurance and that they'd better get going before someone else stole the roadkill for dinner.

So the three went off to collect wolf food. In this case, their prize was a very large elk cow that had been struck the previous evening and had frozen pretty solid during the night. The two women gave Keith the job of handling the chainsaw, probably guessing that he'd want to make a good impression on his first day. He may have had experience cutting wood, but I'll wager this was his first crack at carving up a large frozen ungulate. The most important thing to remember is to stand off to the side and hold the saw at an angle, a rule the girls neglected to tell him. Positioning himself directly behind the saw, he revved up and started cutting. A bright red stripe of frozen elk slush shot up the front of his brand-new Carhartt from his waist to the top of his forehead, much to the delight of the two women, who watched from the sidelines. And to think that after such an introduction Keith remained working with the pack for the next three years. It takes a special kind of person to love this job.

When there was no snow, we could take a four-wheel-drive truck to within a mile of the enclosure and transfer our supplies to an all-terrain vehicle for the final leg. In the winter, however, we could take the four-wheel-drive only as far as Stanley. There our snowmobiles would be waiting for us under tarps covered with ice and snow.

Knowing the ordeal that lay ahead, simply getting out of the truck was a challenge in itself, especially if we had been softened up by a couple comfortable nights in Ketchum. In the dead of winter, the snowmobile's pull-starters were just about impossible to operate. Jim would invariably spend several minutes trying to get those old clunkers functioning while I unloaded the truck. Each snowmobile towed a sled on which we loaded provisions, film equipment, and often a big fat frozen carcass.

Jim drove one of the snowmobiles and I stood on the

back of the sled like an Alaskan dogsled musher. If any of the crew was with us, they paired up on the other machine in similar fashion. Most winter days around Stanley are clear and dry but unbelievably cold. Any exposed skin was burnt by the icy wind as we sped across the blinding white sage flats toward the inviting shelter of our camp, so before setting out we had to cover ourselves in several layers of clothing. I personally wore two pairs of gloves, three or four layers of polypropelene, fleece, and Gore-Tex, a balaclava that covered my entire face, a hat, ski goggles, and heavily insulated boots. Most of the time this was sufficient.

Geographically, Stanley sits in the middle of a high-altitude basin that traps cold air inside a ring of mountains. The area usually records the lowest temperatures in the state, and sometimes even in the entire country, including Alaska! Whatever the temperature was in Ketchum, you could bank on it being at least ten degrees colder in Stanley. Often as I clung to the back of the sled and bowed my head against the frigid air, I wondered if Jim had taken this fact into consideration when he chose the Sawtooths as a site for his project.

Sometimes the wind would whip up a whiteout that would bury the trail and knock down the willow sticks we'd placed as markers. On days like this, Jim seemed to drive by memory. The trail had a few tricks, however. Repeated use packed it into a convex shape, like an inverted rain gutter. If we started drifting to one side, gravity would pull us further off the trail. With the sleds so heavily loaded, we were operating these machines at

the very limits of their power. In winter, the ranch land
that separated Stanley from the alpine forest was an open
and featureless expanse of white. From the looks of it,
one could drive a straight line across the range almost all
the way to wolf camp. But the trail twisted and turned
around irrigation ditches and abandoned ranch equipment that were now buried under the snow, waiting like
landmines. A small mistake could sometimes result in an
hour of digging.

There were a few times when the weather definitely
got the better of us. On one February day, we were returning from spending a few nights in Ketchum. As we
drove north, a curtain of snowflakes began to fall. By the
time we reached the mountain pass that separates
Ketchum from Stanley, the wind was blowing fiercely.
On the rock walls above us, the snow drifted into cor-
nices that cantilevered precariously over the road. The
drive to Stanley, normally just over an hour, took three
times as long. By the time we made it to the snowmobiles, they were unrecognizable mounds of white. The
savage wind had begun to blow the snow sideways, piling
it up in huge drifts along the buildings and fences.

The snow was so fresh and deep that it was impossible to tell our trail from the open snowy fields. Jim could
just barely feel the hard snowmobile track underneath the
fresh powder. As we made our way over a small hill and
out onto the ranch lands, we began slipping off the path.
Jim gunned the engine and the snowmobile, straining
under the heavy burden, fought its way back on course.

Three times we lost the trail completely and the

snowmobile bogged down. Three times we unloaded the sled and dug ourselves out with small backpacking shovels, but we were swiftly losing daylight and had only covered three miles in two hours. As we started to climb out of the flats and up the slope of the forested foothills, the snow became deeper and began to fall harder and harder. We were three-quarters of the way there when we felt ourselves slide into a deep drift. As before, there was nothing to do but unload and start digging. First we unhooked the sled and concentrated our efforts on the snowmobile, hoping that if we freed it we could use it to drag the sled out with a cable. The machine remained stubbornly buried. Every time we gunned the engine, it simply burrowed deeper into the snow. We dug until the last of the gray light faded, working as best we could by the light of our headlamps, choked all the while by the swirling, maddening snow. After nearly an hour, we freed the snowmobile, but by that point we were already soaking wet, mostly from our own sweat.

Between the constant fogging of our goggles, the blowing snow, and the lack of light, it was nearly impossible to see what we were doing. If we continued on to camp from here, we would surely lose the trail again. Our biggest fear was that we would tumble into one of the many creeks that crisscrossed our path. It just wasn't worth the risk to the machine or to ourselves.

We decided to abandon the sled with all our supplies and return to Stanley and try to get a room at the small motel. Thankfully, we had left our camera and sound gear in the yurt, securely guarded by a pack of wolves. We turned the snowmobile around and headed back down the trail, which was already drifting over again but still visible. It was all the more frustrating, knowing that the comfort and safety of camp was only two miles away. Despite the creature comforts of the motel, a hot meal, and a shower, we were eager to get back to our tents.

The next morning the sky was a bright cobalt blue, although the air was much colder, and the new snow creaked under my feet as I walked back to the snowmobile. It was hard to believe that the plains that sparkled so beautifully under the morning sun had been so threatening and infuriating the night before. We started back along the trail, replacing our buried markers as we went. The sled was now nicely stuck in place under a couple feet of new snow. Our bags of clothes, film, and equipment were covered in snow but undamaged. The fresh fruit and vegetables we had brought had not fared so well. The insulated cooler in which we had packed the produce was unable to keep out the deep freeze of a night in the mountains.

I never felt happier to arrive at camp, and the wolves were especially excited to see us. Their hearing is so keen that they undoubtedly heard us approaching the previous night, despite the raging wind. Their overly enthusiastic greeting made me think that they must have been confused by hearing us get so close and then disappear again.

Greeting the pack was always the first order of business whenever we arrived at camp. If we happened to have a carcass with us, we always stashed it about a quarter-mile away. If the wolves could have seen and smelled the food, they would have probably become very agitated. We also made sure to leave all our gear outside the fence and walk in empty-handed to meet them. If we had sauntered in carrying backpacks and hauling sleds, some dangling strap or bungee cord would have been too great a temptation for the curious animals. Besides, we really felt we owed it to the pack to give them our full attention. No matter how pressing the chores might be, or how fast the daylight was waning, we always made time for them before anything else.

After the frenzied hello, they calmed down and we were able to haul our gear carefully into our camp. Nevertheless, we had to be watchful; some of the pack still hung around to see what mischief they could get into, and, of course, Kamots took great pride in stealing things. As always, he enjoyed demonstrating how clever he was. Consequently, while one person pulled the sled with a rope, the other person pushed from behind and prevented any gear from wandering off.

Usually we had two other people with us as part of the film crew. Jake and Patty still joined us when they could. They loved working on the film and being with the wolves and we always valued their input. Jim's daughter, Christina, was Jim's camera assistant until 1995, when she fell in love and moved to Oregon. Jim's new film crew—Burke Smith, Sarah Bingaman, Shane Stent, and second cameraman Franz Camenzind—spent the most time with us at camp in the project's later years.

In naming all the people who were present at camp at one time or another, it gives the impression that we had created a small city in the Sawtooths. In actuality, there were seldom more than four people at camp at any given moment. Taking care of the pack required a 24-hour-a-day commitment, and making a film was a full-time job as well. Burke, Sarah, and Shane split their time between camp and the film production office in Ketchum. Franz came in from Wyoming every once in a while for special shoots that required two cameras. Megan and Keith's duties did not involve filmmaking, so when the film crew was at camp, they could take time off. Everyone knew that relationships could get strained when people are cooped up in tents together for too long, especially during the winter. So we made sure that the crew rotated and that everyone got enough time away.

We did our best to settle into a daily routine. Jim had the painful job of being the first one out of bed to get the stove going. I now believe him to be the fastest fire starter in the country. Crumpled newspaper, kindling, and small logs lay waiting by the stove, ready to be assembled in a flash. Jim would leap from the bed, I'd hear a muttered expletive, the clunk of wood against metal, the hiss of a match, and he would be back. I don't think his bare feet ever touched the floor for more than a second. We dozed off for a few more minutes, listening to the crackle of the fire, letting the tent start to warm up, then it was my turn. I got completely dressed in bed under the mound of warm down, something I had learned how to do in my first week. Then I stuffed my feet into a pair of heavy boots and stumbled up the ladder to the yurt to get the coffee on.

Of course, the needs of the film always took precedence over any daily routine. A film shoot could take place at any hour, any day. Some winter mornings, we would awaken to find the snow coming down in huge flakes, and the wolves frolicking as they always did during a snowfall. When this happened, we'd drop everything and get right to filming, skipping breakfast and leaving the stoves unlit. Sometimes the morning light had a particular golden glow, or there would be a thick and eerie fog enveloping the valley. Sometimes the wolves just seemed to be in high spirits and would be playing or vocalizing. We never failed to suspend all other camp activities for the chance of good filming.

On the other hand, there were days that were so brutally cold that it was just about impossible to do anything. Frequently, the temperature dropped to twenty or thirty below zero and could stay there for an entire week. When this happened, the equipment let us know that this was no time for filming. The combination locks on the enclosure gates wouldn't budge without the aid of a propane torch to defrost the tumblers. Rechargeable camera batteries went dead in just a few minutes, film became brittle, and the camera's operation was noisy and labored. Surprisingly, the cold presented far fewer problems for my sound gear than for Jim's camera, but at twenty below I was perfectly happy to call off shooting. We spent this time huddled around the stove in the yurt, drinking coffee and trying to keep the gear and ourselves warm.

On these frigid days, I was amazed at how the wolves took the temperature in stride, going about their business as if it were any other day. It was a chore for me even to breathe; my nostrils felt like they were freezing together with each breath. Meanwhile, Amani would be dozing in a patch of impotent sunlight, Lakota would be rooting around by himself, thrusting his muzzle into the crusty snow, looking for mice or a scrap of food, and Kamots would be calmly watching over the pack.

These were clearly animals that were made for cold. A wolf's double-layer coat provides superb defense against the elements. Its undercoat is short and woolly, like polar fleece, and contains an oily, water-repellent substance similar to lanolin. The outer layer is made of what are called "guard hairs," long, shiny hairs that break the wind and shed dirt and water. Interestingly, the undercoat is the same color in all wolves: beige Matsi and black Motomo both were an even gray underneath. It is the guard hairs that give a wolf its particular markings, and this is why the wolves appear more striking in winter, when their coats are thick and full.

They never sought shelter from the elements in a den or even beneath the cover of trees. If it was snowing heavily the wolves would simply hunker down, each one curled up with its tail covering its vulnerable nose. Their fur was such a great insulator that the snow didn't melt on their bodies. It just piled up on them until they were nothing more than white mounds in the winter landscape. It was always amusing to see a pile of snow suddenly rise and shake, and a wolf materialize out of thin air.

Days ended early in winter. By two in the afternoon, the sun had already disappeared behind the wall of mountains. The dull light that lingered during the three hours between the premature sunset and total darkness was usually too flat to make filming worthwhile. We filled this time with chores: chopping wood, fixing equipment, and, of course, shoveling snow. Keeping the path to the outhouse open was of supreme importance, as was removing heavy snow from the tent roofs. It was intensely aggravating to deal with the same snow three times, but the new camp setup forced us to do so. First we had to pull the snow off the yurt. Despite the solid construction of this dwelling, we didn't know how much weight the roof could withstand. The snow tumbled down to the deck on which the yurt stood. From there, we shoveled it off the platform to the ground eight feet below, where it formed a huge pile. Unfortunately, the accumulating mound of snow would have given the wolves a means to get up onto the yurt platform and into our camp. I could just imagine them ransacking our tents with all the joy of marauding Huns. So down to ground level we went to dig a trench around our camp.

After the work day and before dinner, Jim wisely allotted time for everyone to take a break and spend two or three hours alone. On winter days, Jim and I retired to the cozy little cocoon of our tent, lit a fire in the stove, and read by candlelight. The orange light reflecting off the canvas, and the hush of falling snow that smothered all sound, transported me back to a time long ago. The modern world faded farther and farther away, until all that remained were the simple joys of warmth, shelter, and companionship.

Jim and I were married on New Year's Eve, the final day of 1994. When I joined him in Idaho I had told myself that it was a trial period, that I could always return to the East, where my family was. But from the moment I arrived, everything fell into place so naturally. Our wedding was a quiet and simple affair at home. Jim's daughter Christina and son Garrick were there, plus two other friends, and the justice of the peace. In a matter of moments, we were husband and wife.

Now our days at wolf camp were like an extended honeymoon. Living in humble tents, isolated among the frozen mountains, surrounded by a pack of wolves, neither of us could imagine wanting to be anywhere else. I smiled to myself when I thought back on how foreign and scary it had been in my mind. Idaho was hardly the far-off and desolate land it once seemed. The great differences between Jim's life and mine, and the imagined sacrifices I would have to make to be with him were all so silly. Now there was just Jim and me as it should always have been, relaxing by the woodstove, sharing this moment of quiet together. I had loved him from the start, and now we were complete.

Around seven P.M., the crew gathered in the warm yurt to prepare dinner. Meals were a communal affair. Although only one or two people could fit in the kitchen area, everyone else sat at the table for the warmth and company. And, of course, there was nothing like wine to keep the crew happy. We found a nice red table wine that we dubbed "Chateau Yurt." We treated dinner like a small celebration at the end of each day, and made an effort to always make it special. Each person had a featured style of cooking. Patty was known for her enchiladas, Sarah for her vegetarian chili, and Christina's pine nut and sun-dried tomato pizza was always a favorite. I was designated queen of the barbecue, even in the winter, specializing in lamb chops and salmon. I found it interesting that the smells of our cooking never excited the wolves in the least. Give them a whiff of rotting deer and they would drool in anticipation, but throw a fresh piece of meat on the grill and they couldn't have cared less. One time I accidentally dropped a corn chip off the yurt platform and into the enclosure, right in front of two wolves resting below. I was irritated at my carelessness, for we never allowed the wolves near any of our food. As the chip landed in the snow, I expected one of them to gobble it up instantly, his taste buds forever corrupted by human junk food. To my surprise they just sniffed it and rolled on it briefly, intrigued only by its sudden appearance and the new scent that it held. Then they turned away, clearly failing to recognize it as something to eat.

Conversation at dinner almost always centered around the wolves. Every day we saw something interesting or amusing in the pack's behavior—Matsi's tenderness toward Lakota, or Amani's infinite patience with Wahots and Wyakin as they took turns latching on to his tail and letting themselves be dragged through the snow. This was our chance to discuss and interpret all the things we saw and marvel together at what fascinating creatures wolves are. The yurt was warm and comfortable, glowing with the light of flickering candles. We lingered around the dining table, casually planning the next day's filming, before heading off to bed.

The wolves' schedule bore little resemblance to our own. They passed through several stages of sleep and activity during both day and night, often with no discernible pattern. How much they slept depended on many factors. After a meal, they would lie around for days, blissfully digesting away. On such occasions, they appeared to be dozing much of the time. Conversely, during the breeding season, or before a meal, they seemed to be constantly alert and active.

We noticed that each wolf had its favorite sleeping spot, which it used whenever it bedded down for some serious rest. Just like dogs do, the wolves turned in circles a few times before lying down. Repeating this action, night after night, they packed down small hollows in the snow which we dubbed "sleep sinks." The wolves took great pains to customize them and make them more comfortable. Willow branches and bark were the preferred materials to get the sleep sink exactly right.

Frequently the pack would bed down at the same time we did but they never slept all the way through the night. We, on the other hand, didn't get out of bed unless we absolutely had to. Everything in the tent quickly froze as soon as the fire went out. If we wanted to have drinking water nearby, we had to keep a bottle in bed with us or it would quickly become a block of ice. Even our breath condensed and formed little fans of ice by our heads and glued our hair to the pillows. But in the dead of night we would hear the pack rustling about, playing and conversing just as they did during the day, completely happy, not minding the cold of night at all. And, of course, every so often the darkness would be pierced by their howling.

Wahots slept as close to our tent as possible. During the day, he was somewhat aloof and unapproachable. He was always present, watching the goings-on, but he never liked to be in the thick of the action. At night, for some reason, he liked to be near us. Perhaps the glow of our lamps and the muffled sound of our conversation were a comfort to him, reminding him of his days as a newborn pup. We were separated only by a chain-link fence and a thin wall of canvas. In reality, he lay just two or three feet away, close enough that we could hear his breathing. When he was inspired to howl in the middle of the night, he could launch us right out of bed.

Befitting his name, Wahots was quite an enthusiastic howler. He was not as melodious as Lakota, but what he lacked in tune he made up for in energy. A howl usually has a definite progression: the alpha usually initiates it, the others quickly join in, and together they bring the song to its crescendo and coda. All the other wolves would stop howling at about the same time, but Wahots never quite got the hang of it. After a few seconds of quiet, we'd often hear him let go a short "oop," before realizing that no one else was joining in. It was like being the only one laughing in a crowded movie theater. At times, I'd swear he was embarrassed.

The air of a winter's night was so absolutely still and silent that the howls seemed to be amplified. Consequently, this became my favorite time of year to record the wolves' vocalizations for the film because the sound was so clean. Before going to sleep, I set up the microphone outside the tent and ran the cables inside to the tape deck. Then I took the deck to bed with me to keep it warm and easily accessible. If the wolves awakened me during the night, all I had to do was push the record button. Then I could lie in bed, comfortable and warm, listening to their songs through my headphones. Each wolf was a different distance from my microphone so each individual howl had a distinct quality. Being the closest, Wahots' howl rang out sharp and clear whereas Kamots' seemed to float in from far away.

Sometimes the howl would spark a rally or a bout of play and we could hear the galloping of paws and good-natured snarling. Other times, each wolf remained in its place rather than running to Kamots. After dark, their howls seemed to be in response to some far-off sound, a barking coyote, or the rustle of an elk somewhere in the forest.

Sometimes I suspected that they were simply checking in on each other, howling back and forth in the dark.

"Are you there?"

"I'm here, I'm fine."

I once read a description of a wolf howl in the night written by a 19th-century mountain man named James Capin Adams. He writes, "It is indeed a horrible noise, the most hateful a man alone in the wilderness can hear. To a person anywise low-spirited, it suggests the most awful fancies, and is altogether doleful in the extreme" (Lopez, p.175).

It just goes to show you how your attitude can completely alter your perceptions. To me, waking up in the middle of the night to the sound of a wolf howling is one of the most beautiful experiences I know, evoking a flood of different emotions. At first, it is a startling rush that shocks you out of sleep. But then the beauty of their voices takes hold of you, as soothing as the sound of night rainfall against a windowpane. In the pitch black, the song transcends space and time. It is the sound of eons, of earth, of life.

Lying in bed on those nights, I sometimes pictured our camp as a ship on the ocean. The vast cold wilderness that surrounded us was as inhospitable as the sea, and we clung to our tiny flicker of life in the darkness. The last note of the wolves' howl would end and then echo back from the mountains in an eerie whisper. Wahots would shift restlessly and let out a deep sigh as he lay back down. Then everything was silent.

Concerns

JIM

The Sawtooth Pack had finally come into its own. It was a real family now, with old and young, males and females, and all the dynamic relationships that a pack can have. And now Jamie and I were in the middle of it. By day, they appeared and disappeared among the willows and pines around us, and by night, the sounds of their conversation filled the air. We were immersed in their lives and they permeated every minute of ours.

Of course, there were many times when we had to leave camp, primarily because we were still trying to sell our second film. Although *Wolf: Return of a Legend* was a success and even won a News and Documentary Emmy, we remained unable to generate any interest in the more personal story of the wolves' lives. Every major company passed on it, usually citing the reason, "There's already been a wolf film." Flying across the country for a twenty-minute meeting was a frustrating and sometimes humiliating process that was exacerbated by constant worries over the pack's welfare while we were away. I was always anxious to get back to camp as soon as possible.

There was not a minute during those six years that I did not think about the safety of Kamots and his family. I could not go home after a week of shooting, relax, and completely forget about the work for a few days. Many a night in Ketchum, I awoke to the sound of wind or thunder. Then I would lie awake, haunted by images of trees falling upon the fence and Kamots fearlessly leading his pack up the mountainside to explore the Sawtooth wilderness.

When we were busy at camp, the worries diminished somewhat. Still, we were well aware of the myriad threats that faced the pack, almost all of which were beyond our control. The wolves, on the other hand, lived their lives and sorted out their social disputes blissfully unaware of the dangers that surrounded their paradise existence.

During the hot, dry summers, the air sometimes grew thick with the acrid smoke of forest fires. At night, we sat in camp and watched the sky glow menacingly red. By day, helicopters buzzed overhead, racing back and forth from nearby Goat Lake with suspended bags of water. The next summer, a huge fire ravaged the back side of the Sawtooth Mountains, and although it was farther away, it made life at camp absolutely miserable. Clouds of smoke poured over the Sawtooths for weeks on end, darkening the sky and dumping a shower of ash on our tents, turning them nearly black. All we could do was watch and wait.

On a much smaller scale, but equally worrisome, the animals with whom we shared the forest lurked in the back of my mind. They were like a wild card that could turn up without warning. I never stopped fretting about the cougar, wondering if and when he might return. More prevalent were the black bears that occasionally entered unoccupied crew tents and rooted around the exterior of our camp, looking for food. I knew that if a determined bear wanted to tear open a seam in the fence, there was little I could do to stop it. All I could do was avoid attracting them to the area. For example, I never gave the wolves more food than they could handle so there would never be leftover meat, and I never placed a carcass near the perimeter of the enclosure, where a bear could see it. And, of course, we always packed out our own garbage and disposed of it in town.

Threats from individuals added still another layer of worry to the mix, just as they had with the cougar film. Many of Stanley's old-timers fear that their way of life is being threatened by the young and often environmentally active newcomers who trickle into the valley in ever greater numbers. The added presence of a group of "wolf-lovers" up in the foothills was, they felt, just one more assault on tradition. From time to time, we would receive anonymous letters in our post office box reading, "Move the wolves immediately or we will!"

There was one local individual who took a particular interest in our project. Although I could never really tell if he had a dislike for us or for wolves, his presence never failed to make me uneasy. A true Wild West hero in his own mind, he was famous for flashy displays of gunplay on Stanley's Main Street following last call at the saloon.

From time to time, he showed up at wolf camp, riding in on his jet-black horse in a trail of dust, sporting a six-gun and dressed fully in black, from his Stetson hat all the way down to his cowboy boots.

The conversation, if any, was generally one-sided. Most of the time he would offer a terse greeting and then just watch us. More often, I think, he watched our assistant Megan. Sometimes he would ask a few questions and then, apparently satisfied, he would nod, spur his horse, and vanish down the dirt trail back toward Stanley.

All in all, this vigilante graced us with his presence four or five times, and it never failed to jangle my nerves for the rest of the day. At the conclusion of one visit, he made his exit with a little extra fanfare, probably for Megan's benefit, yanking the reins sharply to the right and galloping at full tilt through the aspen grove. Unfortunately, we had just had a spell of rain and the trail was a bit more slick than usual. A second after he vanished among the trees, we heard a muffled thud and the sound of hoofbeats slowing to a halt. Before I could stop her, Jamie called out, "Are you all right?" The only reply was silence. Then the hoofbeats started once more, though quieter and slower than before. We did not see him again.

More than any visitors from Stanley, our relationship with the neighboring ranchers caused severe tension. Ranchers traditionally hold some sway with the Forest Service and I feared that our neighbors could shut us down completely if they chose to. When it came to handling this precarious relationship, we took a lesson from

Lakota. We figured if we kept as low a profile as possible on the land and did not make a spectacle of ourselves, we would decrease the risk of a confrontation.

This was another reason that no more than two people, in addition to Jamie and me, were at camp on any given day. The standard crew rotated, so camp was never crowded and there were never too many vehicles parked where the ranchers might see them. I allowed visitors only on rare occasions and tried not to do anything that would attract a critical eye. To some extent, I even tried to keep the location a secret for fear that both wolf lovers and wolf haters would begin showing up and disturbing both the wolves and our neighbors. I did not want cars constantly buzzing through the ranchers' land, and I didn't want the camp to look like a shantytown.

My need for discretion was, sadly, at odds with the needs of the Wolf Education and Research Center, the nonprofit organization I had created. Being inconspicuous was contrary to the goal of a fund-raising organization. They requested that I allow them to supply interns to help with camp duties. It worried me, but in an effort to improve our relationship, I tried to accommodate them.

Unfortunately, these interns seldom appreciated how insecure our position was. I remember one particular college student who continually drove his little red car back and forth across the dirt road from camp to Stanley. He was apparently unable to resist the urge to drive into town several times a day to make phone calls or get a slice of pizza. I couldn't have cared less that his displays of collegiate testosterone were destroying his car's suspension, but I did mind that they were probably further compromising my very tentative relationship with the ranchers.

I was heading to camp with a load of supplies one summer day, when I caught sight of what looked like a huge dust devil spinning toward me. Out of the brown cloud emerged a small red speck of a car bouncing and skidding over the ruts and sagebrush. I was furious. I succeeded in stopping the intern and asked him if he wouldn't mind actually staying at camp during his days on duty and, if he absolutely had to go to town, to please refrain from driving like Mario Andretti in a Dodge Neon.

I reminded him, not for the first time, about my delicate relationship with the ranchers, explaining, "If they get me kicked off this land, the wolves will have nowhere to live and I might be forced to put them to sleep." The intern already knew that releasing them into the wild would have been both illegal and cruel, but his nose was firmly out of joint. It wasn't long before I heard the rumor that "Jim is threatening to kill all the wolves." It still persists to this day in some circles.

Despite my efforts, by 1995, signs of the neighboring ranchers' dissatisfaction with my presence were getting less and less subtle. One day the gate across our access road was closed and locked, never to reopen. Two of the ranchers had had enough of the constant traffic across their land, and frankly, I didn't blame them. From that point on we were forced to detour around their land on an old Forest Service jeep trail. Thankfully, the third rancher who owned most of surrounding land remained friendly. If our relationship with him soured, he could have cut us off from camp completely. More than just a simple inconvenience, this detour prompted two weeks of bridge building so that our ATV would not erode fragile creek beds.

To make matters worse, the next summer a fence that stood on public land was knocked down by the resident elk herd. Even though I was quick to mend the fence, the next day I found a sign, handwritten by a rancher, informing me that I would find myself in the county jail if I broke the fence again. Relations never improved.

There was more to my desire for calm and quiet around wolf camp than simply trying to appease the ranchers. I was also trying to ensure that the wolf pack we were studying and filming maintained as much of its natural behavior as possible. They were such curious animals. A burst of laughter, a revving snowmobile, the clank of a gate usually brought them running to investigate. How could they display their real social behavior with each other if they were continually darting off to see what the people were up to?

Thus I got a bit concerned when a former director of WERC proposed a picnic for all their interns and volunteers to be held at wolf camp. When she suggested it would be fun to set up a volleyball net near the fence, I had to draw the line. I tried to explain that the commotion would upset the animals and irritate the ranchers, but I think I simply came off as the wolf-grouch who wouldn't let anyone have any fun.

Continual misunderstandings with WERC began to truly undermine my confidence in them as permanent caretakers of the pack. At WERC's inception we had agreed that they would take over pack management at the end of the film project. Now I fretted constantly about the future, and what would happen when the wolves were no longer in Jamie's and my care. Perhaps I was overprotective, but I began to worry that the people at WERC did not fully comprehend how much effort we had put into bonding with the pack, how delicate a wolf's trust is, and how easily it can dissolve. I, too, did not fully understand it when I began the project, but I quickly learned firsthand from Akai how terrible it could be when a wolf has no trust in its caretaker.

The unfortunate side effect of my compulsion about keeping a low-key atmosphere at camp was that rumors, like the one started by the petulant intern, were able to flourish. As in any situation where there is a lack of knowledge, rumor and conjecture usually rush in to fill the vacuum. The local grapevine is neither long nor tangled, so sooner or later I was bound to catch wind of all the outrageous things we were supposedly up to at wolf camp.

A memo from the Forest Service arrived in the summer of 1995. It was a general discussion of the conditions of my permit but it also contained a bizarre sentence that seemed to come completely out of the blue. "We are not in the position to approve additions," it read, "and would like to avoid costs associated with considering luxury items such as hot tubs." Apparently I was installing a hot tub and didn't even know about it. Where the story began and how exactly it came across the desk of the Forest Service area manager was a mystery. The minor detail that camp had no electricity or plumbing didn't seem to slow the rumor down one iota.

All this, I suppose, was amusing in some way. It would have been easy to shrug it off as petty gossip were it not for the fact that our special use permit with the U.S. Forest Service hung so precariously in the balance. Every little rumor made the Forest Service think twice about letting us stay in the Sawtooths.

In 1995, while WERC was still raising money to build a new enclosure, I applied for another extension of my special use permit. While tentative, the Forest Service indicated that there were no red flags. But, in June, before the paperwork was completed, the new director of WERC wrote the Forest Service a letter stating that WERC was the rightful owner of the pack and was planning to relocate the wolves that summer. I was at once furious and terrified. What would happen to the pack if I was forced off the land before the enclosure on the Nez Perce property had been built? Where would the wolves live? The Forest Service suddenly found itself in the middle of a custody battle between WERC and me. I had been so worried that the ranching community, with its political pull and hatred of wolves, would try to shut our project down. How ironic it was to find myself at greater odds with WERC, an organization that I had founded and which was ostensibly my ally.

What had started as a simple idea had grown beyond my control. I had created the Wolf Education and

Research Center as a nonprofit foundation to raise money for the pack, to build them a new home, and to educate the public. The board of directors and staff were initially people who had firsthand knowledge of my project and who understood my vision as it pertained to WERC's mission. But each time an employee or board member left the organization, the vacancy was filled by outsiders, friends of friends, who had good intentions but did not share my goal of nonpolitical education. Each new addition brought his or her own new ideas and priorities. My filmmaking business made it unsuitable for me to remain on the board of directors. I tried to attend meetings as an advisor, but with each new face that appeared on the board, I was less and less welcome.

To complete the transformation, WERC merged with a wolf organization in Boise, Idaho, the same highly political group with which I had once rejected an affiliation. When that happened, WERC really became a foreign entity. What was most troublesome was that this group of strangers represented the organization that would eventually take over management of the pack. Like it or not, we were inextricably bound.

My feelings were that WERC would take over the pack when it had furnished a safe home for them, complete with an enclosure that met the standards I had established in the Sawtooths. The new director felt that the wolves were to be transferred at a specific time, period. I dug in my heels and vowed to keep the wolves where they were until the new home on the Nez Perce land was ready.

As I look back on these years, I struggle to find a reason why WERC wanted the wolves so badly and so immediately. Remembering the first days of the project, when crew members bickered over the privilege of sitting next to the pups in the van, I realized that this was the very same problem, only on a much greater scale. No one at WERC ever wanted to see those eight wolves suffer, but they never made it clear just where the wolves would live while they were completing the enclosure.

The Forest Service was caught in the middle of a controversy that it had nothing to do with, but the letter from WERC, combined with pressure from ranchers and hunters and the general atmosphere surrounding wolves in Idaho, provided enough cause to deny my permit extension. The Forest Service decreed that if I wanted to stay on the land for another year, I would have to apply for a brand-new permit. As part of the application process, I would be required to hire an independent firm to conduct an environmental assessment of the project. It was a way that the Forest Service could take a step back and scrutinize our case while still remaining impartial. This study could take months, and there was no guessing the outcome. Sometime in the coming autumn, a team of scientists would appear to decide our fate. If they concluded that the wolves, fence, and camp were negatively impacting the land, we and the wolves would have to leave.

Autumn

JAMIE

The summer of 1995 descended uneasily into autumn. September is a glorious month in the Rockies; the sky is a brilliant blue and the mountainsides flash with orange and gold aspens. But this time, I could almost see the anvil hanging over our heads.

Jim and I both tried to turn our thoughts away from what we couldn't control. We worked intensely on filming and recording sound. When the day was done, we sat on the yurt platform, trying to spot mountain goats on the cliffs above and doing our best to enjoy the last of the long evenings. Sitting there, I could tell that Jim was horribly wracked with worry, for he grew silent and unable to concentrate, playing and replaying worst-case scenarios in his head. As much to himself as to me, he said simply, "What are we going to do?" I looked out at the pack: Kamots, Lakota, Matsi, Amani, Motomo, Wahots, Wyakin, and Chemukh. They were loosely scattered on the ground around camp, enjoying an evening snooze, with no idea that their lives could change at any moment.

In September, the biologists began their study and all we could do was wait to hear their conclusion. We waited. And we waited. Fog gathered in the valley and obscured the mountain peaks. The songbirds departed and all the color bled from the landscape. As if to forecast some impending doom, ravens gathered, sitting in dead lodgepoles like austere judges, watching our every move and cackling earnestly to one another. There is something eerie and almost human about their calls, as if they are trying to warn us of some creeping danger that we are too foolish to see. Of course the raven's sinister appearance has led some human beings to subject it to the same kind of anthropocentric judgment that mankind has subjected wolves to for thousands of years. Fortunately, ravens don't eat our livestock or compete for our deer, so we have mercifully let them live, harbingers of doom or not.

Naturally, there is nothing forbidding about them, and, to be honest, I quite enjoyed having these chatty onlookers at camp during the cold seasons. I saw them as creatures that have many similarities to wolves and to people. They are incredibly smart, gregarious, and even playful. The presence of these birds had very little to do with us, but it had a great deal to do with the wolves. Somewhere deep in ages past, wolves and ravens signed a peace treaty that has held for thousands of years. Native Americans speak about this kinship in their myths, and modern biologists have observed and recorded it.

In the wild, the two species team up to help each other in the search for food, each group relying on the special abilities of the other. Ravens, having the gift of flight, are adept at locating carrion. Wolves have learned to look for ravens to guide them to a meal. By way of reciprocation, wolves tear through tough hides that the birds cannot penetrate. Both reap the reward of the team effort. The scraps that wolves leave behind are more than enough to feed a clan of ravens. Whenever wolves are on a kill, ravens are sure to be nearby, cackling from the trees or boldly pacing the perimeter of the kill site, waiting for their turn.

Some have speculated that there is more to this relationship than simply a case of symbiosis. In some ways, ravens are to birds what wolves are to mammals. Both are among the most intelligent, social, and communicative of their kind. Ornithologist Dr. Lawrence Kilham, in *The American Crow and the Common Raven,* writes of the condition that is unique to social beings: "One of the most difficult of all things to endure for a crow, a raven, a wolf, or a human is to feel alone and separated from one's own kind. A sense of belonging is one of the most universal of all feelings." Perhaps the raven and the wolf actually do understand each other.

The ravens did not share any of this camaraderie with us. They were skittish and never let Jim or me get close enough to even take a decent photograph of them. People, it seemed, were not worthy of their trust. But at least we were allowed to observe at a distance the bizarre confidence they shared with the Sawtooth Pack. On the surface, the truce between wolf and raven seems to have been born out of years of living together. The wolves know that the ravens are too quick to catch, so they simply don't try. The ravens know it, too, but they also know that the rule applies only if they maintain a certain distance. Both creatures are very aware of exactly where this line is drawn, and the ravens are careful not to cross it.

Sometimes when we were feeding the pack, a stray morsel would prove too tempting for a daring raven and he would dart in past the unspoken "safety zone." If this happened, all bets were off. The wolf would turn and snap furiously at the bird, removing a tail feather or two but never inflicting any real damage. I think it was all show. The wolves' attitude seemed to be, "We're predators, we have to try to catch you, and you have to respect us." The ravens at camp actually seemed to enjoy flirting with disaster, making a game out of seeing just how close they could get to a wolf and still escape. I believe the wolves secretly enjoyed it, too.

Amani was snoozing in the grass one day when a raven landed a few feet from his head, bobbing and strutting back and forth. There was no food in sight; the only reason for this adventure seemed to be the sheer pleasure of it. At first Amani showed little interest, so the raven began taunting him with caws and cackles. I saw Amani slowly shift his weight, trying to maintain the illusion of relaxation while positioning himself for a pounce. Suddenly he charged at the snickering bird who leapt backward, flapping wildly. Amani twisted his neck this way and that, futilely snapping at the air. The raven sailed up about ten feet and then glided back to earth a short distance away. No sooner had he landed than he began to prance about again, moving in closer and jeering at the wolf. Again

Amani pretended to lose interest, trying to tempt the bird into a foolhardy display. Once more he pounced, just a feather's width off the mark. This went on for almost twenty minutes before Amani finally got bored with the game and slowly walked away, ignoring the bird's taunts.

We never actually saw a wolf catch a raven, but on two occasions we did find a dead raven lying in the grass, untouched except for a few unmistakable tooth marks. When the wolves managed to catch a grouse or a squirrel they would consume it completely, sometimes playing with their trophy first, tossing it into the air and catching it in their jaws. However, they would not touch a dead raven. It was as if killing the bird had been a terrible accident—the raven had gone a bit too far across the line and the wolf had snapped a little too accurately.

Once I picked up the body of a freshly killed raven and tossed it to Matsi to see what he would do. I half-expected him to ignore it, but instead he delicately picked it up, trotted off a few yards, and placed it back on the ground. The others saw him do this but made no attempt to investigate the body or play with it. Any other small animal carcass, or any new object for that matter, would have been seen as a toy and probably would have sparked a game of keep-away, but the unfortunate raven was treated with a kind of reverence that I did not see the wolves show to any other creature.

Watching the interplay between these two very different species, it occurred to me that they instinctively understood the concepts of cooperation and interdependence better than most human beings do. Here Jim and I were, mired in a custody battle with WERC, plagued by misunderstandings with the Forest Service, battling rumors from disgruntled interns, when all the while we should have been working together toward the same goal. Certainly there were fewer differences between us than there were between a wolf and a raven. Yet these two creatures were far more adept than we were at working together, letting mistakes pass, and respecting each other's boundaries. We could learn a great deal from them.

Throughout autumn, the team of independent biologists appeared at camp to search for endangered flora and fauna, monitor water flow and soil erosion, and conduct a hundred other surveys. The biologists were received warmly by the pack and admitted to looking forward to their visits.

It's funny how different strangers were received differently by the wolves. When some biologists or officials came to camp they wore plain clothes, spoke softly, and were willing to drop their "official" deportment. As a result, the pack greeted them enthusiastically. It was an amusing contrast when other agents showed up in uniform, full of officious posturing, gun belts, and booming voices. The pack would immediately hightail it up into the forest and not reappear until the agents left. When friends who also happened to be officials came on informal visits, without their guns and uniforms, the wolves were once again friendly, but no agent on "official business" ever saw a wolf.

At long last, in the middle of November's bleakness, came the verdict of the environmental assessment. After all our worrying, it turned out to be one of the most humorous and ironic events of the project. The report concluded that the land inside the enclosure had been impacted to a small degree by the presence of wolves, tents, and people. The land outside the enclosure, however, had been severely impacted by the cattle that had been allowed to graze there for years. One of the biologists went so far as to suggest that if there were any endangered plants in the area, the only place they would have any hope of surviving was within our enclosure. She concluded that the land would be better protected if the enclosure remained intact.

It was certainly not the result WERC had been expecting. The Forest Service kept its end of the bargain and granted us a one-year permit. However, it came with a rider stating that after that year, our time was up in the Sawtooths, without any possibility of further extension. We could film for the rest of the following winter, spring, and summer, but come August the wolves would have to be moved, whether WERC was ready for them or not. The project was finally coming to an end.

The Alpha Pair

JIM

The extension to our permit brought with it some much needed calm and security. Even WERC seemed to relax a bit. Confident that they would take over in a year, they finally began to work in earnest toward a permanent home for the pack. Best of all, our assistants Megan and Keith agreed to move with the pack and continue on as caretakers for WERC.

I cannot stress enough the importance of having this consistency. The animals' social nature makes captive wolves very willing to bond with human beings, but just because they have bonded with one person, or four, it does not mean that they are accepting of all people. This characteristic shouldn't be altogether surprising, as people are exactly the same way. Like us, a wolf will recognize certain individuals as friends and the rest as strangers. A new person must be introduced to the wolves slowly, in the company of an already trusted individual. Even then, the wolf may never warm up to or trust that person. There is no way of predicting it. The only dependable way to develop a true bond between a wolf and a human being is for the person to raise the wolf from a pup. Once bonded, the wolf desires the company of that individual just as it desires the company of its own pack mates.

Megan had helped to raise the three new wolves, Wahots, Wyakin, and Chemukh, and was thus bonded to them as strongly as Jamie and I were. Plus, she had slowly grown to know the adult pack over the course of a year. For a while she entered the enclosure only in my company, but soon she was accepted by the pack and able to come and go as she pleased. Megan, in turn, began to introduce Keith in the hope that he would be accepted as a caretaker in the future. Often wolves are more hesitant to bond with men, but Keith was so gentle and displayed such a calm and confident affection for them that they warmed up to him very quickly. We were fortunate that the wolves genuinely liked Megan and Keith, because there was no guarantee that it would happen.

The fact is that you can't switch caretakers as if they were janitors. In his manual on captive wolf management, Dr. Erich Klinghammer writes emphatically, "To remove a keeper with accumulated specific knowledge of pack social behavior borders on the irresponsible." The change must take place gradually, under the supervision of experienced handlers who are accepted by the pack, so that the wolves have a chance to become close, not just familiar, with the new presence. Knowing that Megan and Keith would be moving with the wolves was a huge relief.

With this confidence that the pack would be well provided for in the future, I decided that I would not interfere with their natural urges when breeding season approached. As the females Chemukh and Wyakin entered their second winter, I thought that they might go into heat. It would be early for them, but since there was no older female in the pack, it was probable that one of these two would begin to assert herself as the alpha. I decided that this was too great an opportunity for observation and learning to let it pass by.

WERC indicated that they were willing to accept a larger pack. We even anticipated that the presence of pups might ease the pack's transition to their new surroundings when the time came for the pack to be moved. Our experience watching adult wolves around pups told us that the presence of a few youngsters would definitely give them something to focus their attention on, thus reducing their agitation when they arrived at their new home. So, shortly into 1996, the breeding season began, and the pack showed us another side of its personality, one that was more intense, fascinating, violent, and tender than we had ever seen.

Jamie and I had always believed that Wyakin was a shoo-in for alpha female. As a pup, she had always dominated Chemukh and continued to do so into the winter of their second year. In fact, Chemukh was so shy and submissive and was having such a difficult time assimilating into the pack that we thought she would more than likely assume the omega female position. In the first few weeks of 1996, she was still a timid little wolf, the last to eat and the first to be picked on.

As January came to a close, things changed abruptly, as though a switch had been flipped inside Chemukh's head. Her competitive instinct kicked into high gear, and she decided that it was time to assert herself. Wyakin seemed completely confused by Chemukh's sudden aggression, for although she had been the more dominant of the two, her overall disposition was really quite sweet and gentle. Chemukh, on the other hand, was suddenly all business.

When the rest of the pack chose to dominate Lakota, it was clear that most of their aggression was purely show. There was always a lot of growling and flashing of fangs. Chemukh now began to push her way into the act and changed all that. She would throw herself into the middle of the fray, grab hold of Lakota's thigh, and shake her head violently. Even Amani, whose dominance over Lakota was most severe, never behaved in this way. Chemukh seemed to know that the stakes were high and that she had to improve her status as quickly as possible.

There are plenty of wonderful things to say about wolves, about the way they communicate and care for each other. Unfortunately, the competition for the alpha female is not one of those things. There is no way to sugar-coat it. It is a brutal competition for the right to pass on one's genes. The males are comparatively laid-back, sorting out their status through threats and bluff. The females draw blood.

To say that the alpha male chooses his mate is really an oversimplification. In our observation, one female eliminated her competition, making herself, in effect, the alpha male's only "choice." Chemukh did this in a variety

of ways, the least pleasant of which was to attack
Wyakin's hindquarters, leaving her, I'm sure, in too
much pain to breed.

Jamie and I did try to remain clinical and unemo-
tional, but it was difficult to watch. Plus, we could not
help but play favorites. We really hoped that, in the end,
sweet Wyakin would come forward to claim the alpha
position, but, sadly, sweetness does not an alpha female
make. Wyakin, as spirited as she was, was not up to the
challenge. Chemukh was unrelenting in her offensive,
and when she came into heat a few days before Wyakin,
that really sealed their fates.

Kamots quickly fell under Chemukh's siren spell.
His affections were secured, and we watched Chemukh
transform from a snarling hellcat to a demure little
princess. Suddenly the two were inseparable. Kamots
followed her closely, sniffing and licking her genitals.
They sat for hours side by side, nuzzling and grooming
each other. In a complete reversal of his former behavior, Kamots suddenly protected her at mealtime, driving
the other wolves away and making sure she got plenty
to eat.

Chemukh had completed her job—attracting Kamots—
and now his duties were just beginning. Females remain
in heat for roughly seven days and the other males in
the pack were not about to control their own urges. It
was up to Kamots to keep all other suitors away from his
mate. If any of the males so much as wandered close to
Chemukh, Kamots would attack them with such force as
to make his threats over an elk carcass look downright

playful. The interloper would let out a shriek of submission and retreat in a crouch. He never really hurt another male but he left little doubt that this was very serious business.

For a solid week, the torturous desire among the males was palpable. We have never heard the wolves more vocal. Over and over, throughout the day and night, they would erupt into a chorus of urgent and plaintive howls. Matsi, Amani, and Motomo paced back and forth, just far enough away from Chemukh to avoid incurring Kamots' wrath. From time to time, they would snarl and bicker with each other, looking every bit like greasers at a high school dance. Lakota was so aware that tempers were short that he left the scene entirely and waited for the frenzy to blow over. Wahots hung close by in rapt fascination, but as close to the bottom of the social heap as he was, he didn't dare make waves. In this volatile time, the mid-ranking members of the pack didn't need much provocation to turn aggressive.

All this excitement enabled us to see another side of Wahots' personality. It was strange and wonderful to witness just how much pack hierarchy means to a wolf, even a subordinate like Wahots. He kept a close eye on Chemukh, watching her as she repeatedly mated with Kamots. Unlike the other males, his behavior revealed more curiosity than desire. Kamots had been guarding his mate practically without rest for a week and was completely exhausted. When another wolf distracted him, Motomo saw a window of opportunity, threw caution to the wind, and attempted to mate with Chemukh.

Chemukh wasn't really willing, but she wasn't exactly fighting Motomo off, either. Oddly enough, this proved terribly upsetting to Wahots, who let out a plaintive bark-howl. It was the strangest sound we ever heard him make, a call of severe distress. The noise immediately alerted Kamots, who turned and launched himself at Motomo, growling terribly as he made his attack. The dark wolf practically did a backward somersault off Chemukh and scurried for cover.

That night, Jamie and I were huddled in our bed, staving off the February cold and trying to get some sleep among the choir of desperate wolves. Finally at about two A.M. the pack calmed down and we began to drift off. Suddenly Wahots' same bizarre cry tore us from our sleep. It was followed quickly by the sound of heavy paws galloping across crusted snow, and then a terrible crashing and snarling as Kamots collided with a wolf, probably Motomo once again.

We had become so familiar with these wolves that even in the darkness, without leaving the comfort of our tent, we could picture precisely what was happening. To our amazement, it seemed as though Wahots was actually "tattling" on Chemukh, making sure that Motomo would never be able to mate with her. This little commotion sparked a new round of howling, growling, and complaining that didn't let up until dawn.

For many days, we mulled over the possible reasons why Wahots was snitching on Motomo and Chemukh. He was dangerously close to relieving Lakota of the omega rank and it was possible that he was trying to curry favor with Kamots. Another answer could be that Wahots simply could not stand to see the pack hierarchy violated. Every wolf in a pack knows its place and the places of all the other wolves. Without the hierarchy, the pack falls apart. Wolves may challenge one another within the system but they do not flout the system itself. Wahots knew the rules, and the rules dictated that he could not mate with Chemukh no matter how strong the desire. And if he couldn't do it, by golly Motomo couldn't either.

Wyakin came into heat shortly thereafter, but the males did not pay nearly as much attention to her as they had to Chemukh. For one thing, Wyakin was not advertising herself as "available." In the previous days, Chemukh so successfully dominated her that Wyakin was too afraid to solicit any attention from the males. If a male approached her with intent to mate, Wyakin would run away or sit down and refuse to budge. It was either that or risk having Chemukh bite her hindquarters again.

Kamots had no interest in mating with Wyakin, but he still wasn't going to allow any of the other males near her. Though not with the same conviction, he chased the males away from Wyakin as he had done with Chemukh. This would draw Chemukh's attention and she would lay into Wyakin just for good measure. For the rest of the breeding period, Wyakin kept a very low profile.

It is common behavior in a wolf pack for the alpha pair to be the only two to mate. It keeps the numbers under control, for too many wolves in the pack, especially puppies, would be a liability. Many hungry mouths and not enough hunters means they could all suffer. Instead, each wolf devotes itself completely to the few puppies that are born to the alpha pair, making sure they grow up to be strong and beneficial additions to the pack.

This is not a hard and fast rule. In some packs, the beta pair will be able to breed—it ultimately comes down to what the alpha pair will allow. Generally, their decision will depend on the available prey base. If food is plentiful, the alpha pair may decide that the pack can handle a few extra members and allow the beta pair to breed. When times are hard and food is scarce, even the alphas may choose not to breed. Whatever variables may exist in the wild, however, Kamots and Chemukh held to the standard model and would not tolerate any amorous behavior among the other members.

As the winter months progressed, Chemukh became more and more preoccupied with choosing the perfect site for her den. A den's only purpose is as a place for giving birth and protecting newborn pups. The job of constructing it falls exclusively to the alpha female, for it is her domain alone. Chemukh seemed to have an instinctive set of specific criteria in her head. She would select a spot, dig for a while through the snow and earth, then decide that it was not the right place after all. Perhaps the soil was too loose or too rocky, or perhaps the ground held too much water. Something about it didn't suit her. The rest of the pack dug as well, not that they were helping Chemukh; they just dug shallow pits in any old spot, caught up in the spirit of the occasion.

Having lost the battle for the alpha position, Wyakin

settled gracefully into a supporting role. Like a midwife, she became very attentive to Chemukh, grooming her or just sitting by her side. Kamots, on the other hand, was no longer particularly attentive to his mate. He had done his duty and was back to the business of protecting the pack and patrolling his territory.

Finally, Chemukh settled on a site at the high end of the enclosure in a heavy grove of spruce. A fallen tree had created a natural cavity, a perfect place for her to refashion as a den. In fact, years ago, this had been the exact spot where Makuyi had hidden out. With an air of great importance, Chemukh disappeared into the hole and a second later clumps of dirt began to fly out of the entrance. She kept at her work for several days. We knew the den must be cavernous but we avoided the urge to peek inside lest our presence cause her to abandon the project.

There was still over a foot of crusty snow lingering on the valley floor on April 22, 1996, the afternoon that Chemukh separated herself from the pack and disappeared into the spruce grove. She slipped away so inconspicuously and quietly that none of the other wolves followed, and Jamie and I likewise failed to notice.

The next morning, there was not a single wolf in sight around our camp. We hurriedly threw our clothes on and hiked up to the grove. The pack was milling around the area with an air of great excitement. As we walked to the den, they followed us and peered into the tunnel alongside Jamie and me. Inside, we could hear the delicate cries of newborn pups.

The Sawtooth Pups

JAMIE

The birth of the pups was like an explosion in the pack. The celebration and burst of energy that came over the wolves was incredible. One moment they'd be racing around playing exuberantly and the next they'd be back at the den site, whining and shifting from one foot to the other, barely able to contain themselves.

Jim and I decided it was best to stay out of the way for the first day. We weren't sure just how protective the pack would be of the new pups and we didn't want to find out. We contented ourselves with watching the den from a distance, not trying to film or record sounds. I was as nervous as the rest of the wolves were; in fact, I was even envious of them because I was certain they all knew how the pups were doing.

After the first day, the pack began to return to a normal routine of playing, relaxing, and jostling for social rank. Even so, every wolf, from Kamots down to Lakota, peered into the den from time to time, body tensed with excitement, head cocked, listening to the pups. Wyakin was different, maintaining a constant vigil beside the den. She seemed to be waiting, like a dutiful aunt, to see if there was anything she could do for Chemukh. Still, we never saw Wyakin or even Kamots enter the den. The nursery was clearly Chemukh's territory.

Since the scene around the den had relaxed, Jim and I decided that it was safe to approach. At first, I set up a microphone on the outside of the den and sat nearby with my tape deck listening to the muffled squeals and gurgles that issued from underground. Sensing me above, Chemukh emerged from the den after a few moments to see what was going on. She seemed no more perturbed by my presence than she was by Wyakin's. I was just another familiar face, curious about her new pups and certainly not a threat to her.

Chemukh was still a high-strung wolf, but she had developed a level of trust with me that she shared with no one else. I thought perhaps that, although Jim is a very gentle and soft-spoken man, his size and masculine presence might have been intimidating to her. She might even have been able to sense that Jim was in charge of the project, that the other humans in his company treated him as an "alpha." Whatever the reason, she was much more comfortable around me. It was an unspoken certainty that if anyone was going to crawl into the den to count the pups, it would be me.

The following afternoon, I sat beside the opening of the den and listened to Chemukh and the pups inside. A moment later, she climbed out. She gave me a little whine and a lick on the nose and then sat down next to me, as she had done so often as a pup. I spoke to her quietly, congratulating her on her young ones, and asking her if I could check them out for just a minute or two. I hoped the gentleness of my voice would let her know I meant no harm, and, more important, I wanted to reassure myself that she would not bite me on the behind if I crawled into her den. I scanned her face for any trace of fear or insecurity, but she just looked at me with curious eyes, cocking her head as I spoke. I took out a little flashlight and allowed Chemukh to inspect it to her satisfaction, then got down on my hands and knees and made my way headfirst into the cavern.

The tunnel was at least five feet long and wide enough that I could crawl through it without having to squeeze. Small roots dangled from the tunnel ceiling but Chemukh had managed to avoid the strong, fat roots of the spruce trees. Somehow she had known exactly where to dig. The only odor I could detect was the musty smell of clean spring earth; there was not a trace of any animal odor, at least not to my primitive nose. Chemukh kept a tidy den, cleaning up after her pups and instinctively making sure there was no smell that might attract the attention of bears or other predators.

The tunnel jogged to the left and opened up into a much larger area. There I got my first glimpse of the pups. At first, all I could see was one solid furry black ball that wiggled and whined. A moment later, I was able to make out four little heads with eyes still closed, noses tipped up, sniffing at my unfamiliar scent.

Again I found myself marveling at Chemukh's construction. The rear of the den, where she had placed the pups, was slightly elevated. I had read that wolves do this, but it was still just incredible to see it for myself. Whether consciously or unconsciously, she had formed the floor in this way to keep the pups above any water that might collect inside the den. It was an ingenious bit of engineering. I would love to know if she understood the reasons behind her design or was just acting on instinct.

My entire visit with the pups was less than a minute long. It was enough of an honor just to get a glimpse of these delicate little creatures. I didn't want to try to handle them or see what sex they were; a simple head count was enough. I began to back out through the tunnel slowly. I was so excited that I wanted to rush out and announce the good news, but knowing that Chemukh was undoubtedly waiting outside the den, I made my movements very slow and deliberate. As I surfaced, covered in dirt, Chemukh was waiting for me expectantly. She gave my dirty face another lick, reassuring me that she was not upset, and then disappeared back into the den. Jim and Wyakin both seemed relieved to see me out of the hole.

When we brought the next road-killed deer in for the pack, Chemukh stayed in the den. After eating, Kamots dragged an entire deer leg to the den entrance for her. Wyakin, too, brought food to the black wolf that had until recently been her tormentor. For once, there was no arguing from the rest of the pack when it came to Chemukh getting her fill; she was treated like a queen. Kamots didn't have to enforce this rule. The entire pack was willing to make any sacrifice necessary for Chemukh and the cherished new pack members.

In the first days of May, the last of the year's heavy snow finally receded and Chemukh decided it was time to introduce her pups to the world. One by one, she carried them out of the den and into a little patch of dry grass and sunlight about twenty yards away. Their milky-blue eyes had just opened and they were only beginning to try to stand on their wobbly legs. Finally, we were able to get a really good look at them. There were three females and one male, all black.

Three of the pups looked very healthy, but one of the females seemed terribly thin and lethargic. She did not move around as much as the others and was not as vocal. Jim and I were torn between having a vet examine the pup for problems and simply letting the wolves take care of her.

Statistically, only about half of all wolves born make it through their first year. It is particularly common for some of the pups in a mother wolf's first litter to die, and Chemukh was not only a first-time mother but, at just two years of age, a young one. We had prepared ourselves for the inevitability that some of the pups would not survive. Megan had seen Chemukh carrying something out of the den and deep into the willows a few days earlier. We will never know, but it is likely that she had given birth to a stillborn fifth pup, or one that was so sickly, tiny, and motionless that I had missed it when I peeked into the den. It was a hard choice but we decided that if the fourth pup failed to thrive, there was probably nothing we could do to help her.

It would be weeks before their vision cleared but already the three healthy pups were showing a desire to explore, crawling around on their bellies and sniffing and sucking at everything in reach. As the work of parenting became more of a hassle, Chemukh decided it was time to ditch the role of dutiful mother. The fact is, Chemukh could never pass up a good carcass. Her aggressive rise to the alpha spot may have had more to do with securing a place at the table than breeding rights. When there was food around, her attitude seemed to be, "Pups? What pups?" Kamots continued to use his authority to guarantee that Chemukh would eat first, and she took full advantage of it.

Wyakin saw the vacancy and took the opportunity to step in as a surrogate mother. Watching her, I felt genuinely sorry that she had not succeeded in becoming the alpha, because she really seemed to possess the stronger maternal instinct. Clearly, here was evidence that the alpha female does not necessarily make the most attentive mother. Wyakin constantly groomed the pups, cleaning them gently with her tongue. They made futile attempts to nurse but she had no milk to give. Meanwhile, Chemukh spent her time eating and displaying her alpha status to Lakota and Wahots. After a while she would return to nurse her pups, at which time Wyakin would step back and wait until she was needed again.

It would have been wonderful to let the pack raise the pups completely on their own, integrate them into their society, and teach them the ways of the wolf. Unfortunately, this would have been the height of irresponsibility. It would have meant that one-third of the pack would not be socialized to people, creating a potentially dangerous situation.

Fear of human beings comes naturally to a wolf. Those who have cared for captive packs, like Dr. Zimmen and Dr. Klinghammer, have written that wolves learn to trust people only as a result of being bottle-fed by people from an age of sixteen days or younger. If this process does not occur at the right time, socialization to people will be extremely difficult, if not impossible. Even if its parents have been fully socialized to people, the young wolf will develop an instinctive fear. We had to consider the safety of Megan and Keith, the caretakers who would be inheriting management of the pack in only a few months. Reluctantly, we took over the raising of the pups ourselves, so they would be as bonded to us as the others were. Our one consolation was that this plan was perfectly fine with Chemukh, who by all indications was through with motherhood.

Sadly, there was nothing we or the wolves could do to save the fourth pup, the little female who was so weak and fragile. At ten days of age, when the other pups' eyes were wide open and they were already developing feisty personalities, this little female just lacked the strength to survive. For the first few hours, we bottle-fed her along with her siblings, but she slipped away that night.

The three healthy pups, however, were getting bigger by the day, and we lavished them with attention. We gave them names in keeping with the Nez Perce theme, names that, if not terribly original, had a nice ring. We called the male Piyip and one of the females Ayet, the Nez Perce words for boy and girl. Jim decided to name the other female, the smallest of the three, Motaki, after the playful omega female who was killed by a cougar four years earlier.

When Chemukh was reunited with her pups after our bonding period, her interest in them revived. She seemed determined to reassert herself as their mother, but the pups gravitated toward Matsi, who again had established himself as the pup-sitter and caretaker. The less attention they paid to Chemukh, the more frustrated and desperate she became. She even resorted to downright bribery, presenting the pups with gifts of bones and elk hair for them to play with. Chemukh would drop the new toy in front of one of the pups and then step back, her body tense, trying to incite some play. Once in a while she succeeded, but often it looked as if she were actually annoying her pups. Sometimes they even ran away from her, seeking the protection of Wyakin or Matsi. It was too little, too late. With each passing day, these three belonged more and more to the pack as a whole.

It was interesting to see how each wolf stepped up to deal with the new family members in his or her own way. Kamots remained the chief disciplinarian and establisher of order. Matsi behaved as he had with Wahots, Wyakin, and Chemukh, making sure the pups got a place at every meal and regurgitating much of his own food for them. Wyakin stepped in as the second caregiver after Matsi. Wahots and Motomo were ever fascinated by them and, from time to time, we'd catch them playing with the pups.

By far the most entertaining wolf to watch around the new pups was Amani. We had observed him playing with

Chemukh, Wahots, and Wyakin when they were young, but with Piyip, Ayet, and Motaki, he pulled out all the stops. Some may have been better caretakers, but Amani played with them like no other. He was just shameless, like an indulgent uncle who simply can't say no to the children.

Amani really seemed to enjoy sinking to their level, both physically and mentally. He'd plunk himself down in the grass and they'd rush up to attack him. Motaki would grab him by the tail and yank in one direction, Ayet would seize an ear and yank in the other, and Piyip would pounce on his back and nip at his neck. I couldn't believe the things he let them get away with. Those needle-sharp puppy teeth would puncture my skin at the slightest nip, but Amani just let them gnaw away. While the three pups used him simultaneously as their springboard, chew toy, and surrogate prey, Amani lay in the grass, eyelids drooping, looking as though he were in heaven.

Watching Amani behave in this way revealed just how complex a wolf's personality really is. He was the one that brutalized the omega more than any other. He always seemed to be spoiling for a fight, always ready to display dominance when he could. One minute he could be chasing Lakota into the willows, gnashing his teeth, and the next he would be rolling on his back, looking every bit a puppy himself as Ayet, Motaki, and Piyip squirmed all over him. He did not seem to display any desire to be the pups' teacher or protector, only their playmate. In their company, his often quick temper was nowhere to be seen, and to watch the way the pups treated him left no doubt but that he was their absolute favorite.

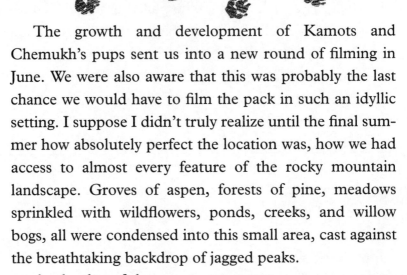

The growth and development of Kamots and Chemukh's pups sent us into a new round of filming in June. We were also aware that this was probably the last chance we would have to film the pack in such an idyllic setting. I suppose I didn't truly realize until the final summer how absolutely perfect the location was, how we had access to almost every feature of the rocky mountain landscape. Groves of aspen, forests of pine, meadows sprinkled with wildflowers, ponds, creeks, and willow bogs, all were condensed into this small area, cast against the breathtaking backdrop of jagged peaks.

As the day of the move grew near, every moment we spent with the pack grew more precious. I took to spending afternoons at the edge of the willows, where Lakota would come and sit beside me. If the pack was quiet, he would stay with me for more than an hour while I talked to him. I told him how bad it felt to leave him, how the pit in my stomach just kept growing. I told him that I would visit him often, and that his trusted friends Megan and Keith would be with him. This talk did little to comfort me.

Eventually Lakota would move away and other wolves would join me for a minute or two. Chemukh, so timid around other people, might allow herself to relax nearby. Her three pups would bound up to me, full of mischief, and make a quick grab at my hair or shoelaces. Motomo would approach and look me over with his intelligent yellow eyes, still trying to figure me out.

Kamots, always the most bold, settled down right next to me with great calm and dignity. As he sat, something caught his attention, a distant sound too faint for me to hear, and he began to howl. The other wolves joined in but did not come to rally around Kamots as they so often did. It was just the alpha and me. In the years I had lived among them, I had never been this close to a howling wolf. Our bodies were almost touching and the air around us was resonating with the power of his voice. I was so mesmerized by the sound and so comfortable with Kamots that what I did next was completely unconscious. I reached out to him and gently placed my hand on his throat. He did not miss a beat. Head thrown back, eyes shut, he just kept singing to the heavens. The effect was pure magic. The vibration raced up my arm, coursed through my entire body and down into the earth. I, too, closed my eyes and let the sound flow through me until the wolf gradually brought the song to a close.

I will always be grateful to Kamots for letting me share this intimate moment, for their howls had always been precious to me. It had been my first contact with the wolves, for on the day of my arrival at camp I had heard them even before seeing them. In their distinct howls I discovered their individual personalities: Lakota's soulfulness, Amani's bravado, Wahots' enthusiasm, Kamots' confidence. In their choruses, I discovered their solidarity, their unity as a pack. Amplified through my headphones, their voices have burned an everlasting impression on my memory. They haunt me now, filling the quiet moments with their singing. I suspect they will do so forever.

A New Home

JIM

We filled those final summer days in quiet reflection, hardly filming, just spending as much time among the wolves as possible. We wanted to memorize their every move and every expression, to imprint their faces in our minds so that they would remain real forever. Most afternoons, I took a book and leaned my back against an aspen to read. From time to time, a wolf would visit and sit near me in its dignified way. Kamots might reach a paw out for me to touch with my own palm, but mostly we just sat together.

In these moments, I realized something I think I had known subconsciously, instinctively, all along. I had insisted on limiting our interaction with the adult pack so that they would grow to accept our presence and behave in a natural way. In doing so, I had also allowed them to keep their dignity, and that, I believe, is what really made the project special. When Kamots sat with me, he did so not because he hoped I might hand him a scrap of food or reach over and scratch his back, but rather because he enjoyed my company. Jamie and I were not the masters of this pack. We did not subjugate these creatures; we strove to know them. We were simply their friends.

The wolves would be making the journey to their new home in transport crates that we borrowed from the U.S. Fish and Wildlife Service. We put a few of the crates inside the enclosure with the wolves so they could inspect them and, we hoped, get a little bit comfortable with them. To me, the sight of those crates resting in the grass, the sun glinting off the aluminum, was an ugly and heartbreaking reminder that the end was drawing near.

On August 6, 1996, we rose at dawn. After a night of no sleep, with a dreadful knot in my stomach, I stumbled through the morning like a zombie; my mind had turned completely inward. Jamie and I sipped our coffee in silence, watching the tops of the Sawtooth Mountains turn a brilliant pink. Nature was putting on a beautiful show for our last dawn with the pack, a parting gift. Nothing needed to be said between Jamie and me. When I looked into her eyes, I could see the anguish and loss that she also was trying to keep to herself. There was at least some comfort in knowing that she understood. We would be leaving not only the wolves but also this place and the life we had created together.

Perhaps a wolf is able to perceive sadness in a person, especially someone he has come to know over several years. But if they sensed our grief, they did not show it.

They greeted their last day in the Sawtooths as they did any other day, as if their lives here would last forever.

We had been over the scenario a thousand times in our minds, knowing exactly what had to be done, but that didn't ease the worry. We would have to sedate the wolves to get them into the crates—there was no other way around it—but they would be awake for the drive. The trip from Stanley to Winchester, Idaho, the site of their new home, could take as long as ten hours along a winding road through remote central Idaho. We would make the journey in the cool of night so that the wolves would be comfortable, arriving before dawn and releasing them at first light.

Our crew assembled and even Val came back to help us. Randy, the veterinarian, was on hand to oversee the sedation of the wolves, and Franz Camenzind was also there to handle the camera. Today I would be fully occupied as the manager of the pack, so I left it to Franz to film this final chapter.

We waited until the heat of the day had nearly passed, when we knew the wolves would be relaxed and snoozing. Jamie and Megan, in a painstakingly coordinated procedure, fed each wolf a piece of meat that contained a sedative. We covered their eyes and gently placed them in the crates. The pups, Ayet, Motaki, and Piyip, we simply gathered and put in a single crate.

Kamots did not want to go under. As the alpha, he had more fight in him than the others did. Perhaps, knowing the safety of the pack rested on his shoulders, he resisted sleep as long as he could. We waited in agony as he stumbled and finally slipped into unconsciousness. In my own heart, I felt the needle-sharp pain of betrayal.

We then placed the crates in the shade and monitored the wolves' vital signs for an hour while the sedative wore off. Megan moved from crate to crate, checking each wolf's breathing and heart rate. When she reached Kamots, I saw her face become tense and knew there was trouble. Kamots' heartbeat was faint and irregular and his breathing was shallow. We had given him a fraction of the dosage of sedative that government veterinarians routinely administer to wild wolves, but he was reacting to it badly. Jamie and I knelt down in front of the crate and watched the faint rising and falling of his chest. More than any of the other wolves, the pack desperately needed him. He was their guardian, their decision maker, their guide. He would be the one to get them through this ordeal and make them feel safe in their new home. We all needed him. Now he, the strongest and surest of all, was the most at risk.

One by one the pack awoke, groggy and dazed but safe. We waited for Kamots to stir, afraid to begin the trip with him still under sedation. It seemed to take forever, but finally his ears twitched and his eyelids fluttered. We could see he was awake, but he appeared unable to rise. We tried in vain to meet his yellow eyes, usually so bright and alert, but he seemed to be gazing at something invisible and far away.

Jamie and I agreed that the best course of action would be to begin the journey and get the ordeal over with as soon as possible. We carefully hoisted the crates into a horse trailer, which the ranchers had kindly allowed us to bring across their land, since we were finally removing the wolves. As the sun began to drop into the Sawtooths, we pulled out across the flats toward Stanley and the north.

We moved at a snail's pace on the jeep trail toward Stanley. Jamie, Franz, and I drove behind the trailer and watched it rocking and shifting ahead of us. When we stopped just short of town so Franz could get some shots of our departure, we took the opportunity to check in on Kamots.

All the other wolves were sitting up in their crates and whining, bewildered but alert. Only Kamots lay immobile, on the floor of his box. While Megan monitored his vital signs, I reached in and put my hand on his neck. "I'm sorry," I told him. "I'm so sorry. Its going to be okay, I promise." Jamie stood beside me and whispered, "Kamots, please wake up. Everybody needs you. We can't do this without you." In the dim light of the trailer, we could see him lying there, unresponsive, motionless.

We drove for another hour in silence, looking at the trailer ahead of us, thinking of Kamots inside. Finally, I signaled for our caravan to pull over. Fearing the worst, I released the latch and carefully swung open the door of the trailer. Kamots was sitting upright in his crate, blinking in the twilight. I put my hand up to the door of the crate and he gently licked my fingers. A collective sigh went up from our small group. He was groggy and confused but he was going to be fine.

We spoke to all the wolves whenever we stopped, and the sight of us and the sound of our voices seemed to soothe them. We told them they were going to a nice place and that all this confusion would soon be over. Staring out through the small holes in the crates, they no longer looked like the wolves I had raised. They had a haunted look, like the collared wolves I had seen being reintroduced into the Idaho wilderness, bewildered, unable to comprehend what was happening to them.

It was still dark when we pulled up to the new enclosure in Winchester. Our headlights frightened a group of wild turkeys who leapt into flight and gobbled a harsh reproach. "Those turkeys are about to have a rude awakening," I thought.

The elevation was considerably lower at the new enclosure. I could feel the thickness and humidity in the air. I wondered if the wolves noticed it, too. It was past four A.M. when we settled down in our vehicles to sleep until sunrise.

The first thing we did when the sun came up was to walk the entire perimeter of the new enclosure. I was alarmed to find gaps in the fence that had not been properly secured. There were holes that were large enough for a pup to crawl through, and it would have taken an enterprising adult no more than a few hours to work one of those small openings into an escape route. Every hole in the fence punched another hole in my own comfort zone. Keith spent the first three hours wiring together seams and tacking down the fence apron while the pack waited.

Finally, at about nine A.M., we carried the crates into the enclosure and lined them up side by side in a grassy field. We let the pups out first. They had taken the entire trip in stride and were eager to explore all the new sights and smells. We thought that immediately seeing the pups free and safe would help to comfort the adults, whose concern for their young knows no limits. Piyip, Ayet, and Motaki bounded out of their crate and into the grass. They ventured a few yards away and then turned back to see where their pack mates were.

Kamots was the first adult to be released. During the night, he had recovered fully and was now back to his old self. For a moment, he held his head low, tucked his tail, and looked around tentatively. It was the only time I ever saw him carry himself this way, like an omega. In his uncertain posture, I could see just how stressful it was for him suddenly to find himself in unfamiliar surroundings. Even so, it took him only a moment to regain his confidence and go straight to the pups. As he inspected each one, they rallied around him in a frenzy of licks and whines, overjoyed to see him again.

The pup Ayet ran over to Matsi's crate and licked his nose through the barred door. Megan slid the door open and Matsi emerged. He enthusiastically greeted Ayet, then the other two, and then lowered himself slightly and licked up at Kamots. We opened the crates quickly now, releasing Motomo and Amani, Chemukh, Wahots, and Wyakin. Each wolf went first to the pups, then to Kamots. It was like an exaggerated version of their morning greeting, but with considerably more whining and licking, as though more information and reassurance was being exchanged.

It was interesting to see how the pups stuck close to Matsi, their guardian, and how he took control of their care immediately. They were terribly fond of their play-mate Amani, and Chemukh was of course their mother, but, in this stressful time, they clung to the one wolf they knew to be a constant source of protection in their lives.

We purposefully let Lakota out last. If he had been able to greet the pups and Kamots before the others had a chance to, it might have resulted in his being punished. Even now he held back. His crate was wide open but he cowered inside, half-afraid of the strange surroundings and half-afraid that the excitement would grow into a dominance display.

The greeting was over and the pack slowly began to sniff the ground and explore the immediate area. Still, Lakota did not emerge. Kamots turned away from the others, walked back to Lakota, and waited beside the crate. The two whined back and forth to one another for several seconds. Finally, Lakota, wide-eyed, poked his head out of the crate and took one tentative step forward, then another, then hurried to his brother. Kamots pressed his shoulder against Lakota's in a gesture of reassurance and together they walked into the meadow.

This was one of the most gentle displays of concern I have ever seen. Kamots was unable to lead the wolves into their new home until his pack was complete. He would not leave his brother behind, omega or not. He under-stood that the wary Lakota needed a little encouragement, and knew how to coax him gently forward. It seemed fit-ting that, as Jamie and I prepared to say goodbye to the pack, they would do something so absolutely touching.

We sat down in the grass and watched them explore.

They took off to one corner of the territory, then returned to see that we were still there, then took off for another. Kamots always led the way, with Lakota in back and the three pups gamboling alongside Matsi. I was expecting that there would be a pack rally, that the nervousness and excitement of the move would spark a chorus of howls. Instead, they loped around the enclosure in complete silence. As I pondered this, it suddenly became obvious. They would keep quiet until they were sure that they were alone, that there wasn't another pack lurking somewhere. They didn't make a peep until they had sniffed every inch of their new home and listened to every new sound that drifted in on the breeze.

Later that afternoon, we gathered in a field a few hundred yards from the enclosure where the Nez Perce Tribe had organized a small ceremony to welcome the wolves. As the drumbeats echoed and the wailing voices rose up into the evening sky, a discordant sound took to the air and mingled with the singing. The wolves, responding to the noise, had begun to howl. Jamie stood there with her sound gear ready, but she was so overcome with sorrow, her eyes so full of tears, that she could not bring herself to record them one last time. After the human song ended, everyone stood motionless and listened until the howls drifted off and all was still.

We spent the next two days filming the pack as they adjusted to their new lives, gathering some final material for the film's conclusion. In reality, I already felt like it was over and couldn't bear to let it drag on. I knew it was time to say goodbye.

Jamie and I sat in the meadow, and Franz filmed us as we bid farewell. We spoke to each wolf as they gathered around us—Chemukh, tentative and shy; Wyakin, flirtatious and feisty; Wahots, intense; Amani, clownish; Motomo, calm and watchful. Lakota approached warily, always careful not to make waves. When he saw that it was safe, he licked Jamie's face and then mine. Kamots, always confident, sat down next to me and, as he had so many times before, reached out his foreleg to me and touched his paw to my hand. This had always been his gesture alone. Only Kamots was bold and relaxed enough to make contact in this way.

Finally I said goodbye to Matsi, sweet and brave, probably the hardest for me to leave. With his gentle, caring manner—the way he looked after the young ones and protected Lakota—he had taught me more about wolves than any other. Even while sitting beside me, getting his neck scratched, he kept one eye on the pups, never forgetting his duty to the pack. "Sweet Matsi," I said to him, "you're always going to be on my mind. You'll always be in my heart. But I think this is going to be fine. I'll miss you."

Matsi turned and trotted off to join the others who were already making their way off to patrol their territory. Watching him leave, I was overcome by a wave of despair. In my heart I knew that the wolves did not understand that we were leaving, and that fact was the hardest to deal with. Their display of affection was not a goodbye, it was the same greeting they always gave us when we saw them for the first time in a day. All they would know is that one day we were there and the next we were gone. They would simply be left to wonder why, if a wolf can even wonder why. I could only imagine that they might feel a sense of something missing, as they had shown when Motaki died. I had spent nearly six years getting to know them, bonding with them, living with them, learning so much of their language, yet there was a barrier that I could never cross. I would never be sure they understood how much I loved them.

My daughter, Christina, and her fiancé, Chad, were waiting for us back at the old Sawtooth wolf enclosure. Already they had begun to break camp, hauling tents and equipment to the house in Ketchum. They had removed the canvas from the yurt, so that now just the wooden skeleton remained. Our little camp had evolved with so much heart in six years: Patty Provonsha's sensitive touches of home and Jake's resourceful designs—the efficient kitchen, the whimsical shower tent—all would be gone in a matter of days.

We drove out to Stanley for dinner since we no longer had any provisions or anywhere to cook. Later that evening, Jamie and I sat on the wooden platform, opened a bottle of "Chateau Yurt," and looked out over the enclosure toward the mountains. It was what we did nearly every summer evening, but this time all was still. There were no flashes of motion in the pines, no sudden whines or yips echoing off the mountains. Nothing burst from the willows and charged into the meadow in a sudden game of tag, and there were no howls to pierce the summer sky, float among the trees, envelop our senses, and then drift away.

From the platform, I could see the worn spots and matted grass where each wolf used to sleep: Wahots by our tent, Kamots under the nearby lodgepoles, Motomo by our camp gate, Matsi and Lakota close together by the pond. It was strange to know how quickly it would all revert to its former state. The grass would sprout in the worn beds and trails, the leftover bones of elk and deer would bleach and turn to dust, the den would fill with earth, and all trace of the Sawtooth Pack's presence would soon be gone.

The long summer twilight faded and the bolder stars began to appear, one by one. Soon they filled the dark sky with a fine mist of light. We climbed down the ladder and crawled into bed for our last sleep at wolf camp.

Jamie's Epilogue

JAMIE

W e awoke to an unfamiliar landscape. In a daze, I helped pack up what remained of camp. My mind was unwilling to let go, to move from the past into the present. As I helped Jim carry a roll of canvas to the ATV trailer, I turned to look at Motomo, half-hidden behind the slender trunk of a lodgepole, watching us inquisitively as he so often did. But it was just a dark shadow.

The long process of editing lay ahead of us, as did many trips to and from Washington, D.C., to try to get our film on the air. At least the busy schedule filled some of the void left by the pack's absence. Armed with samples of Jim's footage and my sounds, we quickly got the attention of several companies, including ones that had previously passed on the idea. We signed a contract with the Discovery Channel for *Wolves at Our Door*, and Jim and I breathed a huge sigh of relief. The wolves' gift of trust had not been in vain. Their story would now be told.

That September, Jim and I were having dinner with

friends at a restaurant in Ketchum, sitting on a patio under a canvas roof. Halfway through the meal, an evening shower rolled over the mountains. Fat drops tapped slowly on the canvas at first. The rhythm grew to a gentle patter, then a steady murmur that muffled our conversation. The wave of sound carried me back to wolf camp, and for a moment I was snuggled in bed next to Jim, cozy and dry in our simple tent. The wolves were waiting out the storm beneath the shelter of the pines. Soon they would be racing through the damp grass and splashing in new puddles. The brief shower passed over and I found myself seated at the table once again, fumbling to find my way back to the conversation.

One of the most common questions people ask Jim and me is, "Do you still go to see the wolves?" The answer is, "Yes, as often as we can." The first time we visited them, four months after they were moved, their reaction was heartrending. They were far across an open meadow as we entered. At first they casually looked our way to see who the visitors were. When Kamots saw that it was Jim and me, he did an absolute double take and came bounding through the snow with the entire pack in tow. Their greeting was so enthusiastic it was obvious that they had missed us.

These times were bittersweet, for with each visit we grew more apprehensive about their welfare. Pack management was changing. WERC's office, a hundred miles away, was dictating the care of the wolves. Our one solace was the presence of Keith and Megan and the stable atmosphere they provided. All the same, Jim and I knew that there was only so much those two could endure, and that awareness terrified us.

There is a saying among wolf biologists that no one who gets involved with wolves walks away unscathed. No matter how one tries to be detached, wolves permeate every aspect of one's life. Once entangled, it is almost impossible to get free. The wolves themselves are not responsible for the damage they do to us. They do not intend to evoke such strong passions in people, but that is exactly what they do. Some of those people want every last wolf dead; others want to bring wolves back at all costs. Some see the wolves as an image of the devil incarnate; some see them as a spiritual guide. The ones who try to find some sort of middle ground subject themselves to fire from all sides.

Jim and I both realize that our lives would be considerably easier if we moved on. In raising and caring for a pack of wolves, making a film, wrestling with a nonprofit organization, and positioning ourselves as lightning rods for the American West's most volatile environmental controversy, Jim and I have broadened the scope of our commitment far beyond the realm of film production. Most wildlife documentary filmmakers choose a new subject with each new film, and we have indeed thought about doing just that. We have typed out proposals on wild horses, sea turtles, lynx, and even snow leopards, but the truth is that there is still so much that we want to say about wolves. As a subject for filming, few other species can claim such a wide variety of appearances and personalities and such an expressive vocabulary of body language and vocalizations. The most intelligent, most social, most caring, most misunderstood, and most persecuted animal on the continent is a pretty tough act to follow. Nor do I think it is time for us to stop speaking for the wolf. We have gained considerable ground toward a greater understanding, but the wolf's future is far from secure. This inspiring creature still needs a voice.

A reporter once asked me, "What did you have to give up to make this film, to live with the pack?"

I replied, "It's not what we lost, but what we gained." Saying this, I cannot begin to calculate what I have gained. They have fulfilled a dream for me, given me a life that is rich beyond any expectation. I will never be free from the Sawtooth Pack and I could never imagine wishing to be.

They gave me so much more than just a glimpse inside their private lives; they also gave me a greater understanding of humankind. One cannot observe a wolf pack without seeing a reflection of ourselves. How closely they mirror our own contradictions and complexities: social hierarchy tempered by compassion, contention mixed with cooperation, the admirable side by side with the abhorrent. They seem to possess so many of the qualities we admire, but one above all resonates strongest, knowing all that has befallen them at the hands of man. Wolves forgive.

Jim's Epilogue

JIM

I look at my yesterdays . . . The hours that made them were good, and so were the moments that made the hours. I have had responsibilities and work, dangers and pleasure, good friends, and a world without walls to live in.

—Beryl Markham, *West with the Night*

In the dark of an early October morning, Jamie and I pulled to the curb in front of Rockefeller Center. Stepping out of the taxicab, I looked up and found myself face to face with a pack of wolves. By the time recognition filtered through the predawn fog in my brain, the wolves were already chugging away down Fifth Avenue in a puff of diesel exhaust. Discovery Channel's publicity department had caught me by surprise. The faces of the Sawtooth Pack had been blown up and plastered on the sides of New York City buses.

The wolves had done it again. *Wolf: Return of a Legend* had been successful, but the massive media attention and ratings that *Wolves at Our Door* was generating surpassed anything that I had ever imagined. The story of two people living with a pack of wolves tapped into a desire, almost a fantasy, that is held in the hearts of many people—the longing to cross the species barrier and to really live with another animal as an equal. Between October and December 1997, Jamie and I were invited to appear on *Today, Good Morning America,* and *Dateline,* were interviewed on *BBC World Radio,* and gave over a hundred other interviews in North America and Europe. We suddenly found ourselves thrust into the limelight as spokespeople for the wolf.

As unprepared as I was for the popular and critical success of the film, I was no more prepared for the harsh remarks it received from a few individuals in wildlife filmmaking. I should have known that the popular appeal of *Wolves at Our Door* guaranteed that it would receive some measure of criticism from the purist fringe. One British producer dismissed it as a "wolf soap opera." To me, he was really saying that our film was an engaging and emotional story that succeeded in touching a great many people. In other words, Jamie and I had achieved our intended goal.

As one might expect, the predominant criticism centered around my choice to use captive wolves in a wildlife film and to make the truth about their captivity part of the story. I suppose I also ruffled some feathers by giving the wolves names. Obviously, we made no attempt to teach the wolves their names, it was merely a way for us to identify them.

Perhaps I could have given the film an air of scientific authenticity by naming the wolves F-22 or M-6 as biologists do. Then again, since it was a "wolf soap opera," I suppose I could have named them Blake and Crystal, or Luke and Laura.

As for me, I never set out to make a film for my professional peers or for scientists. To do so would have been a bit like preaching to the choir. I wanted to make a film for an audience that was sitting on the fence, one that had not formed an opinion about wolves and possibly didn't even watch wildlife documentaries at all. People already know that wolves are efficient predators. I wanted to show the wolf's other side. I wanted these people to look into Kamots' amber eyes and be emotionally moved by a compassionate, family-oriented creature.

After *Wolves at Our Door* aired on Discovery Channel, a Ketchum resident stopped me on the street. "I used to want to hunt wolves," he said solemnly, "but not anymore." He had no idea that they were such social animals, so concerned with family, so much like us. This happened over and over—in Idaho, in Wyoming, and even in New York, strangers approaching us to say that Kamots, Lakota, Matsi, and the others had changed their way of thinking about wolves. This is the greatest compliment Jamie and I could ever have received.

With all that the Sawtooth Pack has achieved, with all that they could still have achieved in the future, how fitting it would have been for this story to have a happy ending. Sadly, true stories have a way of not giving us the ending we want.

Since the wolves were moved, we have visited them on countless occasions, sometimes to take photographs, sometimes just to be with them. For a while, everything seemed to be going according to plan. Jamie and I believed that the wolves we knew so well would live out their lives in safety on the Nez Perce land, under the stewardship of WERC and cared for by Keith and Megan. But this was not the case.

Keith and Megan began to have disputes with WERC over pack management and other factors. The two caretakers whom the wolves knew best both resigned in 1998. Jamie and I were powerless to settle disagreements or ease tensions between the organization and its employees.

It is a testament to wolves' sensitivity that captive packs are so deeply affected by changes in their caretaking staff. This is precisely why we introduced the pack to Keith and Megan slowly, giving them time to develop a bond. Based on my own experience and everything I have read about managing captive packs, I believe that the loss of its two trusted caretakers, and changes in the personnel who were interacting with the wolves, contributed to a declining spirit and cohesiveness within the pack itself. WERC settled into a policy of nonintervention, allowing the pack to sort out its own problems. It was the same approach that I had abandoned years earlier after a series of painful lessons taught me that sometimes a captive pack must be actively managed.

The first of the Sawtooth Pack to die was five-year-old

Wyakin. The sweet and gentle omega female fell in late 1999 to injury and illness that were left untended. When her body was found, her brother Wahots was sitting by her side.

Then Jamie and I had to watch helplessly as stress tore the pack apart. It was more painful than anything I had to endure during my six years living with them, for next among the many victims of this chaos and turmoil was my beloved friend Kamots. The wolf that had been the strength behind the pack—behind me—was found dead the following June.

Only two months earlier, Kamots' formerly stable rule had finally cracked under pressure from Piyip and Amani. He died mysteriously during a five-week period when there was no caretaker present. Volunteers and an assistant threw food over the fence, but no one had enough experience to enter the enclosure and spend time with the pack. The necropsy report indicated that he had been dead for two or three weeks before his remains were found. When I received the news, a piece of my heart went cold forever. For three weeks after Kamots' death, a single wolf was heard howling alone in the night. That wolf was never identified.

The rest was like a chain reaction. With no clear leader, the pack hierarchy crumbled. Noble Matsi had been the beta wolf for so long that he was like a lieutenant to Kamots, but the stability of his position relied on Kamots' presence as alpha more than we had ever realized. When Kamots died, Matsi became an outcast, tormented by the younger wolves. Following an injury, he was removed from the pack and placed in a separate enclosure. Matsi had taught us more than any wolf about companionship, about how deeply wolves need each other. He now lives alone.

Chemukh's alpha status also vanished with the death of Kamots, and she, too, became a pariah. Possibly fearing abuse from her daughters, Ayet and Motaki, she scaled the twelve-foot fence and disappeared into the forests of northern Idaho. She was sighted once or twice during the autumn of 2000, shortly after her escape, but then the sightings ceased. Facing the world alone, she most likely did not survive the winter.

Visiting the pack is hardly a joy now. It is more like a grim duty. We still feel compelled to see the survivors, the members of the pack that managed to avoid the disaster. Motomo's calm demeanor allowed him to rise above the turmoil. He still lives as part of the pack, never the abuser nor the abused, the wolf who appears least affected by these times. And somewhere, still on the fringes, is Lakota, the mildest and gentlest wolf I have ever known. As he aged, he was finally relieved of his omega status, leaving the position to Wahots. It was not that Lakota asserted himself or dominated the younger wolf, he was simply allowed to step aside. I see him now as the wise old man of the pack, for in his life he has seen and endured the most.

The greatest gift Lakota and his family gave me was their trust. Only after living with them for so long did I really understand the value of it. Trust is not a trifle that a wolf gives out freely. It is reserved only for a precious few. It is why Jamie and I will always remember the time we spent with them as the richest, most rewarding, most beautiful experience of our lives. It is also why seeing them now is so painful, for they will never know how we fought for them, how we tried to help but failed. Yet for all that has befallen these wolves, the few that remain still welcome us, remembering their bond from long ago.

The Sawtooth Pack has made its sacrifice and told its story to the world. Kamots, Lakota, Matsi, and the rest have revealed their beauty, their depth, and even their contradictions for all to see. Nothing more should be expected of them. It is up to us now.

Perhaps it was closure we were seeking, or perhaps we were hoping that the memory of better times would soothe the pain of the present. Neither Jamie nor I could really explain why, one autumn day, we found ourselves driving on the old jeep trail toward the site that had once been our home. The willows had grown back in the clearings where the fence used to run, and there was no trace left of our camp, only memories of our tiny yurt, of conversations around the woodstove, and of our friends. In the spruce grove, we found Chemukh's den still intact. I remembered standing under the trees watching in amazement as Jamie disappeared underground, and how Chemukh had stood by with her head cocked in curiosity. Only a few yards away was the small meadow where I used to wait for Makuyi, where one day she had overcome the barrier of fear enough to approach me and gently lick my hand. We walked northeast to the willow marsh where Jamie first met Lakota and where I had let Kamots steal my hat, then to the pond where Matsi and Lakota used to play.

There was a small muddy patch near the creek and,

for a moment, I failed to find anything unusual about the line of large wolf tracks that crossed it. Then with a smile I realized these were the fresh tracks of a wild wolf. They were back in the Sawtooths for the first time in nearly sixty years. This one had probably dispersed from a reintroduced pack in the Frank Church Wilderness and traveled south looking for a mate. The Sawtooth Pack truly had been the forerunners of their wild cousins, not only in this area, but also, I hope, in the hearts of people who once misunderstood them.

Wolves have an uncanny knack for homing in on the scent of other wolves and following their trails. I wonder how this wolf responded when he got to our site and picked up the faded traces of the Sawtooth Pack. Did he investigate the area in silence, wary of encroaching on another pack's territory? Or did he howl in hopes of joining them? Perhaps the scent of his distant kin lingering in the aspen groves and meadows made him feel more comfortable in the new territory, assuring him that, yes, he did indeed belong there. I like to think it did.

Bibliography and Further Reading

Bomford, Liz. *The Complete Wolf.* London: Boxtree Limited, 1993.

Busch, Robert. *The Wolf Almanac.* New York: Lyons and Burford, 1998.

Crisler, Lois. *Arctic Wild.* New York: Curtis Publishing Company, 1956.

Dutcher, Jim, with Richard Ballantine. *The Sawtooth Wolves.* Bearsville, N.Y.: Rufus Publications, Inc., 1996.

Knight, Elizabeth, ed. *Wolves of the High Arctic.* Stillwater, Minn.: Voyageur Press, 1992.

Landau, Diana, ed. *Wolf, Spirit of the Wild.* New York: Sterling Publishing Company, Inc., 1998.

Lawrence, R.D. *The Trail of the Wolf.* Toronto: Rodale Press, 1993.

Lopez, Barry Holstun. *Of Wolves and Men.* New York: Charles Scribner's Sons, 1978.

Lorenz, Konrad. *On Aggression.* New York: Bantam Books, 1967.

McIntyre, Rick. *The War Against the Wolf.* Stillwater, Minn.: Voyageur Press, 1995.

Mech, L. David. *The Wolf.* Stillwater, Minn.: University of Minnesota Press, 1970.

————. *The Way of the Wolf.* Stillwater, Minn.: Voyageur Press, 1991.

Murie, Adolph. *The Wolves of Mount McKinley.* Seattle: University of Washington Press, 1985.

Savage, Candace. *Wolves.* San Francisco: Sierra Club Books, 1988.

Scieszka, John. *The True Story of the 3 Little Pigs by A. Wolf.* New York: Viking, 1989.

Steinhart, Peter. *The Company of Wolves.* New York: Alfred A. Knopf, 1995.

Trivizas, Eugene, and Helen Oxenbury. *The Three Little Wolves and the Big Bad Pig.* New York: Macmillan, 1993.